WOMEN'S
RITUALS

WOMEN'S RITUALS

A SOURCEBOOK

Barbara G. Walker

1817

Harper & Row, Publishers, San Francisco

New York, Grand Rapids, Philadelphia, St. Louis
London, Singapore, Sydney, Tokyo, Toronto

Art throughout by Elizabeth Morales-Denney.

FIRST EDITION

Library of Congress Cataloging-in-Publication Data

Walker, Barbara G.
    Women's rituals : a sourcebook / Barbara G. Walker.
        p.   cm.
    Includes bibliographical references.
    ISBN 0-06-250939-X
    1. Women—Religious life. 2. Rites and ceremonies. 3. Spiritual life. 4. Feminism—Religious aspects. 5. Occultism. I. Title.
BL625.7.W42   1990
291.3'8'082—dc20

89-45520
CIP

90 91 92 93 94 MAPLE 10 9 8 7 6 5 4 3 2 1

Contents

Chapters Listed by Ritual Type

Mental Rituals

Rituals of Play

Guided Meditations

History Reclaimed

Seasonal Rituals

Introduction

Advocates of the burgeoning women's spirituality movement have written many books to guide its followers. They have
covered such subjects as witchcraft, paganism, and Goddess worship; celebration of equinoxes, solstices, and cross-quarter days in
the style of the Old Religions; re-visioned ways to solemnize initiations, weddings, rites of the dead, menarche and menopause rituals; chants, dances, invocations, trance-meditations, and many
forms of magic. These are useful books with intriguing ideas. But
a huge middle-of-the-road majority of women shy away from
such literature. They don't want to label themselves witches. They
don't believe in the efficacy of magic, and they are put off by
some of the outsize claims that are made for it. Perhaps they fear
that certain aspects of "witchcraft" would offend their modesty or
intrude too far into their privacy. In short, there are multitudes of
ordinary, normal, intelligent women going about their business,
giving little thought to whatever they may have heard about
women's spirituality because it doesn't seem to offer anything
they specifically need.

And yet these are the same women who have turned away
from patriarchal religion because they found it unsuitable, un-
believable, or offensive to their female personhood. Many have
inwardly rejected the theologians' father-god as irrelevant to
themselves, even though they might regularly attend a church or
synagogue for the sake of relatives and friends, because it is their
social custom and a primary means of maintaining social bonds.
Their attitude toward traditional god-theology may be agnostic or
simply indifferent—and, if the truth were told, that is the attitude
of most modern churchgoers—but they like the rituals, the music,
the getting together with other people. They feel that religion
must be a good thing because everyone else says so, even if it
doesn't seem to have much connection with daily life.

Still, many feel that this way of taking religion is entirely too
passive. They want to be more directly involved. Many women

express an interest in exploring new kinds of spiritual relation-ships, more supportive of the feminine image. But they don't know where to begin. They are uncomfortable with the idea of joining a "witch cult"—even in the unlikely event that they might find one conveniently nearby. Nor can they collect a group of friends and just suddenly jump up and say, Now we are Goddess worshipers! What then? What does one do about it? How does one express an alternate religion or a quest into new, unorthodox spiritual ideas? Since women's religious customs were either sup-pressed or taken over by patriarchy several thousand years ago, what's left for women to discover?

This book contains answers to these questions. It is addressed to the sort of women who have thought about starting a spiritual-ity group, but can't imagine what kind of activities such a group might engage in. It is addressed to the sort of women whose prac-tical intelligence keeps them aloof from the overly credulous and the hyperenthusiastic; women who are not going to subscribe to irrational or improbable theories, who want to avoid the lunatic-fringe, who are not especially interested in the occult, or who are put off by the seamier connotations of cult phenomena. It is addressed to ordinary, educated women who are conscious of a nagging vacancy in their spiritual experience but don't believe it can be filled by available alternatives.

In order to try the recipes in this book, you don't have to believe anything at all.

All you need is a group of interested women, any number from about five to fifteen, who agree to get together periodically in a convenient place and do some ritualistic things, to see how they feel about it. There is no prescribed order of events, no rigid format, no single "right" way. The rituals in this book are sugges-tions offered in the spirit of experimentation, always subject to creative modifications.

Such a group of women may grow together, passing by com-fortably gradual degrees from the tyro stage to a keener aware-ness of what women's spiritual interrelationships can mean, to a surer pathway toward the much-neglected inner feminine ideal, and consequently to a more confident self-image.

Much has been written metaphorically about self-empower-ment and emotional self-healing. In contrast, this book is mini-mally metaphorical. It suggests things to do. The doing may engender metaphorical interpretations, or arouse surprisingly deep feelings; but the results are not part of the prescription. Every group is different. What works for one group may not work for another. There is a choice.

For many centuries, men have been devising the religious rituals of our civilization. They have written formal prayers, invocations, and other liturgical speech. They have composed anthems, hymns, processionals. They have invented ceremonial gestures and procedures. They have designed and built ritual spaces, utilizing every talent of the best available architects, artists, and craftspeople. They have set up vast, complex structures of hieratic action having no purpose except formal celebration of male-centered religious beliefs. In a very real sense, the actions create the beliefs. The practice of religion is ritual, and every ritual *is* a human invention.

In our Western culture, men alone have claimed the right to invent, teach, or lead religious rituals. Women have been almost totally excluded from the process. Even when patriarchal religious authorities took over older ceremonies that once celebrated the Goddess and were first created by her priestesses, men erased the signs of feminine authorship and changed the gender. Even when priests adopted female dress in token of spiritual power, they claimed it had been their custom from the beginning. Even when men plagiarized ancient scriptures written by women, they substituted "God" for "Goddess" and pretended that their rituals were founded on directives from "him."

When women continued their own ancient ceremonies privately, outside the framework of male orthodoxy, they were labeled witches and made legally subject to torture and murder by the male establishment. In such crude, brutal ways have men enforced an exclusive right to perpetuation of their own religion through ritualistic behavior patterns.

Contrary to the sexist claims of our priesthoods, however, the capacity to invent and enjoy ritual is not gender specific. The creation of ritual is a universal human impulse. (Indeed, it is seen among animals also.) We all do and say things without perceptible practical reasons, other than to reassure ourselves with empowering or repetitive thoughts and behaviors. The comforting reassurance of repetition is the real secret of the appeal of every formalized religion.

When denied their rightful part in creative ritual-making, women have been forced to adopt whatever the men produced and to train their own emotional responses accordingly. Today's churches and temples have been immeasurably enriched by the unacknowledged input of women, who faithfully decorate, support, proselytize, raise funds, serve refreshments, swell the chorus of liturgical song, and still slavishly accept their second-class status as "noncreative" pillars of the church. Yet the rituals of such churches are not women's products. They are not based on women's true spiritual needs. They do not harmonize with women's deepest thoughts. They have disguised or buried the female symbolism that underlies their so-called mysteries. They are cynically exploiting the mighty spiritual powers collectively embodied in women, which they do not deserve to use, because their patriarchal system has been the primary source of women's oppression.

For such reasons, the modern women's spirituality movement questions male claims to authority in the creation of ritual as well as in all other theological matters. Many women have discovered in themselves the capacity to devise beautiful, satisfying ceremonies for personal or group use, which please them more than the traditional posturing of self-styled spiritual fathers. This form of creativity now pours forth with immense vitality from those women who have rediscovered its inner wellsprings, who have found the courage to reject patriarchal habits in favor of their own emotional and esthetic instincts.

Drawing from the Goddess religions of antiquity, from the frank Mother worship of the pagan or the primitive, and from their own personal sense of what is both spiritual and fundamentally female, women have begun to create their own corpus of ceremonial procedures. This can provide future generations with workable alternatives to those patriarchal practices that have inflatedly claimed the title of "religion" for themselves alone, decrying all others—especially those of women—as witchcraft and devil worship.

The Goddess is not a devil. She is now, for many women, a focus of their long-suppressed intuitions and a major symbol of their self-empowerment. She is the Mother who accepts their feminine personhood, in contrast to the Father who rejected it. To them her image has a better feeling about it than the God image. Therefore rituals based on this Goddess image are proliferating.

Through them, women may find both themselves and each other in fresh, exciting ways.

Most important of all, women are beginning to take into their own hands the creation of a new morality that may prove to be the only real salvation of the human race, which stands teetering on the brink of male-engineered apocalypse. In view of the fact that hardly any human effort can be more essential than this, there is every reason to pay attention to women's spiritual insights, feelings, and practices. If traditional religion seems dull, pointless, or irrelevant in today's dangerously male-dominated world, a new and vital spirit may be found in the seeds that women are currently learning to plant, hoping for a future harvest of peace. In this respect, historical patriarchy has failed us. To the women who are now rethinking spiritual values, it seems we have no choice but to try something else.

The human psyche apparently loves ritual and is reluctant to live without it. Children automatically invent rituals for themselves, until they learn to replace their own creative workings with society's "accepted" ones. At this point the ritual becomes more sophisticated, but some spark is lost. A certain spirit of wonder disappears, never to return.

For many women, the spirit of wonder departs when they begin to realize that their Judeo-Christian religious training involves men primarily and selectively, with little or no theological sanction of the feminine image, except in very restricted ways. Women can be wife of the flesh, mother of the flesh, temptress particularly of the (male) flesh, or purified virgin renouncing the flesh; but she is not "made in the image of Goddess." She is not the Daughter of Goddess. She cannot see a divine counterpart of herself. Christian women are encouraged to revere and serve a Father-Son image that is essentially a deification of men's Oedipal jealousy: the Father commands the Son's agonizing death, and the Son tamely obeys, like a good soldier following the orders of his superiors (pseudofathers) in the chain of command. That men can be trained to do this is what makes war possible. History confirms that patriarchal religion has always been a training ground for war. The most warlike societies were (and are) those in which patriarchy is pronounced most divine.

Feminists reject the rituals of a patriarchal society or a male-dominated religion. Yet the human desire for ritual doesn't evaporate because the "accepted" rituals are found unacceptable. More appealing substitutes might be drawn from the real ideas and experiences of real women. Women grope in the dark, because the past traditions that sprang from genuine feminine spirit were either buried or hopelessly corrupted by patriarchal authorities who stole them, turning what had been invented for the service of the Goddess into a new interpretation to serve their God.

It might be said in passing that certain elements within the framework of established religion are trying to do this all over again. Seeking to revitalize the worship of the male God, certain churches are trying out the ritual practices of neopagan, feminist spirituality because people seem to like them. The church, as always, wants to find out what sells, in order to attract more customers. Feminists need to be aware of this cynically exploitive trend, to keep their spiritual discoveries (or rediscoveries) away from the patriarchal machine.

One important element that was quite lost during the suppression of feminine spirit was the sense of play embodied in ritual: the feeling that it can and should be fun, that jokes and laughter have a real function in formation of interpersonal bonds, and that having fun together is a vital—if often unacknowledged—constituent of any practice of love. Men often become overly serious about rituals, even when they put on silly hats and identify themselves as members of secular fraternal organizations. Women tend to be more playful in the making of ritual, willing to let it feel good, willing to laugh. This is not shallow or frivolous. It may be necessary for the sense of inner release in many individuals, who were taught from childhood that laughter is unseemly and out of place in church, although weeping is allowed. We have been trained to approach religious customs with excessive physical and mental control, in the patriarchal style. The ways of the ancient matriarchate were different.

The suggestions in this book need not be taken over-seriously, nor do they require commitment to any particular system of belief or nonbelief. Women's rituals are for any women and all women. Even though patriarchy preempted rituals in the first place from matriarchal roots, women's rituals are not rivals of women's other convictions, whatever they may be. It is an insufferable arrogance for any organization to claim an exclusive right to ritualize, or to set up its own forms as the only correct ones. Because ritual is an integral part of human behavior, it belongs to every human being.

Therefore this book presents suggestions rather than rules. These are suggested answers to the question women ask themselves and each other when their groups begin to form: Now what? What shall we do? How shall we do it? What is "correct" or "not correct"? Do we dare to be inventive? What if we don't have any creative ideas?

Rather than bog down in endless discussions over minor technicalities, it is best to jump right in and *do* some rituals, to see how they work and how they feel. A given ritual may work one way for one group, another way for another group. Flexibility is important. Experimenters should feel free to adapt and innovate. We've been taught that rituals must *represent* something; but sometimes the reality works the other way.

One can easily view any ritual as a kind of game, and vice versa. Rituals and games overlap in many ways. Women's rituals can be seen as games without competition, having no winners or losers, only participants. Even today, uncivilized societies demonstrate ritualistic games in which all players cooperate rather than compete. Sometimes such games are plainly recognized as media for teaching and practicing spiritual principles, like the Game of Rebirth associated with Tantric Buddhism.

An important rediscovery made by the modern women's movement is that fun can be enlightening, and enlightenment can be fun. Historically, when religions were taken over by men, they tended to lose the light touch and to become grim, serious, ascetic, or even painful in both imagery and practice. Much emphasis was placed on self-denial and suffering, self-abasement and guilt. Enjoyment became sinful. Initiations often became agonizing endurance tests. It was generally assumed that the spirit couldn't grow without renunciation of the flesh, which usually meant injuring it.

The women's movement has largely denied such doctrines. After centuries of suppression, the feminine spirit rises again to assert that divinity is discoverable through the senses; that laughter is not hostile to spirituality; that play can have profound resonances in human psychology; and that members of a spiritually oriented group need not lead or be led, win or lose, but may cooperate in the creation of a group feeling to which each participant may relate in her own way.

Meaning develops out of doing. Those who are open to possibilities will find that any ritual act can have many layers of meanings. Women of the modern world seek their own meanings in rituals that feel right to them, that do not damage the feminine spirit, and that can be democratically shared. Many of the gamelike procedures minutely detailed in this book can provide doings for the evolution and enhancement of new, woman-centered meanings.

Finally it is necessary to understand the subtle but important difference between meanings and beliefs. For many centuries, religious authorities have insisted that no one can be "spiritual" without belief in the literal truth of their more or less astonishing creeds. Unbelief has been a pejorative term, almost synonymous with devil worship (even though the latter would involve belief too). Unbelief has been equated with immorality or crass materialism, as opposed to spirituality—despite the obvious fact that some of the world's most moral people are nominal unbelievers.

Some people fall through the cracks of traditional beliefs because they reject, say, the violent war god of the Old Testament, or the primitive creation myth, or a virgin birth story, or the idea of transubstantiation, or any of a dozen other equally improbable doctrines that have been perpetrated by patriarchal theology. Traditionalists are anxious to label such people immoral or crassly materialistic; in short, unspiritual. More recent alternative views of spirituality may urge belief in similarly fanciful notions—ghosts, horoscopes, magical healings, unknown dimensions, Atlantis, UFOs—as if spirituality must be virtually synonymous with unquestioning gullibility.

These matters should not be confused. *Spiritual* does not necessarily mean credulous, shallow, or naive. On the contrary, the deepest spirituality springs from the deepest thought. A profoundly spiritual ritual may have nothing to do with otherworldliness at all, but may celebrate the sacredness of the real and the natural: woman, earth, flesh, daily living, human relationships. The sense of holiness within everyday things is a characteristic of women's spirituality, as opposed to the typically patriarchal separation of body and spirit, earth and heaven.

Women are concerned not to reject Mother Earth but to love, honor, and protect her; not to despise the flesh but to delight and comfort it; not to ignore the mind's common sense but to use it. Women's rituals can have these very legitimate aims without any recourse to irrational beliefs. That is why the new feminist spirituality is for everyone, regardless of belief or unbelief. It can be successfully related to traditional or nontraditional faith, or to none. Just as ritual is not the same as churchgoing, so belief is not the same as spirituality.

The rituals suggested in the following pages are direct, personal, involving, sense oriented, thought provoking, and conducive to a new spiritual sensitivity toward the real worlds: both the outer world of nature and the inner world of self-discovery, where all deities have their true existence. Women's spirituality can frankly acknowledge that these are the worlds where we live, and where all rituals, ultimately, take place. Perhaps it is not merely fortuitous that the word *ritual* is contained in the word *spiritual*. Sense of the sacred is contained in the human spirit, and in human actions, and in human desires. If rituals make these matters clear, then one of their greatest goals has been achieved.

The Environment

Women's meetings are held in all sorts of places: outdoors and indoors, private homes and public buildings, wild woods and city apartments. There is no official environment. Each group makes do with what's available. The following remarks on environment are guidelines toward an ideal of sorts, to define aims as much as immediate possibilities.

If meetings are held in private homes of members, there must be no interruptions or intrusions: no phone calls, no doorbells, no visitors, no family demands for the duration of the meeting. All other household members who are not involved in the meeting should remain unseen and unheard, out of the way, and if possible out of the house for the evening. Arrangements should be made for fathers or other caretakers to attend to small children. In other words, nothing should be allowed to break the concentration of the group.

In warm weather, meetings can be held outdoors: in someone's yard, garden, woodlot, meadow, or field if available. Public places like parks, campgrounds, or picnic areas are usually unsuitable because privacy can't be assured. Since an outdoor meeting is subject to vagaries of the weather even in summertime, shelter should be available in case of a sudden rainstorm.

A satisfactory environment might be found in a public building, within a convenient distance for all members. Possibilities include all-purpose rooms in schools, universities, libraries, churches, town halls, community centers, clubs, or commercial buildings. If the group has money to spend, it might even rent a meeting room in a hotel or motel when free space cannot be found. Usually, though, something can be found in almost any neighborhood.

Cleanliness and comfort are the primary requirements for any indoor space. The room should be large, so group members can move about freely. The room should be well carpeted, for sitting or lying down. The working space should be empty of furniture except for a central altar table about knee high. A round coffee table serves quite well. On this table, members can place their candles, crystals, talismans, personal treasures for show-and-tell, or decorations of the season: spring flowers, summer fruits, autumn leaves, midwinter holly.

Some groups keep a special cloth for covering the altar table, so anything can be converted into an altar anywhere—boards on bricks, a trunk, a packing crate, even a large cardboard carton. Such a cloth might be handwoven or hand embroidered by group members; or it could be a purchased cloth with initials or personal symbols painted on by each member with fabric paints or indelible markers; or it might be a cloth of plain solid black, white, or red (Triple Goddess colors). The altar cloth could be a shawl, an afghan, a bride's veil, a wizard's cloak, a tapestry, or a handmade rug. It should be made of an organic material, such as heavy silk, linen, cotton, or wool, rather than a synthetic fabric.

If a special altar cloth is used, measures should be taken to protect it from candle drippings and other stains. Narrow candle sticks generally are to be avoided in favor of the cup-type candle holder or the kind of candlestick that has a flaring concave base to catch dripping wax. If there are no candlesticks, candles can be set upright in small tin cans with their labels washed off, or in small juice glasses. A candle set into a blob of melted wax in the center of such a container will burn just as brightly as one in a sterling silver candlestick.

The altar covering doesn't have to be a cloth. A large flat mirror or plate of glass makes a pretty tabletop, reflects the candle-light, and is impervious to wax spills. A special piece of wood, a roll of parchment, or a slab of stone will do for an altar fixed in its place—outdoors, for instance. Remember, tombstones originated as family altars on which descendants made offerings to the spirits of their deceased ancestors. Indoors, a coffee table with a polished marble top can make an excellent altar. It can't be easily carried from one place to another, but it also can't be burned or stained, and it is easily cleanable.

If the group doesn't find or create an altar table, then a simple cloth laid on the floor or ground will do. Outdoors, a small flat area may be smoothed out and surrounded by a circle of stones. A large log section, set on end, also makes a nice altar. It's important to be flexible, and to realize that you may use any materials that come to hand. The creativity of group members will inevitably suggest improvements and embellishments.

Groups lucky enough to have their own permanent space can create a real shrine full of personal meanings. They can hang their own paintings, photographs, or mandalas on the walls. They can store their robes or other ceremonial garments handily. They can drape the room with garlands, curtains, or group webwork. They can place Goddess statues in the corners and directional symbols at the four compass points. Around the walls they can place bookshelves for feminist publications and reference books; stereo equipment for meditation background music; glass cabinets for displaying crystals and other objects of contemplation; vessels for seasonal flowers, incense, or votive lamps. The center of the floor might be occupied by a special rug—a circular shape is both unusual and appropriate—or by a permanent pentacle. There could be soft indirect lighting for times when the candles are not burning. There could be storage space for eating utensils, tools, musical instruments, or record files. A beautiful, quiet, spacious room equipped with everything necessary for women's rituals is not available to most of us, but it can be kept in mind as a future goal.

To achieve an ideal environment would require money, effort, and ongoing commitment. Today, churches usually siphon off that kind of commitment among women, many of whom seek their own spiritual fulfilment in voluntary services to church organizations run by men. Europe's many Goddess temples were destroyed or taken over by Christianity fifteen centuries ago. Consequently women no longer have spaces that they can call their own. Women's spiritual environments need to be recreated and revisioned, in consideration of what they used to be, and what they might be again.

Two or three thousand years ago, women's rituals were conducted in splendid temples dedicated to their Goddess. Women's holy dances were performed on marble floors among beautiful carved pillars, illuminated by jeweled lamps, before magnificent statues of the original Queen of Heaven, crowned with stars, enthroned on the moon, holding forth her gifts of fruit and flower, animal and child. She was invincible, subject to no god. On the contrary, all gods owed filial devotion to her and swore by her name. Priestesses governed her worship, settled legal and moral problems by her authority, taught and counseled and administered her religion throughout the ancient world.

Most of that was destroyed in several centuries of relentless attack by early Christians, who were adamantly opposed to every manifestation of the Goddess, and determined to set up a wholly male-identified religion. Christians tore down her temples, passed laws to make her worship illegal, persecuted and killed her priestesses, burned the books from her sacred libraries, melted down her gold and silver lamps, stole the jeweled eyes and ornaments from her images and battered the remains to powder.

After a thousand years of official dominance, Christian churches were still fighting her, because common people tried again and again to restore some vestige of their beloved Holy Mother to popular consciousness. Offered the Virgin Mary as a substitute, they enthusiastically adopted and adored her even though the church insisted that she was not divine. Remnants of the true, ancient, divine Goddess worship were condemned as witchcraft. Even a mention of her name could be interpreted as a trafficking with devils and a capital crime.

In such ways, the female deity has been erased from women's knowledge. Yet, even without knowledge, many women yearn for some version of that primal image that gave dignity and holiness to the world's mothers, sisters, daughters, grandmothers, female judges, leaders, artists, thinkers, arbiters of morality and ethics.

Even today, many women deeply sense the wrongness of male morality with its punitive, warlike gods, its ascetic sex fears, its focus on death, and its hostility toward nature and the living body. Male morality chose to view the natural environment—the living Mother Earth—as inert material to be used and exploited, just as male theologians officially declared the living womb in a woman's body an inert "soil" in which the lordly male seed could grow (preferably into another image of the father). Such views disparaged both woman and the earth, to the point of denying the essential fact that the very existence of "man" is entirely dependent on both.

In a sense, then, Environment and Woman have been identified with one another even under patriarchy—which is not entirely illogical, because every man's primordial environment is a woman. Women are born of woman too, and can relate to the idea of feminine surroundings as extensions of their own bodies, their own sense of enclosing and being enclosed. Woman is skilled at creating a sacred space around herself. This fact is still vaguely recognized by the kind of truism that says a home can't be home-like without a woman's touch. Can we recall soldiers being inspired to fight by images of the church or the synagogue? No. The images are of Mom and apple pie: the warmth of her fireside, the fragrances of her kitchen.

Women in the Western world are encouraged to create this sacred space primarily for others—husbands and children—rather than for themselves. But an increased awareness of ritual environment brings many women back to the long-suppressed desire for a personal shrine in the home setting. Christian customs of furnishing the home with icons, crucifixes, and other holy images were originally adopted from pagan matriarchal customs of home worship. The clan mother's hearth fire was once a sacred place, under the eye of her Goddess in some form, with relics of ancestral ghosts and tribal deities whose spirits attended the family feasts. Talismans, amulets, soul symbols, objects of divination, and seasonal decorations like spring flowers and midwinter greens were taken into the pre-Christian home by the woman who owned it.

Women often recreate such ancient customs by establishing not only a "house" environment to be lived in, visited, and appreciated by others, but also a personal environment like a small shrine within the house. Such a shrine can be as simple as a single shelf, table, or bureau top; or it can dominate a whole room that is devoted to its maintenance, furnished with special lights, cushions, seats, pictures, and mementoes. Virginia Woolf called it "a room of one's own." A woman needs her own private corner, where she may contemplate those things that are important and meaningful to her.

In such a place one can set up a home altar covered by a special cloth or provided with candles, incense holders, smudging vessels, lamps, or perfume vessels. On the altar one might place fresh flowers, leaves, herbs, special stones, crystals, jewels, seeds, nuts, tarot cards, Goddess images, photographs, driftwood, art objects, gifts to be consecrated before giving, reminders of absent friends, and any other items of personal interest. The altar is a focus—a Latin word that used to mean a housewife's central hearth, her hub of food and warmth. The altar is a place where one can be alone and quiet for a few minutes each day, to refresh one's inner resources, to think one's own thoughts.

The home altar or shrine is a place where a woman need never please anyone except herself. Whatever items she brings to this place should be her own choice and no one else's. The assortment may be changed whenever and however she wishes. Similarly, the space used by a woman's group should express the tastes of group members only.

Just as men preempted the right to sanctify altars representing the male-created God, so women must reclaim their right to sanctify a place representing the divine spirit in and of themselves. Just as women were forbidden to approach the altars of the men's God, so the spiritual environments of women must be free of male intrusion. That is not to say that men should be excluded from knowledge of Goddess spirit, or from rituals that will help them. But the new flowering of feminine consciousness is still a tender and tentative bud. It must grow in its own way without male interference, until it becomes strong enough to provide the morality of tolerance and love of life that the male-dominated world has lacked for two thousand years.

Women need to make their own rules for a while. Women need to determine for themselves the circumstances under which they will meet, how often they will meet, what they will do, and what their goals will be. Women need to reclaim their spiritual history and practice their own ceremonies, recognizing their own priorities. Women need to think creatively about the foundations of morality and ethics in our culture. The world sorely needs a keener sense of human beings' responsibilities toward themselves, each other, and their home planet. Women, left to themselves, may find this sense through their own inner connectedness. Now it is necessary for women to discover how their own intuitive morality can be externalized, codified, and honestly practiced in the everyday world.

Silence

Most women are quite articulate. Their everyday method of maintaining social contact is a stream of talk. Many believe a long lapse of conversation in a social setting is awkward and embarrassing, and they try to keep it from occurring.

The conscientious hostess typically dreads an extended silence, which she interprets to mean that her guests are not comfortable, not enjoying themselves. A chorus of babble and laughter is the sound of a good party. Even two or three women, getting together for a social occasion, will allow few lulls in their talk. Some women are virtually addicted to talk. In their homes, they keep right on talking whether other family members are listening or not. They chat incessantly with friends on the telephone. When alone, they will even turn on radio or television just for the illusion of an answering voice. They believe that silence is a sign of displeasure; to refuse to speak to someone is an insult. They express friendly intentions by saying "I'll talk to you again soon," or "Let's get together and sit down for a nice long talk."

But there can be such a thing as too much talk. Though most women keep up conversations without perceptible difficulty, it does use a certain amount of emotional energy. Talk can be taxing even when it seems effortless. The constant talker drains her inner resources without realizing it.

One of the functions of a spirituality meeting is to teach women that they can turn off the stream of talk sometimes and still feel at ease with one another. After a little practice they might even find that being silent together is more relaxing and reassuring than talking together. A period of silent meditation in the circle can help establish a sense of peace, centeredness, and group focus.

It's a good idea to begin each session with five or ten minutes—whatever length of time feels right—of silent being-together. This tends to settle everyone down and intensify awareness of the place, the other people, and one's own inner feelings.

During silent meditation, trivial cares of the day begin to recede from consciousness. Each participant can relax into what is, for many women, a fairly unusual state of mind: knowing that the moment holds no interpersonal obligations at all, not even the implied obligation to hold up your end of a conversation. No one expects anything of you. You can just breathe, and be.

When a group of women tries this for the first time, some may feel uncomfortable. A few may feel constrained to break the silence with nervous remarks or giggles. It's not easy to break the habits of a lifetime, and some habits demand small talk as a way of relating. But this constraint will pass. After a few sessions, even the most dedicated talkers may find themselves looking forward to these moments of being quiet in the presence of others. Sometimes it helps if the group will try to breathe in unison, or if participants close their eyes. Sooner or later, all will discover the soothing quality of collective silence. By not speaking, each woman says to the others, You don't have to perform for me. I accept you as you are.

When the time comes to break the silence, one person may begin quietly humming, singing, or slowly intoning the ancient sacred syllable Om (Aum). The others can join in. No words or harmonies are needed. A mere vocal drone, emptying the lungs, is enough. The sound might grow gradually into a great shout, or it might stay low-key, like a collective moan. Sometimes it feels good to join hands around the circle and slowly raise the arms while the sounds are made. The important thing is that each person begin making a sound whenever she feels ready, go on making any sort of sound she likes, and let her sound die away slowly when it pleases her to do so. All this may be done sitting or standing, keeping still, swaying, or otherwise moving around the circle if movement seems to be called for.

The important lesson to be learned from silence or from inarticulate sounds is that no one will be expected to keep up social appearances. No one has to behave like a good hostess or a good guest. No one has to be "on stage," meeting certain standards of performance in order to be accepted by the others. It is permissible to be self-centered for a change, instead of worrying about social responses. The only obligation any one person has to the presence of others is to refrain from judging them adversely.

It's amazing what a refreshing revelation this can be for some women, especially the ones who think people will not like them if they allow the conversation to lapse.

Centering

A short period of silence at the beginning of a ritual meeting is a good time for each participant to practice the inner readjustment known as centering. This is especially important for women, who tend to lead other-directed lives in which they must constantly place the needs of others ahead of their own needs. Centering is a way of calling one's perceptions and powers back into their home within the self, where they can be used to enhance personal creative thoughts and responses.

There are many methods of centering. Different individuals choose different methods. A simple, basic procedure is to close the eyes and concentrate on a point somewhere within the actual body: deep in the pelvis, perhaps, or in the solar plexus just below the breastbone, or in the geometrical center of the head. Some people may prefer to keep their eyes open and concentrate on some external point, such as a candle flame, or an upper corner of the room. Some like to focus on the various glints and reflections within a transparent crystal. A comfortable, cross-legged sitting position seems to suit most people.

A good way to start the process is to find the pulse, either in the wrist or in the carotid artery of the neck. Feel the pulse until the heart's rhythm is well in mind. Then begin slow breathing, determined by the heartbeat. Inhale for six beats, hold for three beats, exhale for six beats, hold for three beats, and repeat. The pattern may seem hard to control at first, but after several minutes it becomes so easy that the breaths can be lengthened to four beats each, or even longer. Moreover, there is a synergistic effect on the heartbeat itself. It slows down. All body processes tend to relax slightly but perceptibly, in response to deliberate, conscious slowing of the breath. One also becomes more aware of the heart's rhythm. As the slow breathing continues, most people find that they can feel the heart's "inner dance of life" without feeling a pulse with their fingers.

During centering, one person may lead or read a guided meditation such as the following:

"As you slowly breathe in and out, each time a breath goes out of the body send away with it another portion of physical or mental tension. Send away worries, preoccupations, reminders, duties. Gradually exhale everything that bothers you, everything that tightens your muscles or nerves. Breathe it out and let it go.

"Visualize your own internal structure as a spiral pathway to a small, bright light in the center. Each time you breathe in, the light spreads outward a little more along the spiral pathway. Illumination grows with each breath, expelling the darkness. Soon the light will permeate your whole being. Imagine yourself afloat in light, partaking of the quality of light, becoming both the source and the essence of light.

"See your inner self bathed in a pure white light, or if you prefer, in luminous rainbows of multicolored light. Allow yourself to become engrossed in images of light. Let the light fill all parts of your spirit just as your blood fills all parts of your body, being directed by your heart, which is in turn connected to your breath."

Upon a prearranged signal (perhaps a gong stroke or a chime), participants may try breathing together with the help of a simple traditional chant. On the first exhalation, all together intone the Sanskrit version of the primal word, or "mother of mantras" (*matrikamantra*), that is, the Goddess's word *om:* Ooooo-ohhh-mmmmm. On the second exhalation, all together articulate "I am": Iiiiiiii-aaammmmmmm. The group may go on breathing out alternately "Om" and "I am" for as long as it feels satisfactory. The tradition for this is many thousands of years old, and is viewed by oriental sages as a common expression of the divinity within the self.

Invocation

According to Wiccan precedents, it has become more or less customary for women's groups to invoke the elements as the first standardized ritual of each meeting. This doesn't mean the real elements (such as hydrogen, oxygen, phosphorus, iron, sulfur, carbon, and so on through the whole Periodic Table). It means the four classical pseudoelements that ancient people everywhere in the world used to consider the universal building blocks of matter: earth, water, fire, and air.

Why such an invocation? Why should women, seeking hidden truths about themselves and their society, refer back to archaic false views of the real world?

An answer lies in the original thought behind the concept of these four ancient pseudoelements. Though it has been largely forgotten, this original thought is still valid today in a metaphorical sense, just as it was thousands of years ago.

The four elements of antiquity were chosen for the one function that they have in common, as perceived by humans. Each represents a traditional way of disposing of the dead. People could be buried in the earth, set adrift on the waters, cremated by fire, or exposed to carrion birds of air, in the manner of the Parsees or Native Americans. Unless the culture condoned cannibalism, these were the only possible methods of dealing with a corpse. In each case, returning the dead to an "element" symbolized the return to the universal womb for later rebirth. Our Neolithic ancestors everywhere believed that they would be literally born again, out of the same matrix that received them after death. Since any reincarnation—birth or rebirth—depended on the miracle of maternity, funeral ceremonies nearly always referred to the chosen element as a uterine Mother spirit.

The dead were envisioned as living within the universal womb, waiting their chance to enter a new human mother. Spirits-in-waiting thus became "elementals," which used to mean ancestors. They had gone into the environment, to become part of it. The environment was therefore a collective living entity, the personified Great Mother who was of one substance with all her children.

In our own century there are still many peoples, such as Native Americans, who have preserved some beautiful expressions of this reincarnation idea that once made the mother-planet Earth and all her living children an almost seamless whole—constantly changing individual forms, but identical in essence. The environment was respected because it was thought vastly sentient, filled with the souls of the deceased (human or animal), as well as the spirit of the Mother herself. The whole planet was personified as the Goddess whose bones were rocks, whose flesh was fertile soil, whose breath was life-giving atmosphere, whose vital heat was fire, whose uterine blood made the "living waters" (the primordial idea behind baptismal rebirth in water), and who was forever birthing new forms and taking the old ones back into her substance. To offend, pollute, or heedlessly exploit any part of this vast entity would have been unthinkable according to prepatriarchal systems of morality. Even the classical gods of patriarchal Hellenic Greece were subject to her. She was Gaea who mothered them all and whose invoked name held them to their promises absolutely and without any possibility of deception.

Whatever our modern philosophy, we can all relate positively to the still reasonably familiar concept of Mother Earth, Mother Nature, the beauty and power of the natural world, the mysteries of the cosmos that only an intense human hubris could ever pretend to know. This is the valid meaning of "elemental" invocation for women of today. It is a reference to the primordial holistic attitudes that were lost when patriarchy began to divide the world into We and They, spirit and matter, soulful "man" and soulless "brute creation," the latter existing only to be used by the former.

To honor the elements in this symbolic form is not wholly invalid from a scientific viewpoint, either. Everything that lives and dies really does become dissolved into its constituent atoms. Everything organic or inorganic is constantly reabsorbed in the cosmic cauldron, created and recreated from the same mix of atoms. In a sense, then, it is true that all our forebears and all the cultures of the past remain physically with us as part of the living environment, just as the flesh of animals and plants that we eat will become ourselves for a while, and eventually will return to the earth again to rejoin the perpetual molecular exchange. Our ancestors evolved concepts of the endless, timeless, cyclic dance of ongoing creation, an eternal shuffling of elements wherein life forms appear and disappear, each according to its allotted span. Our ancestors (or ancestresses) were wrong in detail but not in essence. This "archaic" view actually has more scientific validity today than the crude myths of a one-shot creation and a universal doomsday that Europe's patriarchy inherited from Zoroastrian Persia.

Invocation of the elements, then, is a reminder of all who have gone before us, with their collective hopes, dreams, failures, and accomplishments: a vast mental image to be condensed into a single fourfold symbol. One of the usual ways to ritualize this sense of vast times and spaces is to relate each pseudoelement to one of the four directions, which have always been identified with the four winds, the four "corners" of the earth, the four guardian spirits, the four quarters of the year with their equinoctial and solstitial festivals, the four seasons, the four ages of civilization and of each individual, the four primary colors, the four bodily "humors," the four suits of the Tarot, and so on through many other quaternary concepts. Some said the Goddess, like the Native American image of Spider Woman, initiated creation by spinning her two threads to cross at the world's center, thus dividing all things into quarters. Ancient cities were laid out on this same plan, which is why various districts of cities are still called quarters whether they are so or not.

Different traditions assign different elements to the directions. Earth is usually but not always placed in the north. Air is usually but not always in the east. Fire and water seem to alternate between west and south. The Tantric tradition, stemming from India with its southern ocean, assigned the south to water, the western sunset land to fire. The suits of the tarot cards had roots in the Tantric worldview and were supposed to represent the elements, whose mingling was mirrored by shuffling the deck. The suit of cups stood for water, wands for fire, pentacles for earth, and swords for air. In ordinary playing cards, the modern descendants of the Tarot, hearts correspond with cups, clubs with wands, diamonds with pentacles, and spades with swords. Some women's groups use card suits to mark off the borders of their ritual space, according to this system.

In deference to the tradition that sisterhood should be non-hierarchical, four different people may choose to invoke the four directions or elements in turn. Or a single person may walk around the outside of the circle to face all four directions, one at a time; at the next meeting a different person does it.

Some material symbol of each element may be held up for contemplation with the appropriate invocation. For instance, earth can be represented by a potted plant, a clay vessel, a pentacle, a stone, a sculpted figure, a handful of soil, or anything else that seems appropriate. Water is usually a cup containing plain or salted water. Fire is a burning candle, a lamp, or a wand representing the torch of enlightenment. Air might be a bird's feather, a fan, a pinwheel, a balloon, a bit of thistledown, or the ritual knife that echoes the tarot sword.

There is no fixed rule about which direction should begin, or which way the invocation should pass around the circle, though the usual progress is counterclockwise. That is the lunar, "widdershins" direction typical of the pre-Christian Old Religions of Europe. Invocation customs are developed according to the needs and desires of each group, so there can be no formulae—only guidelines.

A specific example might go something like this. The woman who chooses to represent earth may take her symbolic object and stand outside the circle in the northern quarter, facing either in or out, and say: "I call upon the Goddess (or spirit, or power) of the North, golden spirit of earth and creation, principle of fertility, power of regeneration and renewal. Help us to be mindful of the Earth our Mother, to heal her wounds, to live in peace together as her children. Help us to understand the processes of life and death, seedtime and harvest. Be with us and bless our circle. Blessed be." Other participants then echo: "Blessed be."

The woman choosing to represent water may then take her cup to the southern quarter, and speak to this effect: "I call upon the Goddess (spirit, power) of the South, blue spirit of water and of birth, the principle of love that sustains all things, giving and flowing throughout our bodies and throughout the living world. Help us to give and receive, help us feel the ebb and flow of nature, help us to sustain and be sustained. Be with us and bless our circle. Blessed be." All echo: "Blessed be."

Next, the woman choosing to represent fire might take her candle or other symbol to the western quarter and say: "I call upon the Goddess (spirit, power) of the West, red spirit of fire and passion, blood and wine, sexuality and vital heat, driving forces of the id, powers of aspiration, ambition, ecstasy, warmth, and joy. Help us to control and direct our emotions to creative ends. Help us to live more fully. Warm our hearts and our hearths. Be with us and bless our circle. Blessed be." All echo: "Blessed be."

The last woman, choosing to represent air, might take her symbol to the eastern quarter and say: "I call upon the Goddess (spirit, power) of the East, white spirit of winter, recession, suspension, and contemplation, the wise and ageless Crone, who knows the mysteries of eternity. Help us to breathe freely, to drink the winds and yet find the still center. Help us to know liberation. Help us to perceive with crystalline clarity what we need to know. Help us to think swiftly and see without distortion. Be with us and bless our circle. Blessed be." All echo: "Blessed be."

Finally the central altar can be invoked and consecrated as a temporary symbolic meeting place of all these elements. Each person in the circle may speak a few words about it in turn, or may take this time to place on it some personal talisman to remain there for the duration of the meeting. The center is the personal space for each participant, and for all collectively. Eyes will be focused throughout the meeting upon the group of lighted candles, the flowers, the ornaments, or the personal objects that group members have brought to share with one another. The center draws all gazes together, symbolizing the meeting of the minds of all those present.

The foregoing are sample invocational speeches and actions. They are by no means intended for memorization or literal repetition. They are only to give beginners an idea of the sort of thoughts an invocation might call up. As different people express their ideas of what they would like the group to think about, the same group might do a different kind of invocation with each meeting.

During the invocation, group members may stand around the altar and turn, individually, to face each direction as it is greeted. In some groups, it is customary to extend the right hand in each direction, pointing either with the first two fingers, or with a personal ritual tool such as a wand or knife (athame). For invocation of the center, the arms may be crossed over the breast in the "Egyptian" manner, as shown by ancient Egyptian deities holding their symbolic scepter and flail. Members may wish to hold the knife in the right hand, the wand in the left, when in this position (see "Tools," pages 142–48).

An important traditional symbol of the fivefold invocation is the pentacle, long associated with Goddess worship, and for that reason often condemned officially by pejorative names such as devil's cross, goblin's foot, or witch star. The pentacle is simply a classic five-pointed star formed by a continuous interlocking line. Five is a traditional female number, and continuous-line figures were once believed to lock out evil influences. Some people suggest that the Christian custom of crossing one's self was originally copied from the pagans who traced a pentacle on head, arms, and breast as a charm of self-protection.

If the points of the star are numbered clockwise from the top, 1, 2, 3, 4, 5, then the interlocking line passes from 1 to 3 to 5 to 2 to 4, and back up to 1.

The invocation of the center can be elegantly enacted by each pair of the four callers (north-south, then east-west), facing each other across the central altar and simultaneously tracing two

opposite pentacles in the air, back to back. If wands or athames are used for this, the effect is even better.

Both persons begin at the top (position 1), pointing their fingers or tools together, then continue to trace their pentacles in unison but in opposite directions, as happens naturally when participants are facing each other, and both begin by pointing downward to the right. Such imaginary pentacles drawn in the air at arm's length usually appear to be about a yard in diameter.

Another way of drawing the pentacle resembles the Catholic gesture of crossing one's self—for the good reason that the early church copied this gesture from pagan religions in the first place. As performed today, the official 'sign of the cross" simply repeats the ancient figure 4, "sign of Hermes," taken from Neoplatonic or Gnostic worshipers of Hermes as the Logos-god, some sixteen hundred years ago. At the time, the female consort of Hermes was the Goddess of Crossroads and of the underworld, Hecate, who was later diabolized as a queen of witches. Hecate's sacred number was 5 as opposed to the Hermetic 4. Her sign was a pentacle. Presumably her female worshipers crossed themselves with the pentacle, which is why medieval clergymen insisted on calling it the Witches' Cross.

This feminine version of self-blessing is done as follows: With the right hand, touch forehead, left breast, right shoulder, left shoulder, right breast, and forehead again to complete the pentacle. Participants may perform this gesture in unison with a chant, such as: "To my Goddess I dedicate mind, heart, action, support, will, and the soul that combines them."

Expression of invocational ideas, keyed to elemental symbols, calls group attention to collective goals. Freedom and flexibility in procedure are important to women, many of whom have been trained to listen to formalized liturgical speeches by male religious authorities, intoned before audiences who don't participate except for brief formal responses. For women's groups, general participation and consensus can make a vital difference. In a circle, no one assumes a leader's position. Each woman by herself is a high priestess and a living representative of feminine divine energy.

To invoke this awareness—by any means that comes to hand—is an excellent reason for establishing a women's spirituality group in the first place.

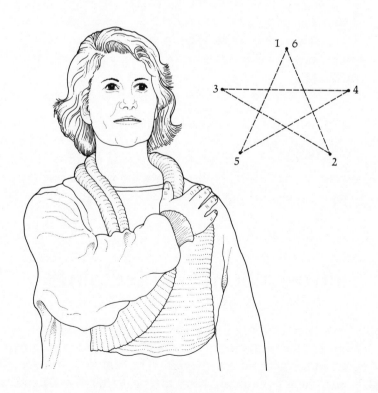

Another kind of invocation is customary at the very end of a ritual meeting, to close the formal portion of the proceedings. The same people who addressed the elements in the beginning might address them again at the end, this time not calling them into the circle, but rather thanking them and bidding them farewell. Other group members stand and face the directions, as before. Alternatively, one or two people may walk around the circle, making protective pentacle signs in the air as a wish-symbol for everyone's safety and health.

One of the most pleasing ceremonies for closing is a traditional "fairy" chant that invokes the Goddess by way of the four elements. All members join hands around the circle and recite in unison; or, if some don't know the words, one person may speak a line at a time, and the others repeat:

> By the earth that is Her body,
> By the air that is Her breath,
> By the fire that is Her bright spirit,
> By the living waters of Her womb,
> The circle is open, but unbroken.
> The peace of the Goddess go in our hearts.
> Merry meet, and merry part, and merry meet again.
> Blessed be.

It's usual to raise all the joined hands high in the air while speaking the final "Blessed be." This gesture is sometimes called "building the Temple." As a natural expression of communal feeling, it almost always elicits smiles. Participants who feel particularly *en rapport* after this may want to finish with hugs all round.

Introductions and Blessings

When a circle contains newcomers, or people unknown to each other, introductions are needed. The simplest introduction ritual is for each woman in turn to speak her own name, all around the circle. To fix the names more firmly, the entire group may repeat each name in chorus after its owner has spoken it. The group may repeat each name three times, or may add a few words such as "Welcome, dear sister," or something similar. An elegant way of doing the introduction is for each woman to *sing* her own name, making a few tuneful notes at random from its syllables; then the entire group repeats the same little name-song.

An introduction technique combined with unification of the group is the round-robin blessing, which may be used at every meeting whether newcomers are present or not. It's nice to have a special goblet or chalice for this purpose. This cup may be filled with rose water, seawater, springwater, or plain tap water with any desired additive: salt, herbs, a crystal, a few drops of perfume, a flower, or a bit of vegetable coloring to suit a seasonal color theme.

If participants are all known to each other, vessel and blessing both pass counterclockwise (widdershins, moonwise). The first woman takes the cup, dips her finger in it, and with her wet finger traces a crescent moon on the forehead of her neighbor to her right, saying, "I bless you, Helen (or whoever), you are Goddess." She then hands the cup to Helen, who turns and blesses *her* right-hand neighbor in the same way, and so on around the circle, until each woman has been blessed by her left-hand neighbor and the cup returns to its starting place.

If participants are not all known to each other, the vessel passes counterclockwise while the blessing is retrograde, so as to serve as an introduction. The first woman takes the cup, dips her finger in it, and with her wet finger traces a crescent moon on the forehead of her neighbor to her left, saying, "I, Carol, bless you, Diane, you are Goddess." Then she hands the cup to Helen on her right, who says, "I, Helen, bless you, Carol, you are Goddess." Then Helen hands the cup on to her right-hand neighbor, who proceeds to speak her own name and bless Helen in the same way, and so on around the circle, until each woman has been blessed by her right-hand neighbor and the cup returns to its starting place. With this system, the first woman needs to know only one name beforehand, that of her left-hand neighbor. All other names are learned along the way.

The repetition system may be combined with the blessing, so that each name is repeated by the entire group as its owner is blessed. The woman herself may repeat her own name in a self blessing, such as, "I am Diane; I am Goddess." Then the group can echo this. There are many ways of opening a meeting with recognition and group acknowledgment of all participants, and these pleasant rituals should be preserved. After all, one of the best features of women's circles (in contrast to men's churches) is that no one remains anonymous and all are made welcome in and as their individual selves.

There are good reasons for the use of the word Goddess in these blessings. Though many people today envision divinity (if they envision it at all) as either androgynous or sexless "spirit," the fact remains that *god* is a masculine noun, which has always carried exclusively male connotations. Man, not woman, created his God in his own image. Those who contend that each human being contains a spark of divinity might still describe that spark as God, which implies that the spark is masculine, by dictionary definition, even within a woman.

To change the word to Goddess is thus more than a mere quibble. It means a fundamentally altered attitude toward the feminine principle: an attitude harking back to those ancient times when the Divine Female seemed just as real as, and even more powerful than, her male consort. Her priestesses were often believed to possess—or to be possessed by—the Goddess's spirit, in the same sense that prophets or saviors possessed the spirit of God. Leading priestesses often assumed the Goddess's name and persona, so that their actions were transcribed into myth and folklore as actions of the Goddess herself.

Moreover the divine spark within each woman was perceived as distinctly female. Romans called this spark every woman's *juno*, corresponding to a man's *genius*. The latter term is still with us, of course, although patriarchal society has forced the former term into oblivion.

For any woman to recognize herself or another woman as Goddess is to state that femininity is as honorable, as holy, and as worthy of recognition as any deity made in the image of man; and that this quality dwells in all ages, sizes, colors, and shapes of women. When a woman cites the Goddess image, it subtly changes her perception of herself and her neighbor. The change is eminently useful to a ritual group, because it implies a sense of the numinous in every woman—a sense that western patriarchy usually denied. It sets her free to act as her own priestess and

spiritual agent, needing no male intermediary. This is a fundamental tenet of women's ritual procedures.

CHANT

(To be sung or spoken repetitively, a number of times over, after
the blessings have gone all the way around)

> I am the Mother's daughter,
> She knows me.
> We have met our Goddess,
> We are she.

Smudging

Smudging is the delineation of a sacred space by some kind
of sweet-smelling smoke. Native Americans used tobacco, offering their lighted ritual pipe to each of the four directions in turn,
then upward to Father Sky, then downward to Mother Earth. Old
Testament priests cooked meat on their altars, for a "sweet savor"
and "an offering made by fire unto the Lord" (Exod. 29:25),
believing along with their pagan contemporaries that gods were
attracted by the odors of roasting flesh and actually lived on the
airy essence that rose into the air with the smoke. It was also a
universal custom to attract the attention of deities with other
sweet smells: perfumes, incense, burning spices. Burnt essences of
all kinds were used throughout the Middle Ages to cover the less
attractive smells of unwashed bodies and of careless housekeep-
ing in churches. Thus it has long been believed that sweet-
smelling smoke "purifies" the space. This is the principle that
underlies smudging.

As it is practiced today in women's circles, smudging means
passing around a small vessel of smoking incense or fragrant
herbs, so that each participant may cense herself. She may draw

the smoke over her head, or pass her hands through it, or pass the vessel around her body, or breathe in the scent, or all of these. The burning material may be commercial incense or home-grown herbs, dried and ignited. Sage makes an especially pleasant smoke. To light a smudge, allow the material to burn briskly for a few seconds, then gently blow out its flame, so that it continues to glow and produce a column of smoke.

Smudging may be done at any point during opening ceremonies, or it may be used to scent the environment. One woman may carry the smudging vessel around the space, offering it to each other woman for censing as she passes by. Vessels should be suitably fireproof and made of nature-symbolic materials such as earthenware, shell, or hollowed stone. Test the vessel to be sure that it will not become too hot to hold.

The Talking Stick

Some women's groups have adopted the useful Native American custom of the talking stick. During powwows, the sacred stick or rattle was passed around the circle. Only the person holding this object was allowed to speak. Everyone took a turn as the stick was passed from hand to hand. In this way, each person had a chance to say whatever was on his or her mind, and to speak without interruption until finished. Those not holding the stick could practice silent restraint, and marshal their thoughts for orderly presentation when their turn came around again.

The talking stick is especially good for those group members who might be too retiring to speak at all, or who find it hard to break into a lively conversation among others more accustomed to dominating the the talk. Quiet individuals often have a lot to say when handed the talking stick—and with it the undivided attention of the whole group. Habitual interrupters may find the discipline of the talking stick difficult at first, but certainly it can only improve their conversational skills; for the knack of patient listening is one of the best of social graces.

It helps a group to have one particular object to use as a talking stick at all meetings. The object can be literally a stick: an interesting piece of driftwood, a natural branch, a carving, a wand, a pestle, a rolling pin, or a rod specifically created and decorated for the purpose. It can be a length of broomstick or dowel on which each member has cut her own notch or painted her own stripe. It can be anything else as well: a stone, a crystal, a shell, a paperweight, a Goddess statuette, a rattle, a drum, a bowl, a knife (preferably sheathed), an ornament, a doll, or a stuffed animal. It can be anything, but it should be something fairly durable. A flower, for example, wouldn't do. Ideally the talking stick should be something esthetically attractive, nicely balanced for holding in the hand, neither too large nor too small, neither too light nor too heavy. It should be pleasing to the touch, because women like to play with the stick while they speak, turning it over in their hands, absently stroking or fingering it. This seems to help the thought process.

The talking stick can be kept in the custody of one member, who then becomes responsible for bringing it to meetings; or it can be kept in a special place along with other group tools, available to all. It should not be anything intrinsically valuable if it is kept in a more or less public place.

Some meetings can consist almost entirely of talking-stick talk, especially those meetings where women exchange ideas about their goals, troubles, hopes, and fears, or discuss what they expect to be the group's place in their lives. The holder of the talking stick may say anything she wants. She can share a favorite poem, review a book, present a philosophical idea, relate a dream, or talk about a recent insight or daily experience. She can tell about her summer vacation. She can describe a situation that needs resolving. She can express feelings of frustration or anger, happiness or pleasure. She can talk as if to herself. Listeners should wear expressions of sympathy and attention, and should refrain from criticizing what anyone chooses to say.

Possession of the talking stick doesn't mean one is forced to speak, however. If a woman feels that she has nothing to say when the stick comes to her, she simply passes it on silently to the next person. When everyone has spoken as many times as she wishes, and the stick has gone once around in silence, then it is time to lay the talking stick aside and pass on to other observances. Sometimes, during talking-stick sessions, one woman will suggest a ritual that she would like to try, and the group may drop everything else and try it, forthwith.

The talking stick does not work well for a group of more than about fifteen women, simply because it takes too long to go around. Larger groups could be divided into smaller circles for the purpose of using the talking stick, and each circle could have its own individual stick. This works best if a particular project or topic of discussion has been designated, so that the subgroups can later rejoin the whole circle and share their group conclusions with the entire gathering. Another good way to handle the problem of a large group is to pass the talking stick all the way around just once, allowing each person a chance to speak of her current aims, feelings, or outlook, or perhaps to express her perception of the group's present or future directions and goals.

Use of the talking stick should always be as free as possible, without restriction of any speaker's subject matter. Once in a while, a group may include a compulsive talker who keeps the stick too long and chatters on until everyone else is virtually anesthetized with ennui. The only way to deal with this is to set time limits, with a clock or egg timer. However, such artificial restrictions are to be avoided unless there is no alternative.

Show-and-Tell

Most of us played the childish game of show-and-tell in grammar school. We took favorite toys or other objects to class, and described them at the teacher's command. The adult show-and-tell game is superficially similar but considerably more meaningful.

Women bring objects to their spirituality group meetings and describe them voluntarily, not by anyone's command. They are things women want to display and share. Usually they are personal treasures, with unique histories and specific memories.

Women generally find each other's personal treasures fascinating. People reveal significant parts of their personalities in showing the things they love and telling why they love them; and women are nearly always interested in personality configurations. Some groups find the show-and-tell game so intriguing that they play it at almost every meeting.

As a rule, the objects rest on or near the altar, thus generating visual appeal at the focal point of the circle. For example, among the common show-and-tell articles are crystals of quartz and other minerals. A number of sparkling crystals arranged among the candles can create a very attractive altar.

Other commonly used articles include the following. Jewelry: especially antique or heirloom jewelry passed down through the owner's family or acquired for special occasions. Natural objects: stones, twigs, pine cones, acorns, roots, seeds, flowers, leaves, shells, gourds, feathers, driftwood. Things inherited from relatives: a grandmother's thimble, a great-grandfather's watch fob, a great-aunt's good luck charm. Things made by one's children. Things made by oneself: drawings, poetry, beadwork, needlework, pottery, woodcarvings, and other crafts. Favorite tarot cards. Figurines. Photographs. Dolls and other toys. Love gifts. Mementoes of journeys: sand from the Sahara, water from the Ganges, a pebble from the Athens acropolis. Household ornaments of special connotations. Interesting items from any kind of a personal collection.

It is usually understood that a show-and-tell item may be passed around the circle for everyone to feel and handle, unless the owner specifically asks that it not be touched. If the hands-off request is made, it is always honored.

An object chosen for show-and-tell becomes doubly meaningful to its owner. First, it brings to the communal altar the owner's own feelings for it, adding emotional or esthetic overtones to the physical focus of the meeting. Second, it carries away new overtones as a result of having rested on the altar and having been appreciatively shared. Afterward the owner can remember that it served as an altarpiece, and that her spiritual sisters concentrated on it, handled it, and blessed it with sympathetic attention. It becomes sacralized. I know several enthusiastic collectors of crystals who habitually carry each new acquisition to a spirituality meeting, not only to share their own pleasure and interest, but also so each crystal can be exposed to the combined and focused energies of a woman's altar.

Perhaps the best kind of show-and-tell item is one sufficiently unusual so that information about it will add to everyone's general background knowledge. The owner should try to identify the item as closely as possible. If it is a shell, for example, find out what kind of shell it is, what kind of animal inhabits it, and where it is found. Leaves, flowers, and other natural objects should always be identified. Antique objects should be dated if possible, and any available information about them should be explained. Thus, like the schoolroom version of show-and-tell, the adult version too can enhance knowledge. A ruby ring is interesting when the owner says it was a gift from her grandfather to her grandmother; but it is even more interesting when she explains that ruby is the red variety of the mineral corundum, and all other colors of gem corundum are called sapphire.

Finally, let it be emphasized again that there should not be anything compulsory about show-and-tell. Some people might prefer to be an audience rather than one who shows and tells. Some might want to bring to the altar just a simple handful of daisies in a jelly jar, saying nothing about it. Whatever one wants to do—let it be.

If a special time is set aside for the show-and-tell part of the meeting, it's pleasant to round off that time with a descriptive summing up of all the objects that have appeared, imaginatively relating them to each other. Remarkable correspondences of choice will sometimes appear, or interrelationships will be found that seem to reflect significant ideas for the group. This exercise can be a lot of fun, too. A brief show-and-tell session at each meeting can enhance good understanding among members, provide "omens," consecrate personal possessions, foster mutual learning, teaching, and communication, and keep up members' personal interest in one another.

At the end of a show-and-tell session, participants may join hands and salute all the objects together with a brief chant:

CHANT

Hail, my creature,
Hail, my treasure,
Greet my sisters,
Bring them pleasure.

About Plants

Most women enjoy flowers. Nearly always, someone voluntarily brings a few garden flowers to grace the altar at a meeting. Characteristic blooms appear in the spring, summer, and fall seasons. Winter altars may feature pine cones, dried arrangements, mistletoe, or sprigs of holly. This last is particularly appropriate for women's gatherings, because holly used to be sacred to the Norse underground Goddess Holle, or Hel, after whom both the tree and the underworld were named. It was once thought that all humans came from her subterranean womb, and returned thence after death; the holly's red berries represented the sacred, life-giving, child-forming uterine blood that she gave to all women.

Though we may think garden flowers the most decorative items in the plant kingdom (or queendom), we might remember that Nature doesn't favor them over any other plant. Nature doesn't deal in comparative standards of beauty. We can learn from a new consciousness of Nature that any growing thing has its own esthetic qualities. Elegant hothouse hybrids are lovely; but wildflowers, herbs, and weeds can supply a gathering with a sense of the green world of Nature just as well.

Fallen autumn leaves can be as colorful as roses. The joy of spring can be represented by willow catkins or onion grass as well as by crocuses. Florists sell flowers for fat prices, but Mother Nature's woods and fields provide beauty for free: dandelions, violets, buttercups, asters, cornflowers, Queen Anne's lace, daisies, clovers, and infinite varieties of pretty leaves.

Women with special fondness for herbs and plants may want to devote a whole meeting to exchanging information, specimens, seeds, recipes, gardening hints, herb teas, books, and pamphlets. Someone might do some research on healing herbs, both the ones that really work and the ones that enjoy undeserved reputations. Such information is always useful.

One way to commemorate a meeting about plants is to create group sachets. Each member contributes her choice of sweet herbs (lavender, thyme, sage, and so on), fresh or dried flower petals, citrus rind, or other naturally scented material for a potpourri, plus a small piece of cloth and a string to tie it up. All ingredients are mixed together in the bowl, then distributed around the circle. A portion is tied into each individual cloth for a sachet.

Some groups like to have something of a natural vegetable nature on the altar at every meeting. It can be very simple: a handful of grass, a scatter of petals, a weed from a sidewalk crack, a sprig from any hedge, bush, or tree. When Earth or Nature is personified as the Goddess whose body mothers every living thing, it's pleasant to contemplate a few samples of her products, to be mindful of the constant miracle of ongoing life.

CHANT

Green growth, green growth,
Flesh and hair and dress
Of our universal Mother Earth.
O Terra Mater, bless us always
With green growth.

Celebrating Trees

Ancient Europeans revered trees as symbols of the mother-hood principle and the goodness of nature. Our Yule (Christmas) tree is a remnant of their tree worship. They were keenly aware that trees contributed much to human lives: refreshing shade in summer; natural beauty; fruits, nuts, and other foods; materials for protective dwellings; furnishings; tools; boats; vehicles; house-hold articles; and fuel for cooking and warmth. Early civilizations knew their heavy dependence on trees. Modern civilizations also depend heavily on trees, but often fail to recognize the fact.

Unlike moderns, the ancients consciously honored the essen-tial contributions of trees to human survival. In the Middle East, India, and Egypt, the Great Goddess herself often appeared as a tree. People generally regarded trees as maternal deities or forest spirits, to be respected even when their lives were sacrificed for human use (pagan woodcutters never felled a tree without first begging its forgiveness). Female tree spirits lived on in myth and folklore as dryads, the Greek version of the tree-worshiping druid priestesses.

Today, when the world's few remaining forests are being ruthlessly destroyed, we need more than ever to redevelop some of the ancient reverence for trees. A tree ceremony helps to raise consciousness of the vital importance of trees and the holiness of their prepatriarchal connotations.

For a tree ceremony it is best to choose a private outdoor space with flat ground surrounding a sizable freestanding tree. First, the group may form a "fairy ring" by sitting in a meditation circle around the tree. When she feels ready, each woman in turn stands up, goes to the tree, and puts her arms around its trunk, hugging it in silence for as long as she wishes. When all have tak-en a turn at hugging the tree, they share their feelings about it. The group may pass around a talking stick made of one of the tree's own fallen twigs, a scrap of loose bark, or other arboreal debris.

After each one has spoken in honor of the tree, all join hands, rise, and dance widdershins (counterclockwise) around the tree, to the accompaniment of a chant:

> Hail, Forest Mother,
> Beautiful tree,
> Gracious protectress,
> We honor thee.

After the dance, the circle may contract and converge on the tree, so that all may hug it together, either continuing the chant or simply humming. Then the group may sit in a tighter circle around the tree, either facing it or placing their backs to it, and again speak in turn of their feelings about this particular tree or about trees in general. A star formation works well for this: Let each woman sit with her back to the tree and extend her legs, so that each foot touches the neighbor's foot. This formation may be held for another meditation period.

Before bidding farewell to the tree, group members may each pick a single leaf from its branches or from the ground, to take home and press. The event can be commemorated by a ribbon left tied around the trunk, or by a circle of pebbles or other tokens left on the ground around it—but *not* by any symbols cut into the bark, which is an injury and a desecration.

The ceremony of celebrating a mature tree may be followed by the planting of a young tree, which is similarly honored and encouraged by ritual.

Some groups may have the opportunity to use the same special tree for seasonal festivals, marking its times of budding, leafing, fall color change, and winter dormancy.

The Bowl

Some groups regularly use a special ceremonial bowl or similar vessel, approximating the temple basin that the ancient Egyptians called *shi*, copied by biblical writers as the brass "sea" in Solomon's temple (1 Kings 7:23–26). Such vessels were filled with water for lustrations, baptisms, and ritual purifications of all kinds. They were the pagan forerunners of the Christian holy-water font. Like these forerunners, the font still represents a womb, although the patriarchal church deliberately underemphasized this archaic feminine symbolism. The font is specifically referred to as the womb of Mary, "fecundated by sacred fire" when the phallic paschal candle is plunged into it.

However, in ancient matriarchal temples, the womb-vessel had its own inherent fertile power. Its holy waters were considered spiritually revivifying in and of themselves, because they represented the energy of the birth-giving Goddess. The bowl filled with water or other fluid has symbolized the womb and the feminine principle from the earliest ages, when women of primitive village cultures were coiling the first clay pots.

A ceremonial bowl can be made of wood or natural stone or some other nature-emblematic material. Since it stands for the all-producing womb of Mother Earth, it is especially appropriate if handmade of earthenware, preferably by a female potter.

The bowl can hold water, wine, or juice for formal drinking together, each woman dipping her own cup with words of dedication. Conversely each woman may pour water from her cup into the bowl with words of consecration and promise, so the combined waters represent the group's combined intentions. For example, the group may express concern for the natural environment through a bowl ritual. One woman says, "I denounce the hunters and will challenge their right to enter the woodlands," as she pours her water into the bowl. The next says, "I will support community recycling programs," as she pours. The next says, "I will use only organic fertilizers in my garden," as she pours. Another says, "I will never wear a coat made from an animal's skin," as she pours. When all waters and pledges are combined, the water can be poured out on the Earth as a promise to her.

In the same way, the bowl can serve as a receptacle for unwanted qualities or blockages. One woman states that she pours away avarice; another pours away impatience; another pours away weakness or passivity; another pours away her past errors, until each has renounced something that troubles her and poured water into the bowl in token of her renunciation. Then the bowl can be emptied into a "hole of oblivion," or into a toilet, to signify that the unwanted things are flushed out of one's life and a fresh start can be made.

The bowl can also be used for the baptismal sign of new birth, just like the holy waters of the ancient Goddess temples. In memory of the Goddess as "Mistress of Earth and Sea," the bowl can be filled with salt water and sprinkled with herbs. One member of the group can carry it around the circle to each other member in turn, holding it while she blesses herself with the water. Since each woman is her own priestess, no other "officiating" authority is needed. We bless and consecrate ourselves.

CHANT

Holy womb of water,
Vessel of our birth,
Keep us ever mindful
Of our Mother Earth.

The Personal Gift

This ritual is for a group whose members know each other fairly well.

Write the name of each member on a slip of paper. Fold and seal each slip. Put all slips in a chalice. All members draw at random from the chalice, one slip apiece. The slips are opened to make sure no one received her own name. If someone did so, return the slips for another drawing. Keep a record of whose name was drawn by whom, if desired.

For the next meeting, let each person bring a gift for the one whose name she drew. The gift must be created with the giver's own hands, out of materials costing less than one dollar (or any other agreed-upon total), and must express the personality of the recipient, as viewed by the giver, in some meaningful way. When all gifts are presented, each member in turn tells the group her thoughts about creating the gift she gave and her response to the gift she received.

This ritual requires perfect attendance for at least two consecutive meetings. If one member should be absent from the gift-giving session, the gift intended for her can be given to the one who would have received a gift from her, had she been present. But the substitute gift may be in some way inappropriate, so this creates a vacancy in the ritual and every effort should be made to avoid this.

Another kind of gift-giving can be purely imaginary: the giving of *qualities*. Each woman asks herself, "What quality do I have in my own personality that would be useful to X if I could give it to her as a gift?" Each person in turn explains what she would give, and perhaps why. The usefulness of this exercise is twofold. It enables each woman to discover and name aspects of herself that she can respect or admire; for if a quality is good enough to be given as a gift, then it is good. Many woman are taught that the affirmation of their good qualities must come from others instead of from themselves, and so they undervalue themselves. The exercise also enables each woman to feel the support of other women who understand her weaknesses and wish to offer help.

When one member of the group has a birthday, the others might like to prepare small gifts or brief celebratory poems in that member's honor.

Another occasion for personal gift-giving might be made when one member of the group faces some trouble or life crisis, such as ill health. Little gifts like stones, herbs, craft objects, and other mementoes can be passed along to the person in difficulty, after having been blessed on the collective altar and dedicated to the group's wishes for improvement in her circumstances. Often such objects bring real comfort and a better mental outlook because of the affection and trust associated with them.

Group members may wish to exchange gifts from each one to every other one, so that each may have the same assortment of objects to carry about in an amulet bag, as a reminder of all her sisters together. These should be small, light objects, such as seeds, beads, shells, small crystals, locks of hair, miniature pentacles, dollhouse utensils, buttons, and so on. Each group member provides as many identical objects as there are people in the group, and gives one to each. Everyone then has the same collection, which symbolizes the group as a whole.

If a group has money to spend, members may want to purchase identical pieces of jewelry such as rings, pins, or symbolic pendants. But the matter of money should be delicately handled. One of the most refreshing aspects of women's spirituality groups is that it usually costs nothing to belong to one. Those who want or need to save their money should never be pressured to spend it. A significant reason for the very existence of women's groups is that they want to reject the greed and ostentation of male-dominated established religions, with their implied hierarchies of relative wealth.

Therefore gifts involved in ritual giving should be kept modest in regard to dollar value. That's why natural things (which can be gathered for nothing from the woods and fields) or handmade craft items are often preferred. A ring, anonymously manufactured and bought in a jewelry store, may be more valuable but is certainly less expressive of the giver than a ring carefully braided from a lock of her hair!

Let it be kept in mind that the best gifts women can give each other are the gifts of attention, sympathy and caring—that is, the gifts of love, which are too often in short supply although our intensely materialistic society is all too lavish with unneeded luxuries.

CHANT

The Mother is the giver,
We value what she gives.
Her earthen power has given
Life to all that lives.

Weaving Sisterhood

All stand in a circle, spaced two arms' lengths apart, facing inward.

The first leader steps forward, turns right, and walks in front of the person to her right. Then she walks behind the next person, then in front of the next, and so on, weaving in and out of the circle in the widdershins (counterclockwise) direction. When passing in front of someone, she touches that person's forehead with her right hand. When passing behind someone, she touches the back of that person's head with her left hand.

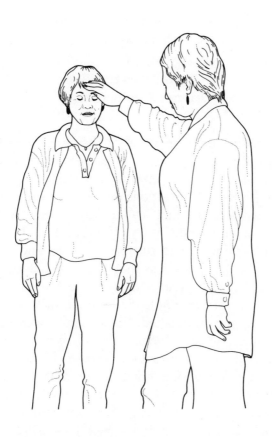

During this progress around the circle, all chant or sing:

> Sisterhood we weave,
> Moonwise go the strands,
> Nightweb we receive,
> Fabric of our hands.

When the leader returns to her place, she turns left and weaves the circle again in the deasil (clockwise) direction, reversing all motions. If she passed in front of the last person on the previous round (the person to her left), she now passes behind that person. If she passed behind on the previous round, she now passes in front. She touches foreheads with her left hand, backs of heads with her right hand.

During this second progress around the circle, all chant or sing:

> Sisterhood we weave,
> Sunwise go the strands,
> Dayweb we receive,
> Fabric of our hands.

If the circle is small, the ritual can be repeated by each participant in turn. If there are too many present to make this feasible, perhaps the ritual may be repeated four times, by four different people who stand in the positions of the four cardinal directions.

As a variation, the first leader may carry a ball of cord or yarn to lay down a pathway on the ground as she goes. Picture the women walking in and out of the circle, and imagine them making a trail with the yarn as they move. The thread will form a wavelike floor pattern, enclosing each person in a lozenge and making a "web" of the whole circle. Ends may be tied together when the weaving is finished. Subsequent "weavers" can step along the same pathway. Finally, threads can be cut in front of each person and the individual pieces taken home to serve as private ritual reminders of sisterhood connections.

Another popular variation of the weaving ritual is the random web. Each participant brings her own skein of yarn or cord. All sit or stand in a circle, and toss the skeins to each other at random across and around the circle. Upon receiving a skein, each woman passes it once behind her body and then sends it on to someone else. As the strands unwind from the skeins, a large free-form web is created gradually in the center of the circle.

A dozen or so two-ounce skeins of ordinary knitting worsted wool used in this manner will create a surprisingly strong web, capable of holding the weight of a human body with ease. Therefore, when all the yarn is used up, the group can experience an exercise of mutual trust and unity by lifting each woman in turn as she lies in the middle of the web, which the others lift above their heads by its edges. The sensation is fascinating for both the lifters and the liftee. It doesn't take too many people to raise the weight of another person easily. It's always surprising to find how light even a heavy person can feel, when many are helping to lift. (If ten lift a 150-pound person, each is really lifting only 15 pounds!) It's also surprising to lie in the middle of such a web and find its apparent fragility transformed into dependable strength.

After the web has been created and used, it can be hung on a wall or bundled up in a solid mass and made into an icon.

Another type of web can be laid out on the floor or ground in the shape of separate spokes of a wheel, like the framework of a

spider's orb web. Each spoke leads from the center to one of the participants, and is pinned down or otherwise fastened at her place. Then all participants can sing a weaving song to accompany a weaving dance. All dance in along the spokes to the center, join hands and circle once around, then return to the outer circumference along the *next* spoke beyond the pathway each woman took originally. In the course of the dance, everyone passes in and then out of the circle as many times as there are spokes, progressing spoke by spoke back to her original position. Here is a chant to accompany this exercise:

> Wheels of time are turning, turning, turning,
> Solar fires are burning, burning, burning,
> Mind of mine is learning, learning, learning,
> In my round of days.

During the course of this weaving dance, each woman may carry her own ball of thread and lay it along the periphery, so as to approximate the wheel formation of the spider's web. It is useful to remember that the Great Goddess of past civilizations was usually depicted as a weaver of the wheel web of fate, and even had several spider incarnations. Her classical name was Arachne and she was one of the aspects of that divine weaver Athene, although the myth as revised by men made them separate rivals. Some believe this story of their rivalry was artificially deduced from an icon that showed the Goddess side by side with her arachnoid weaving form.

The web symbol stood for the Goddess and her consecrated women in antiquity throughout many cultures. This symbolism expressed—and still expresses—the idea that the Goddess is the hub (omphalos) of the universe; and the nearer each individual woman comes to this central mystical revelation, the nearer she comes also to all the others who are simultaneously approaching along their own spokes. Thus the web rather neatly depicts the image of women-together representing Goddess spirit. A hub is a central place where all paths meet. Women alienated from one another are far out on the spokes, unable to make contact. Women conscious of their own divinity, however, have drawn closer to other women and so created that divinity among themselves.

CHANT

We are the web,
We find our center
By coming closer.
The center is our truth.

As a final exercise, participants may gather together at the center of the web and embrace one another by putting their arms around each other's shoulders all the way around the circle. This little tight circle can move to the chant by gently swaying, or else by stepping slowly sideward in the counterclockwise direction.

Self-Expression

This ritual is fun, both for the experienced group and for beginners who may be not yet well acquainted with one another. The prerequisite is a large assortment of artifact materials: colored paper, glue, scissors, wire, string, crayons, markers, clay, plasticene, ribbon, rickrack, yarn, cloth scraps, beads, thread, needles, paint, cards, cardboard, small toys, artificial flowers, real natural objects like leaves, twigs, seeds, stones, shells, herbs, feathers, also costume jewelry, old stockings, aluminum foil, bits of glass or metal, sequins, fringe, and other trimmings. All this is placed in the center of the circle.

First, each participant takes pencil and paper, and writes down the words "I am . . ." In silence, each continues for a paragraph or two, writing her own opinion of her personality, feelings, needs, wants, virtues, faults, interests, relationships, current or past situations, favorite symbols, spiritual identification, how she is perceived—or thinks she is perceived—by others. When all have done this, each in turn reads aloud what she has written, without further comment.

Then each participant takes materials from the assortment in the center of the circle, and constructs an object that seems to express some aspect or aspects of her self. A fair amount of time should be allotted to this, and it should be done with a minimum of talk, no more than "Pass me the red ribbon," or "Are you finished with the scissors?"

No instructions are given as to the type of object to be created, or its size, or its meaning, or its future use, or any other limiting factors. Each participant takes whatever she feels like taking, and puts her choices together in any way that appeals to her. This is not a craft competition, or a how-to class, or even a sharing of technical expertise. It does not matter how things are assembled. The only authority to be consulted is the creator's own inner inclination.

Any group may include experienced craftswomen, as well as those who say they are "all thumbs," and all degrees of creative ability in between. Such distinctions are irrelevant here. No matter what the level of skill may be, each object will express something that its individual creator wishes to express. The ritual is designed to objectify the creator's intentions and personal meanings, not her technical accomplishments.

Those who finish their creations before the others must sit quietly, and refrain from distracting their companions with small talk. Insofar as possible, silence should be maintained throughout the whole exercise. One aim of such a ritual is to help individuals who may feel excessively dependent, and must consult someone else's opinion of everything they do, like the overanxious child who constantly seeks approval. This difficulty is frequently found even among grown women. In a ritual situation where there are no recipes and no one judges any right or wrong way, the dependent individual can learn to give more attention to her own inclinations. Therefore participants should be cautioned *not* to consult one another, *not* to ask or to give suggestions or advice.

The next step comes when all have finished working, or when sufficient time has elapsed. Thirty to forty-five minutes is about right for most groups; but if a majority require less or more time, let it be taken. Objects are then placed in a circle, each one in front of its creator, and the talking stick is passed (see pages 32–34).

Holding the stick, each woman describes the symbolism of her object, her feelings and thoughts while making it, what aspects of herself it may express, and how she perceives her connection with it. Others may comment if they wish, before the stick passes to the next creator.

This ritual is versatile. It serves well for a getting-acquainted session, and also proves useful for deeper, more serious analyses among women who are actively engaged in learning about themselves. It is both supportive and self-expressive. It provides each woman with a visible reminder of her own and others' insights, because her object will go home with her and may be kept in her own private space. If she does not wish to keep it, she may dispose of it in any manner that seems good to her: take it apart, give it away, leave it by a certain tree or building, throw it into a stream, burn it as an offering, bury it, hang it outdoors to be exposed to the weather, or even—if it represents some undesired trait or problem—violently destroy it as a personal ritual purgation. The point is that the object is created in any way that pleases its creator, and may also be uncreated according to her wish alone, without direction from any other source. It is surprising how many women discover within themselves a deep, unsatisfied need for such absolute autonomy; and a ritual that provides it is always rewarding.

CHANT

I am she who made you,
You are mine,
You are me,
I am myself,
I am.

Dancing

Women often want to add physical movement to a chant or song, because movement feels good and enhances group unity. Dancing need not incorporate any formal step patterns at all. Participants may skip, shuffle, jog, march, cross-step, two-step, or just quietly walk in rhythm with a chant. Following are some simple rhythmic steps that can be done to almost any vocal sounds, by anyone who is able to walk. Instrumental accompaniment is optional. Sometimes a drumbeat is helpful. Tambourines and finger cymbals also can be used by nonmusicians. Ankle bells can give a nice touch when all participants are moving together in the same pattern.

Women's dances traditionally circle widdershins—that is, counterclockwise, following the retrograde course of the moon. In the following examples, movement goes in this direction: toward your right, as you face the center of the circle. Dances usually begin with participants holding hands in a circle and facing inward. Hand holds may be dropped for clapping, twirling, or any other individual maneuver. In addition to holding hands, there are other ways of keeping contact with one's fellow dancers. Here are some of them:

1. *Arm hold.* Each woman grasps her neighbor's nearest shoulder or upper arm.
2. *Shoulder hold.* Each woman reaches all the way across her neighbor's upper back to grasp the far shoulder (or the arm) of the next woman.
3. *Elbow link.* Each person puts her left hand on her left hip, and her right arm through the elbow of her right-hand neighbor.
4. *Front crossover.* Each person stretches her right arm over the left arm of her right-hand neighbor, and her left arm under the right arm of her left-hand neighbor, to grasp the hands of the *next* woman on each side..
5. *Back crossover.* Same as front crossover, except the hands reach behind the backs of neighboring women, to join at the small of the back.
6. *Belt hold.* Each person ties a cord or sash around her waist, which is grasped by her neighbors on each side as she also grasps theirs.

STEPS

Toe-heel walk. This is simple, slow, and elegant. Walk around the circle, taking 2 beats for each step. On the first beat, point the toe to the ground without putting weight on the foot.

On the second beat, set the heel down and shift weight. The hips automatically turn from side to side as you do this stylized walk.

Syncopated kick. Walk slowly around the circle, at each step lifting the opposite knee and clapping the thigh with both hands, in rhythm. Be careful not to kick your neighbor.

Hip sway. This is a simple walk to the side, with most of the movement in the body rather than the feet. If desired, it may be done with hand clapping or finger snapping at each step.

1. Step to the right on the right foot, leading with the right hip and leaning the upper body far to the left.
2. Bring the left foot in close to the right, leaning the upper body the other way and sticking out the left hip.
   Repeat 1 and 2.

Grapevine. A very old, traditional folk dance movement, undoubtedly inherited from pagan harvest dances. It is easy and graceful, with flowing back-and-forth half-turns of the body and as much hip movement as you want to put into it.

1. Step to the right on the right foot.
2. Cross the left foot in front of the right, and step on it.
3. Step to the right on the right foot again.
4. Cross the left foot behind the right, and step on it.
   Repeat 1 through 4.

Briar rose. A slightly more staccato step with less travel than the grapevine. Each beat should be preceded by a slight, quick bend of the knees, marking the offbeat, to achieve a syncopated effect.

1. Step to the right on the right foot.
2. Cross the left foot diagonally in front of the right, pointing the toe to the ground without putting weight on it.
3. Extend the left foot to the left side and again point the toe to the ground without putting weight on it.
4. Cross the left foot in front of the right, and step on it.
   Repeat 1 through 4.

Ocean wave. This is a simple crossover step enhanced by a slight pause.

1. Step to the right on the right foot.

2. Lift the left foot into the air and hold it diagonally across the right leg.
3. Holding the left foot up, give a slight bounce with a bend of the right knee.
4. Cross the left foot in front of the right, and step on it.
    Repeat 1 through 4.

Past and future or **looking backward.** A traditional movement found in many Greek and Balkan folk dances.
Beats 1 through 4: same as Ocean wave, above.

5. Step to the right on the right foot, turning the body to face diagonally left.
6. Lift the left heel and point the left toe to the ground without putting weight on it.
7. Shift weight to the left foot, turning the body to face diagonally right.
8. Lift the right heel and point the right toe to the ground without putting weight on it.
    Repeat 1 through 8.

TOE-HEEL WALK

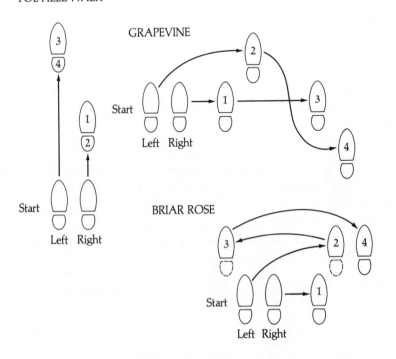

Heel-and-toe. This is a time-honored folk dance step that can develop considerable verve when done to a fairly rapid tempo.

1. Keeping weight on the left foot, extend the right foot to the right with the toe up, heel down on the ground.
2. Keeping weight still on the left foot, cross the right foot in front of the left and strike the right toe down to the ground.
3. Step to the right on the right foot.
4. Bring the left foot in close to the right, and step on it.
   Repeat 1 through 4. Note: this pattern may also finish with a two-step, right-left-right (the traditional "heel-and-toe, away-we-go"), in order to repeat to the other side. If so used, it will combine with some other intermediate pattern in order to travel around the circle.

The shuttle. This can't be done holding hands, since participants turn alternately outward and inward while traveling widdershins around the circle; so the hands are free for clapping, striking cymbals, reaching overhead, waving banners, or any other motion, as desired.

1. Step to the right on the right foot.
2. Bring the left foot in close to the right, and step on it.
3. Step again to the right on the right foot.
4. Pivot 180 degrees on the right foot, with a slight hop, to face outward from the center of the circle.
5. Step to your left (same direction of travel as before) on the left foot.
6. Bring the right foot in close to the left, and step on it.

HEEL & TOE

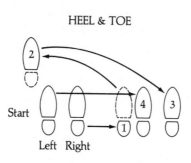

7. Step again to your left on the left foot.
8. Pivot 180 degrees on the left foot, with a slight hop, to face inward toward the center of the circle.
   Repeat 1 through 8.

Weaving or Maypole dance. Step patterns are not important here. What matters is the dancers' orientation in space. The Maypole dance is identical with the square dancer's "Grand Right and Left," which was derived from it. In order to do it properly, there must be an even number of participants. Each may hold the end of a long string, ribbon, roll of crepe paper, or ball of yarn attached to something in the center: a real Maypole, or a tree, post, or pillar. Strands will braid prettily around the object if they are attached high up, and the dancers keep track of their directions.

Start by facing one another in couples around the circle, so half the participants are looking clockwise, the other half counterclockwise. Each person moves forward, passing right shoulders with the one she is facing. Then she will be facing another, with whom she passes left shoulders. The next pair will pass right shoulders again, and the next left shoulders again, and so on, until all strands are wound up after having been thus carried over-and-under throughout the dance.

The foregoing are only suggestions in outline of the kinds of dancing that a group might do. Many other possibilities abound. Dancing can be as formal and "rehearsed" as the group might wish; or it can be absolutely patternless and spontaneous, each individual doing her own thing to a repetitive chant, drumbeat, or handclapping, which may simply go on for a while until it stops of its own accord. Some groups prefer a quiet, calm, meditative period of free movement; others might enjoy leaping and shouting, flinging themselves about in cathartic abandonment. Some occasions seem to call for one type of dance, other occasions for a different type. The important thing is to feel free, inventive, and comfortable in one's own body so as to enjoy whatever the body is doing.

The Star Flower

All sit on the ground (or floor) in a tight circle, facing inward, knees slightly bent, feet together in the center. All feet should touch, side by side. A large group may encircle the altar and still have all feet in contact. A smaller group may use an open area away from the altar. In this case, the central space should contain some symbolic article: a candle, a pentacle, crystals, a vase of flowers or leaves, a bowl of water, seeds, or fruit, etc.

All join hands—left palm up, right palm down—and bend forward to touch the feet, all heads down between the arms. After a few moments of silent meditation in this position, the group may begin a soft hum, which grows in volume as the backs slowly straighten, the heads begin to rise, and the joined hands begin to reach upward. It should be done very slowly and smoothly, keeping in mind the image of a flower in its unhurried opening. At the peak of the movement, when all joined hands are reaching straight up, chant:

> As the star flower opens
> To the sun, wind, and visiting bee,
> So let us open hearts and minds
> To all the world that we see.

The movement may continue. After reaching as high as possible, with hands still joined, all slowly roll back and lie down flat. The joined hands now reach outward along the ground, so the formation is like a many-pointed star as seen from above. Lying still, relaxing, participants may now speak as individuals, sharing their feelings about the formation and its symbolism; or they may simply keep silent and breathe together, sensing their unity as well as their diversity.

This is a good exercise for soothing and centering, bringing group members into spiritual rapport, and helping to envision goals.

Chantmaking

Chantmaking is an interesting and sometimes amusing exercise that stimulates creativity, and may provide a group with its own collectively invented liturgy. It is a simple process of using the circle to construct sentences or sentiments, each member in her turn adding a word or phrase.

When any member considers that the chant has reached an appropriate stopping place, she may finish it by saying "Blessed be" (the equivalent of *amen*). At this point, those who have spoken repeat what they have said, to fix the phrases in the minds of the others. Then the whole group together repeats the entire chant, perhaps to the accompaniment of rhythmic clapping or drumming. The chant is written down.

After this, another chant can be created in the same way, beginning with the person who ended the first chant, and continuing on around the circle. By such methods, a group can build up a repertoire of chants appropriate for every occasion.

Here are some examples:

FIRST SPEAKER: "Hail, Goddess . . . "
SECOND SPEAKER: "Who inspires and inspirits . . . "
THIRD SPEAKER: "Fill our hearts . . . "
FOURTH SPEAKER: "With powers of love . . . "
FIFTH SPEAKER: "Let us overcome . . . "

SIXTH SPEAKER: "All our obstacles . . . "
SEVENTH SPEAKER: "Blessed be."

The chant is repeated and written. Seventh speaker now becomes first speaker.

FIRST SPEAKER: "Our Mother . . . "
SECOND SPEAKER: "Loves us . . . "
THIRD SPEAKER: "Our sister . . . "
FOURTH SPEAKER: "Needs us . . . "
FIFTH SPEAKER: "From Mother to sister . . . "
SIXTH SPEAKER: "We carry the torch . . . "
SEVENTH SPEAKER: "We bring fire . . . "
EIGHTH SPEAKER: "To the hearth . . . "
NINTH SPEAKER: "We bring love . . . "
TENTH SPEAKER: "To the heart . . . "
ELEVENTH SPEAKER: "Blessed be."

The chant is repeated and written. Eleventh speaker now becomes first speaker.

FIRST SPEAKER: "I am Woman . . . "
SECOND SPEAKER: "I am Child . . . "
THIRD SPEAKER: "I am Crone ..."
FOURTH SPEAKER: "I am the Holy Triad . . . "
FIFTH SPEAKER: "I will fulfil my destiny . . . "
SIXTH SPEAKER: "Blessed be."

The chant is repeated and written. Sixth speaker now becomes first speaker.

FIRST SPEAKER: "Never give up . . . "
SECOND SPEAKER: "Never give in . . . "
THIRD SPEAKER: "Never say die . . . "
FOURTH SPEAKER: "Never go back . . . "
FIFTH SPEAKER: "Blessed be."

The chant is repeated and written. Fifth speaker now becomes first speaker.

And so on.

Variation: if group members prefer to sing their phrases instead of speaking them, then chantmaking becomes songmaking.

Making Mandalas

This is an entertaining exercise that can be full of childlike fun as well as psychological insights and personal symbolism. Materials are simple. Each woman should be provided with a blank page on which a large circle has been drawn with a compass. White poster board is probably the best medium, because artwork done on a carpeted floor needs a rigid surface to work on. In addition to the blank circles, participants will need a large assortment of crayons, colored markers, pens, or any other appropriate drawing and coloring materials, which are shared around.

With, perhaps, a quiet musical background, each goes to work on her own mandala, filling her circle with any shapes and colors that come to mind. Designs may be as simple or as complicated as the individual wishes. The whole point of a personal mandala is that it should spring from unconscious symbolism in the same way as the drawings of children. Artistic talent is not required. Anyone can make a mandala. Designs may not even require recognizable pictures. The circle can be geometrically divided up into areas of different colors, which can be labeled with written words. Suns, moons, stars, triangles, stick figures, clouds, wavy lines, circles, mazes, spirals, crosses, hearts, handprints, floral designs, zigzags, or any other shapes can be chosen from infinite symbolic possibilities.

After all mandalas have been completed, each in turn shows her work and explains to the group what she thought or felt about its creation, and what, if anything, her symbols are intended to mean. Other members then offer comments, which may well provide further insights into the mandala maker's objectives. Symbolic shapes have powerful and sometimes unexpected psychological connotations. What we choose to draw in our blank circles can show us how to know ourselves better.

The final disposition of the mandalas is up to the group. Members might hang them on the wall, at least temporarily, just as children's artwork is displayed in the classroom; or they might trade about and give them to each other; or each might take home her own mandala for further contemplation.

Guided Meditation: The Heroine

Women's groups often employ guided meditation, that is, a collective vision described by one person while the others listen, feel the sensations as described, and picture the scene within their minds' eyes. As a rule, one approaches a guided meditation by assuming a comfortable position, closing the eyes, and relaxing while the speaker's voice suggests quiet, peace, receptivity, and release of muscular tension. Then the speaker begins to describe the scene, journey, or happening that becomes the meditation experience.

The content of a guided meditation is open to anybody's vision. It is limited only by the boundaries of the imagination. If a group enjoys this sort of ritual, there can be a guided meditation at every meeting, with a different person acting as speaker each time. Good sources of material are portions of stories and personal fantasies, remembered dreams, and wishes of the "wouldn't it be nice if . . . " variety.

The following images are often used as meditation material: visions of encounters with the inner Goddess; a meeting with a special, magical women's circle in a transcendently beautiful place; an enlightening pilgrimage to a secret shrine; a journey into some enclosed chamber, cave, pyramid, or temple adytum where symbols of peace, healing, and self-validation can be found.

The following meditation is a bit different. It draws upon the kind of heroic adventure fantasy that boys take for granted in their literature and entertainment, while they are growing up in our patriarchal society to believe in personal victory through aggression. Girls may desire similar heroic fantasy experience, but the society gives them few models to follow. Hence girls are often denied the self-empowerment that is psychologically implicit in fantasies of triumphant battles against forces of evil. That's why this meditation sounds like a typical hero/monster encounter that almost any man would recognize, although it might feel a little strange to women. But take note of the subtle differences in symbolism. Try it once, and see if this kind of vision might be what you need to help realize your own inner strength. Let a reader present the material at a group meeting, or read it onto a tape that can be played at the meeting.

Lie down or sit comfortably. Rest your body. Breathe deeply. Each time you breathe out, let go another bit of muscular tension along with the breath. Think in turn of your face, jaw, neck, shoulders, arms, fingers, back, abdomen, hips, thighs, legs, feet, toes. Relax each part completely as you focus on it. Breathe quietly. Let your mind be clear and receptive.

You are sinking down, down through the ground, through the rocks of the earth, down into a hollow place deep underground, an underworld, another country: the land of inner space. It is a wilderness of tumbled stones and craggy hills without vegetation. The sky is full of dark, blowing clouds. You are standing naked in a bleak stony landscape with a weird reddish glow of light about you.

Despite your nakedness, you don't seem vulnerable. You are tall and strong, with keen eyes and tight, smooth muscles. Your long hair blows in the wind. You feel ready for whatever may happen.

You see a white figure coming toward you very fast. As it approaches, you see that it is a beautiful unicorn: a horse as brilliantly white as sunlight on snow, with silver hooves, a twisted silver horn on its forehead, and deep plum-colored eyes. The creature stops in front of you and lowers its head. With one light, powerful leap, you vault onto its back. It twists its neck around, and looks at you affectionately with its big purple eyes. You grasp the long silky mane. The unicorn sets off at a smooth gallop.

You feel the animal's warm, silky coat under the tight grip of your strong thighs. The hair of its mane ripples in the wind like banners. Its hooves seem hardly to touch the ground. You have a wonderful sensation of flying.

Your unicorn stops in front of a wall of red rock. There is a door in the center of the wall. You slide down off the animal's back and approach the door. As you come nearer, it begins to open. Behind the door there is a dark cave, with a point of white light glowing in the center. You enter the cave and see a carved stone altar with a sword stuck point-down into its top. The sword is silver, long and straight, with a crystal in the hilt. The cave is illuminated by the crystal, which glows as brightly as a white flame.

You reach up and grasp the hilt of the sword. The blade comes easily out of the stone. The sword feels comfortable and perfectly balanced in your grip. You know you can use it expertly.

You leave the cave and remount your waiting unicorn. Again your steed gallops off across the rocky land. After a while you see a curious dark hump just over the horizon. You thought it was a mountain, but as you draw nearer you see that it's a gigantic living man-shaped creature, so tall that clouds drift around its chest. It rises higher and higher against the sky as you come closer. When it towers up before you, like a great cliff, you can see that this dark giant has a peculiar composition.

You know this is Purusha, the Collective Man. His giant body is made of millions of ordinary men, all compacted together like the cells of a normal-sized body. Each component lives and speaks, so there is a perpetual hum of vocal sounds issuing from every part of the giant. In the head, far up against the sky, his eyes pierce the clouds like spotlights of angry red. His huge mouth opens, showing vicious fangs as long as tree trunks, releasing a roar that shakes the earth. It is Purusha who keeps this land barren and dry, who cracks the rocks and poisons the soil, who swallows and absorbs every man who ever tried to do battle with him.

You know Purusha is very dangerous, but you are not afraid of him. Your unicorn gallops right up to one of his foothill-sized feet. Swinging your sword high over your head, you attack the huge Achilles tendon at the back of Purusha's heel, which stands out like the bole of a giant redwood tree. Far in the air above you, Purusha's outraged roar sounds like thunder. His enormous hand comes down to swat the tiny thing that hurts him, just as you would swat a mosquito. Your unicorn dances aside as lightly as a feather, carrying you out of range of the swinging hand, which is acres in width. The wind of its passing almost blows you off your seat on the unicorn's back. But you hold on, and immediately return to hack again at Purusha's heel with your magic sword. Somehow you know that like the mythological Achilles himself, this giant too was left heel-vulnerable by his mother. Perhaps she knew you would come.

The giant tendon snaps at last. The vast column of leg totters. Now Purusha must put all his great weight on the other foot, which you can see a mile or two away over the rocky plain. Your unicorn sets off toward it in a blur of speed, dodging the repeated swings of the monstrous hand that tries to swat you.

You arrive at the other heel and begin slicing into it with your sword. The giant's roars become deafening. The whole sky reverberates. Purusha's fist smashes into the ground near you, making a hole like a meteor crater. Your unicorn avoids the flying rocks, and returns to the attack. The magic sword severs the giant's other heel tendon. He begins to topple over, no longer able to stand on his legs. A mountain is falling down out of the sky.

Now your unicorn must fly faster than ever before, to get out of the way of that immense falling body. Like lightning you dash away from the area where Purusha will come down. He hits the ground. Thunder and earthquake resound all around you. The giant passes through the surface of the plain like a stone falling into soft mud. His body buries itself with the impact. Gigantic house-sized boulders fly up and cover him with a huge cairn. A new range of tumbled mountains now rises over his body where there was once a flat desert.

The earth settles back again. The clouds of dust and rock recede. The giant is buried. The great eater has been eaten.

Your unicorn carries you up to the pinnacle of a high crag where your head almost touches the swirling clouds. You lift your sword toward the heavens. Suddenly a brilliant white beam of light comes down from the sky and touches sparks from your sword's point. The light envelopes the sword, your body, and your steed. You stand aglow in brilliance against the dark clouds. Down the beam of light glides a gleaming gold crown set with mystic jewels. The crown settles on your head. It fits perfectly. It gives you the power to rise up gently into the air like a soap bubble.

Thus ascending, you reach down to give your unicorn a parting pat. The creature flicks its tail, tosses its head to bid you farewell, and trots off down the mountain trail. You rise higher and higher, leaving the underworld space, coming back through the earth to your own time and place, your own body.

In your hand you carry the crystal from the hilt of your magic sword. It will remain with you and serve as an emblem of your power. Feeling relaxed, at ease, and victorious, you return to your present life.

After this meditation, the group may honor the heroine with a chant:

CHANT

I am a woman warrior,
Training myself to be strong,
Seeking to lighten the darkness,
Seeking to right every wrong.

Celebrating Heroines

Who are our heroines? Feminists often lament the lack of strong, independent female role models in our traditions, thanks to patriarchal historians' emphasis on male role models presented as heroes. Female figures, on the other hand, tend to be martyred or victimized, like Joan of Arc, Boadicea, Heloise, Anne Frank, or countless deliberately invented female saints tortured to death in their spotless intransigent virginity. Passive, long-suffering (if fictional) sainthood has been held up as the best possible feminine image. But those women who were real martyrs, the independent and intelligent ones tortured and burned as witches in their millions, are largely unknown to a world that erased even their names from its history.

It is instructive for any group of women to pass the talking stick around and share personal impressions of what might constitute a heroine. In telling their stories, women help each other develop more positive concepts of female strength and power. The following are typical examples of women's responses to the idea of celebrating heroines.

"My heroine is Catherine the Great of Russia. Male historians have always put her down, because she was sexually liberated. She took men at her own pleasure, the same way male rulers have always taken women. To the traditional male way of thinking, this made her evil. Isn't it odd that women who behave like men are so often considered evil? What does that really say about men's behavior? Actually Catherine was a good ruler, much better than some of the awful, cruel men tyrants who came before and after her. She was intelligent, energetic, and basically devoted to the welfare of her people. Any king in history who behaved the way most queens have behaved has been honored as a hero and a great, good ruler. So I think Catherine's honor is long overdue."

"My heroine comes out of a comic book. When I was a kid, I wanted to be Sheena, Queen of the Jungle. She was not only tough and strong and gorgeous, she was also morally impeccable. She was always on the side of justice. She defeated all her enemies, who were also by definition the enemies of Goodness. Nobody could mess around with Sheena. Besides, she loved the wild animals and they loved her. They defended her. As an animal lover, I could relate to that too."

"My heroine may sound improbable: Carry Nation. Yes, the original 'battle-ax' who went around trashing saloons with a hatchet. Carry was given very bad press by the men who wanted to hang on to their weekly or nightly binges, and were terrified by the idea of any woman with a weapon in her hand and the willingness to use it. Carry has been painted as an uptight spoilsport Victorian prude. Mostly, though, she was a progressive feminist who realized that drunken men were regularly beating up helpless women and children all over this country, even killing them all too often. She thought the elimination of saloons would help save women from the violence. She focused on that, although of course the problem went even deeper. She was intrepid. She faced every danger, and both verbal and physical assaults by men. She was jailed many times for upholding her concept of what was right. And she laid the foundation for political change."

"My heroine is another who faced a lot of nasty opposition in order to relieve women's pain: Margaret Sanger. She saw poor women suffering and dying of excessive motherhood imposed on them by men. She fought all her life to give those women the (then illegal) birth control information that they needed and craved. She faced everything the men could do to her: vandalism of her printing office, physical threats, vilification, jail, exile. She never quit. After years of heartbreak, she won. The laws were changed because of her crusade. In her old age, she was honored as one of this century's greatest saviors of women. She should never be forgotten."

"My heroine is a family figure, my great-grandmother Helen. She was just what you think of as the epitome of the pioneer woman. She traveled in a wagon to a new homestead in the wilderness, where she birthed six children and helped my great-grandfather hack a farm out of the primeval forest—sometimes hitching herself to the plow when they were too poor to afford a horse. After a mule kicked her husband in the head and killed him at the untimely age of thirty-four, she carried on alone. She worked the farm and made it pay, and kept the house, and raised her kids, all at once. She allowed herself only five-and-a-half hours' sleep every night, and she never sat down without some work in her hands. Once her house burned down. Another time she lost all her crops in a flood. She rebuilt and she replanted. She refused to accept defeat. Not many men could have done what she did single-handed, or lived the life that she had. She was tough as nails, a real heroine. She also educated the children herself, when there was no school. They all went to college eventually. She lived to be over ninety, still on her farm and taking care of herself and her house up to the last three days of her life."

"My heroine is Amelia Earhart, because she was the first great woman pilot and ever since I was a little kid I wanted to learn to fly. I think she was a martyr too, because I subscribe to the theory that she was on a secret spy mission for the government when she vanished, or was shot down, or was captured—whichever way it was. Of course that has never been officially acknowledged, so she has never been posthumously designated a national heroine. In any case, she was an extraordinary woman."

"My heroine is Alexandra David-Neel, the brilliant Frenchwoman born in 1868 who lived much of her adult life as an itinerant Buddhist pilgrim in the most remote areas of India, China, and Tibet. She was the first European woman to enter the forbidden city of Lhasa, having disguised herself in beggar's rags. She spent years traveling on foot through the world's most inhospitable mountains among bandits, hostile armies, and other dangers. She became a world authority on Tantric Buddhism and wrote many books and articles that gave Western scholars some of their earliest views of the subject."

"Who is my heroine? Hippolyta, the Horsewoman, Queen of the Amazons in Greek myth. The later Greeks claimed that their hero The-

seus kidnapped and married her; but I think they lied, because patriarchal writers always lied about the women in their legends. Hippolyta
would never have married an Athenian; she would have died first. I
read a lot about her when I was a youngster, and always wondered what
her real story was."

"My heroine is Marie Curie, the first woman scientist to be recognized by all the world as a true thinker. Unfortunately she, too, died a
martyr, poisoned by the radiation that was the subject of her lifework.
But her intellectual brilliance was honored, she received Nobel prizes
and grants to found her Institute, she became great in the popular sense
by sheer hard work and clear thinking. To me, that's heroic."

"I have millions of heroines: all the so-called witches killed by the
churchmen because they were midwives and healers, because they
helped women enslaved by patriarchy, because they dared to criticize
the church's greed or aggression, because they got more respect from the
common people than the clergy got. European society wiped out most of
its really intelligent, creative women during those centuries. Even if we
don't know their individual names any more, we should remember
them."

CHANT

Celebrate the heroine, honor the heroine:
Healer, thinker, adventurer, fighter,
Wise woman, strong woman, life-giving woman,
Woman of spirit, woman of power, woman of peace.
All hail, all honor, blessed be.

A Ceremony of Dolls

We all need to recognize and nurture the child within us,
even when we are grown-up people with serious responsibilities.
It's refreshing to become childlike for a time, to play, to caper
about, to dare to enjoy childish things again. In this light, a ceremony of dolls can be fun. It presents an opportunity to recall a
pleasant aspect of childhood.

There are all sorts of dolls that women might bring to a cere-monial meeting. Women who collect dolls, of course, have a wide choice of candidates. Some women have old dolls that they have preserved from their own childhood, or from the childhood of children who are now grown. But there are many other possibili-ties. Many woman have anthropomorphic or theriomorphic fig-ures as parts of other collections, such as teddy bears, marionettes, Toby mugs, miniature ornamental gargoyles, owls, frogs, or other animals; a "kitchen witch"; a gingerbread man; a souvenir kachina or similar doll; models, carvings, pottery fig-ures, paper dolls, toys. Almost every household has something that can serve as a doll.

It is possible to make one's own doll in a few minutes out of rags, corn husks, wooden clothespins, pipe cleaners, wire, and many other materials, including a simple paper doll created by cutting a figure out of a newspaper or magazine picture and mounting it on thin cardboard with rubber cement. A doll can be anything. One of my favorite childhood dolls was nothing more than a towel with a knot tied in the center. A face was painted on the knot. Cloth above the knot represented long hair; cloth below the knot represented a dress.

Once the group has agreed on a doll ceremony, each member brings one or more dolls—crude or elaborate, old or new, home-made or manufactured, it makes no difference. In fact, variety is desirable. Dolls rest in the altar space during opening rituals. Then, after the manner of show-and-tell, each doll is individually described, and passed around the circle for inspection and com-ment. The comments begin to establish a personality profile for each doll as perceived by the group.

Then comes a reenactment of little-girl doll play, with adult psychological overtones. Each woman moves her doll about, speaks for it, interacts with other dolls on its behalf, and in gener-al plays the doll's part in a miniature improvisational theater. It is usually best if only two or three at a time interact with one anoth-er, while others act as an audience—though the latter may become involved, and make comments.

Variety suggests a characterization for each doll in these mini-dramas. An elegant, expensive antique doll in satin and lace might play the snobbish lady, behaving arrogantly toward the humble rag doll. The paper doll might try to put on airs, only to be discovered as a thin pretense, all facade with nothing behind it. The teddy bear might play peacemaker and try to reconcile differences; or it might become a snarling wild animal. The kachina might claim mighty spiritual powers. The littlest miniature doll might try to hide, or frisk about playing tricks on others. The baby doll will require mothering. The child doll may be a sweet little angel, or a brat. The commercial teenage fashion doll (such as Barbie) will undoubtedly reflect an immature personality and interests.

This kind of play is fun, and also rich in psychological insights. Doll play can act to open up the quiet, retiring member who seemed too shy to contribute much. Sometimes it brings forth unexpected depths in certain individuals, or seems to relate either directly or indirectly to events in the women's own lives.

As a climax of the ceremony, members might make an expendable and temporary sort of doll out of wax, bread dough, rolled-up paper, plasticine, rags, paint, and such, to serve as a "poppet"—that is, a scapegoat figure to be destroyed by the group in a symbolic purging of evils. Or one member may offer her own homemade creation to serve as a poppet. Each member names an evil that the poppet is to represent: nuclear war, pollution, greed, drugs, violence, sexist attitudes, personal hangups, hurtful behavior patterns, and so on. Then each member "kills" the poppet in some way: sticking pins into it in the classic witchlike manner, tearing it apart, shredding it. Finally it is altogether destroyed and disposed of. If made of edible material, it can be divided up and eaten by all, thus literally internalizing the group's wishes.

Closing rituals might be conducted by the dolls themselves, with the same doll voices and doll attitudes that developed during play. This is a ritual with much general potential for creativity and many symbolic overtones, which will vary according to the general nature of the group. It is also fairly certain that the owner of a doll that has participated in the ceremony will always afterward view that doll in a rather different light than before.

CHANT

Hail, Child,
Past maiden self I see,
Come out to play;
Come forth, and say
The hidden words to me.

A Ceremony of Stones

According to the Greek version of the ubiquitous flood myth, the Goddess Themis taught the surviving couple to repopulate the world after the Deluge by tossing "the bones of their Mother" behind them as they walked. They understood that the Earth was their Mother, and her bones were stones. During their magical journey, the stones handled by the man became men; the stones handled by the woman became women.

This story was drawn in part from the primitive notion that bone is a foundation for forming the child in the womb. Ancient Sumerians thought a mother could create her child's skeleton from one of her own ribs. They named the Birth Goddess Nin-ti, "Lady of the Rib." The same tradition clearly influenced the biblical fable of Adam's rib, though the birthing miracle was deliberately reassigned to a male. The idea that Mother Earth's children can be made from her stone "bones" is related to the prevalent identification between her skeleton and the rocks, in myths and religious histories all over the world. We still speak of "rock-ribbed" country.

Often stones themselves were worshiped as living embodiments of divinity. Cybele, the Great Mother of the Gods, was incarnate in a black stone. The god Mithra was given birth from a mother stone, the *petra genetrix*. A stone Goddess, the Hag of Scone, used to govern the choice of Celtic kings; she still sits under the British coronation throne in the form of a large stone. In biblical times, any Middle Eastern deity could be manifested as a stone (Greek *baetyl*, Hebrew *beth-el*, "dwelling of a deity"). The great Triple Goddess appeared at Orchomenos as three ancient standing stones. From time immemorial, Indo-Europeans worshiped in circles of standing stones.

Being mindful of such worldwide reverence for mother stones, women today may plan a ceremony around these "bones of Mother Earth." Each member of the group should collect and bring a bagful of stones, of any convenient size from golfball to softball. If the ceremony is to be held indoors, all stones should be washed clean beforehand. Participants should choose solid, firm-textured stones, rather than the friable, crumbly kind that can leave a mess on floor or carpet.

On arrival, stones can be piled all together in a heap near the altar. To establish the outside circle, each member in turn may take one or two of these stones from the heap and lay them somewhere on the periphery of the space, meanwhile pronouncing a wish, a hope, or a dedication in honor of which each stone is placed. Turns can continue around until all stones are used, or a small heap may be left for other purposes.

Finally the stone circle is closed, while participants meditate on the ancient temples where the Goddess was worshiped within larger circles of the same material. If the site is outdoors where the stones can be left permanently in position, then this placing of them is in effect the building of a temple, where the same circle can be used over and over, thus acquiring its own tradition. However, a feeling of security and protection can be generated by the stone circle even when it is temporary.

Sometimes an indoor stone circle can be moved outdoors at the end of the meeting and left permanently surrounding the entire building. When the indoor circle is dismantled, stones can be divided among all participants and carried outside, to be dropped one by one during a circumambulation ("walking-around") of the whole structure. Remember, stones should not be placed on grass that has to be mowed, or anywhere else where they might cause inconvenience. Place them under bushes, or up against foundation walls, where they will be out of the way.

During the meeting, members may speak in turn of their feelings about stones, perhaps as models for personal qualities like strength, endurance, dependability, and so on. Some may wish to read poetry related to the subject. Instead of a talking stick, a special stone may be passed from hand to hand to designate each speaker. Group chants can be accompanied by "rock music," created by each member clicking two stones together in rhythm.

A stone ceremony is a good opportunity for special personal stones, gems, and crystals to be brought and placed on the altar. Their owners may wish to describe them, or pass them around the circle for comment and energy input, in the show-and-tell manner. As an experiment in nonvisual experience, try passing stones around the circle with all eyes closed, describing to one another how stones are perceived by their feel alone.

Another way to use stones in ritual is to build a cairn; that is, a rockpile made as vertical as possible by careful balancing of its component stones. The ancients built cairns for many purposes: to mark paths, boundaries, or burial places; to leave messages; to warn away intruders; to commemorate special events; to symbolize the group unity of the builders. If women have a place where they can build a cairn and leave in *in situ*, then it can be visited afterward and used again for ceremonies of rededication or renewal. A cairn can be made quite permanent by pouring cement down in amongst its stones.

If the cairn must be built indoors, or must be removed after the ceremony, it can still serve as an altar for one meeting. Candles can be set upright on its stones. Clay figures or dolls can perch on it. Colored ribbons, shells, or strings of beads can decorate it. It can be danced around, sung to, named, labeled, or photographed for a record of the group's activities.

Another way to use stones is to create a labyrinth, with just one route in to the center and out again, suggested ceremonies of enlightenment and regeneration to most of our ancestors on every continent. Having created a spiral or any other form of a mystic path, group members may walk through it one at a time, expressing their personal sense of its meaning.

When gathering up stones to take them away after completing a stone ceremony, plan to do something special with them. Even when stones cannot be left in place, as an outdoor circle or cairn, their final disposition should be something of personal significance. One woman might take her stones to a lake, stream, or seashore, to drop them into natural waters. Another might toss them, one at a time, in various directions while walking through woods. Another might paint eyes on some of them and keep them as "pet rocks." Another might put them in her garden, window box, or patio. Another might make an individual stone circle in her back yard. Another might dig a hole in a certain favorite spot, and bury them. At the next meeting of the group, each woman may tell the others what she did with her portion of stones. It might be a good idea for each woman to choose just one stone to keep for her very own, to place on her individual altar, as a reminder of her relationship to the group and its activities. A small stone can be a wonderfully soothing object to hold and handle, or to contemplate as an aid to meditation. This is the real secret behind the eternal popularity of "lucky stones."

And remember what enormous spans of time are involved in the formation of any stone taken from any part of Mother Earth's fertile flesh. Hundreds of thousands, perhaps millions of years. Many stones are nearly as old as Earth herself. To hold one in your hand is like holding the essence of Time. A flower, an animal, or a human being is born yesterday, here today, and gone tomorrow; but a stone is forever.

CHANT

Old, old, old one,
Forged in the Earth's hot blood,
Bone of her bone, stone of her stone,
Let us feel the vastness of Time
In your unyielding substance.

A Ceremony of Cards

Many people are fascinated by the symbolism of tarot cards: an ancient symbolism, touching upon images that express the collective unconscious through many centuries of history. Such cards are good ritual tools. The richness and depth of their meanings can help create new insights. They are useful even to people who know nothing of their historical background, because there can be strong psychological responses to their imagery on the intuitive or unconscious level.

Of course, it is much better to have more information rather than less. Prior study of the Tarot's ideological roots is highly recommended.* This gives an enhanced appreciation of card symbols and a more varied choice of connotations and interpretations.

It's best to have several decks of cards available for a card ceremony. One deck can be used to enclose the ritual space, a suit

---

*See Barbara G. Walker, *The Secrets of the Tarot: Origins, History, and Symbolism* (San Francisco: Harper & Row, 1984).

laid out in each quarter to invoke elemental connotations: cups in the south, wands in the west, pentacles in the north, swords in the east. The altar might be draped in black, the color of the unconscious, and furnished with black and white candles to express time as the alternation of night and day.

Major Arcana or trump cards can be laid out between the candles in any of several traditional shapes, such as the infinity sign (a figure-8 formation), or the Yoni Yantra, a female-symbolic triangle with seven cards on each side and the zero card (Fool) in the center. Since the yantra or symbolic shape was invented in the first place as an aid to meditation, it might be well to begin the ritual with a meditation guided by someone who has studied the background meanings of the symbol.

There are many different card layouts used by "readers," for purposes ranging from mental centering and enhancement of awareness, to the crudest kind of commercial fortune telling. For a group ceremony, the cards can be approached in a somewhat different way. Psychological insight is the primary goal of the ceremony, so there is considerable verbal sharing of ideas.

After the usual opening rituals, a deck of tarot cards can be shuffled and passed around the circle, face down. Each person draws one card at random and places it before her, still face down. When all have drawn their cards, the cards are turned face up simultaneously and are mutually studied in silence.

Then the talking stick is passed around. Each woman in turn states how and why her particular card might be applicable to some aspect of herself, her life situation, her past or her future. This is followed by a second circuit, in which each woman states her impressions of the others' cards explaining why she agrees or disagrees with previous interpretations, and adding her own thoughts.

This exercise demands tact. Adverse criticism must be avoided even if an individual card seems to express someone's less pleasant characteristics. All should remember that nobody's perfect, and that the purpose of the ritual is to help, not to hurt. Some women are all too adept at putting others down, while making a pretense of sweet concern—the I'm-saying-this-for-your-own-good syndrome. This should be recognized and renounced. A ceremony of cards requires honesty, but not brutality. Participants should finish with better understanding of and sympathy for others as well as themselves.

A more complex variation of this ritual calls for each individual to draw three cards. The first card drawn is designated Body, and placed to the left side. The second is Mind, placed in the center. The third is Spirit, placed to the right. Cards are interpreted accordingly. This expanded version works best if each participant brings her own deck of cards from which to draw her triplet.

There is a more voluntary card ceremony, in which the drawing is not left to chance (or to the Goddess Fortuna), but is self-regulated. Each participant chooses a card that she finds appealing, as a representation of some aspect of herself, some ideal image, some hope or aspiration, or even some handicap or problem that she faces: anything that seems to be of personal concern. Each participant in turn presents her chosen card to the group and tells why she chose it. Others respond with a discussion.

Another kind of card ritual is storytelling, which can be a lot of fun. Having drawn one, two, or three cards at random, each participant tells a brief story made up on the spur of the moment, based on the cards' images. Others in turn may continue the same story, working their own cards' imagery into it; or they may invent separate stories of their own. Card images can also serve as inspiration for a short guided meditation led by each participant in turn. After all the stories have been told, the game may finish with a general analysis of what has been expressed, learned, allegorized, or demonstrated through the medium of storytelling.

The elemental connotations of the suits can be used in combination of meditation and self-expression. Each set of fourteen cards can be laid out on the floor of the ritual space, at each appropriate corner, in a small circle about a yard in diameter. Then each participant in turn walks around the space, stepping into each of the four small circles and pausing there to speak of her feelings about the qualities and meanings of the "element." The following speeches are examples:

"Now I am in the house of cups. I feel the flowing quality of water, how it seems to yield and retreat, but its persistence is strong enough to crumble whole cliffs. Water is like love. The tighter you grab it, the faster it disappears; but an open, relaxed hand can keep it cupped forever. I think I try too hard to grab love. I need to be more easygoing. I feel that the house of cups is a place of relaxation, very beautiful, with pale blue translucent walls, marble pools with water lilies, and the sound of waterfalls everywhere. Water is restful and maternal. All life began in the sea, and we are still always born from waters."

"Now I am in the house of wands. This is a place of power, filled with fire, lightning, electricity. There are sparks snapping all around me. It's hot. The heat drives people, it makes them uncomfortable until they get moving. I often need something electric—galvanizing—to stir me up. I need to feel power. Sometimes it's exhilarating to be driven toward a goal. Energy springs from this place. I see tall red candles in golden candlesticks, and red curtains that wave and bristle with vibrations. I want to be able to control the lightning of my own energy."

"Now I am in the house of pentacles. I am underground, in a cave. It's dark. Everything is hidden. Yet I can see stars in the darkness, golden stars. Like thoughts shining deep in the darkest part of the mind. Or maybe it's outer space, or a concept of outer space that shines in the dark. It's very mysterious. I feel that the stars might speak to me if I could understand. The pentacle lies at the core of the earth. It's a mystery, and it will always be a mystery. I am drawn to it because it is central to everything. It is the answer that we always want but can never know."

"Now I am in the house of swords. It is silvery, icy white, and cold. An ice palace, full of sharp points. This is a scary place, but I feel that if I learn its secrets I can overcome any fear. I think facing and overcoming fear is what this place is all about. A sharp, clear, precise mind has no cloudy fears, no half-formed shadows lurking around the edges. I should keep to the point, cut through the nonsense, be sure and true like a blade. Then I will be fearsome instead of afraid. I will not go wrong. I will not be blunted or diverted. I will know what I want."

A similar process of envisioning and drawing counsel from the vision can be applied to the card triplets in combination with the storytelling idea. Having drawn three cards, each participant labels them past, present, and future, then proceeds to describe impressions of the card based on experiences or feelings from her own past, present, and projected future. Sometimes the visions may be intensely personal and specific; sometimes they may be more abstract. Each person decides for herself how she will treat the material of which the card reminds her.

As a final exercise, each person might draw one last card at random from the pack and study it for a moment in order to carry away that particular image and its connotations. For the next day, or the next week, or whatever period might be agreed upon, she thinks about that card in relation to actual happenings in her daily life. In what ways does it seem relevant? What kinds of insights might the image provide, that she would not have noticed if she hadn't been thinking about it? How does the card image become transmuted into personal thoughts in accordance with actual events? Who or what does the card represent, or seem to represent?

At the next meeting, members share their thoughts and experiences in relation to their selected cards. This ongoing ritualization of responses to the cards provides an excellent way for the novice to become familiar with tarot cards and to understand how they are used as tools of insight.

Guided Meditation: The Greater Secrets

With the disappearance of the Tarot's trump cards called Major Arcana (Greater Secrets), the remaining suits evolved into the modern bridge deck. All the cards of the trump suit were eliminated except the Fool (Joker), by order of church authorities during the fourteenth and fifteenth centuries. These authorities assumed that rival religious teachings were embodied in the trump cards. There are reasons to believe that this view was essentially correct, and that those rival religious teachings had to do with the suppressed religion of the Goddess.

The first trump card, the Fool, without either number or information, presumably represented the uninitiated novice about to pass through the sequence of instruction in heretical Mysteries. Some think the Fool was allowed to remain in the deck—though not to play—for the very reason that his card had nothing to teach that churchmen could find objectionable. In much the same way, traditional pagan Mystery figures became the fools or clowns of Carnival and the *commedia*. Certainly the final image of the trumps, that of the Naked Goddess, indicated that progressive Tarot teachings would have taken a direction opposed to Christian patriarchy.

It is interesting to construct a guided meditation from clues provided by the Major Arcana sequence, just as these same cards might have represented a sacred processions, or a series of holy icons within a temple passage. The subject of the meditation begins by personifying the Fool, then passes through the Greater Secrets numbered one through twenty-one: the Magician, Papess, Empress, Emperor, Pope, Lovers, Chariot, Justice, Hermit, Wheel, Strength, Hanged Man, Death, Temperance, Devil, Tower, Star, Moon, Sun, Judgment, World. The meditation is a life journey as well as an exercise in imagination. Upon later consideration, the sequence may reveal deeper meanings, especially with a deck of tarot cards to trigger the memory.

The reading begins.

You feel happy because you are starting on a journey, even though you are not very well prepared. You have no supplies except a few odds and ends that you carry in a bag over your shoulder. You aren't even sure what's in the bag. You don't know your ultimate destination. Still, the sun is shining, and a white butterfly leads you, demonstrating trust by opening its frail wings to the vagaries of the wind. You follow the butterfly, paying no attention to a dog who snaps at your heels and seems to warn you of dangers ahead. You are young and thoughtlessly cheerful. You take joy in moving on.

Eventually you meet a strange man who catches your attention by performing magic tricks. He wears a curious broad-brimmed hat. He manipulates symbolic articles in interesting ways. He has a cup, a wand, a sword, and a coin marked with a pentacle. You believe he could reveal some hidden secrets to you. When he invites you to go with him, therefore, you consent and follow him.

He leads you to the mouth of a great cave. Just within the entrance, a veiled woman is sitting on a throne between two pillars. She holds a book filled with mysterious writing. She greets your guide as a friend. She studies you carefully, then grants permission for you to enter the broad, arched gateway into the cave behind her.

Soon you come to an underground alcove, through which a stream is running out to the open air by way of a large rift in the rocks, with the sound of a rushing waterfall. Sunlight pours in, illuminating another throne where another woman is seated. She wears a silken gown and a crown of stars. She holds a stalk of wheat. Flowers and ripe fruits are piled around her. Beyond her, through the opening in the rocks, you can see green fields rippling in a summer breeze. She smiles on you graciously, and gives you an apple, which mysteriously cleaves itself in halves in your hand, so you can see the pentacle within its core.

Your guide takes you on to another chamber open to the air. A richly dressed man is sitting on a large salt cube, holding a three-pronged scepter. The scene beyond him shows precipitous, barren red sandstone cliffs, where shrieking crows and jackdaws circle in the updrafts. The man looks sternly on you and searches your mind with his penetrating, powerful gaze. You feel a twinge of fear. With a slight, imperious twist of his wrist, he dismisses you.

The wizard next takes you to a very lofty chamber of Gothic pillars whose tops are lost in darkness. A man in ecclesiastical vestments is sitting on a throne, with two monks or acolytes groveling worshipfully before him. He fixed you with a piercing stare and raises the cross-crowned staff in his left hand, to bless or dismiss you—it's not clear which. His attendants watch you narrowly as you depart.

The next chamber seems to have a wedding in progress. An elder woman in a jeweled gown is directing the responses of a young couple who stand before her, holding each other's hands. They seem very much in love. Over their heads, half hidden in the shadows, an image of a winged love god aims his heart-tipped arrows at them. As the couple kiss at the climax of the ceremony, you have the curious impression that they have united with one another in every way possible for a man and woman to unite—in complete sexual, spiritual, and emotional harmony. They seem almost to have merged blissfully into one person having the characteristics of both sexes.

The young man is transfigured. He seems to have grown suddenly, to have become surrounded by an aura of light. He glows with power. He is like a god. He rushes toward you and seizes your hand. You can't break his grip. He drags you away at great speed, toward a far corner where you see a great golden chariot, with two horses hitched to it: one black, one white.

The young man leaps into the chariot, pulling you after him. The horses start off at a frenzied gallop. Their speed is terrifying. You cling to the side of the swaying chariot, fearing a fall. The young charioteer stands proudly upright, disdaining to hold on. His hair whips about in the wind. A canopy the color of the sky, sprinkled with stars, floats above his head.

With horror you notice that he has no reins to guide the horses. Moreover, as you look out over the animals' plunging backs, they seem to turn into something other than horses—lion-bodied sphinxes, perhaps. They are pulling apart in different directions. Sometimes they resemble one grotesque beast with two heads at opposite ends of the body. The proud young charioteer seems not to notice any of this. Suddenly the beasts altogether separate. The chariot crashes down in ruin. Then, for a while, you know nothing more.

When you awake, you find yourself in another rock chamber before another throne. A stern-looking woman sits holding a pair of balances in one hand and a huge sword in the other. Above her head, a painted eye glares down at you with almost hypnotic power. The woman points her sword in a sharp, severe gesture. Out of the shadows, a hooded, cloaked old man shuffles in the direction that her swordpoint indicates. You feel compelled to follow him.

The old man goes into darkness, tapping with his staff like a blind person. But he is not blind. He holds up a small lantern to light his way. Its feeble rays do little more than silver the edges of his long white beard. You can't see much of the dark rocky path that he follows through a world of featureless black silence.

Eventually you hear a grating noise in the distance, like a gigantic machine working inside the echoing cave. As you approach, it grows louder and louder until it seems you are almost on top of it. The old man turns a corner and holds his lamp higher. You see that his walking staff has suddenly turned into a large snake, or perhaps two snakes intertwined. He has stopped in front of a huge wheel that turns in the dark abyss.

Strange misshapen figures are riding the rim of the wheel as it rises on one side and descends on the other. When they are carried down past the floor level, they fall wailing into the dark pit. Suddenly one of them grabs you and pulls you onto the rim of the wheel. You are rising, rising, with a euphoric sense of weightlessness, to the very summit of the arc.

But then you begin to descend. You become frightened. What lies below? What is waiting for you, down there in impenetrable blackness? The wheel turns inevitably over your perch. You find that you can't hold on any longer. You let go and fall, wailing like all the others.

You recover from a kind of swoon, becoming aware of the fearful roaring of a lion. You open your eyes. There is the beast right in front of you. The lion is accompanied by a tall, commanding woman who wears exactly the same kind of broad-brimmed hat as your original magician-guide. You look at her more closely. Is she the magician himself, in a female disguise? No. She seems to be a different person, though she resembles the magician well enough to be, perhaps, his sister.

She suddenly seizes the snout of her lion in both hands. Looking intently at you, she pulls the lion's jaws apart. You understand her meaning: you must "enter the lion's mouth." Something dangerous is about to happen.

You are enveloped in darkness. You feel yourself lifted and carried by many hands. Your wrists are roughly pulled behind your back and tied together. Something is wrapped around your ankle and drawn tight. Then, to your dismay, you are turned upside down and hoisted into the air by this ankle. You dangle in considerable discomfort, the blood rushing to your head, the pulse pounding in your ears.

You are left alone in darkness and utter silence. You can do nothing for yourself now. Someone else must come to your rescue; but there is no one anywhere near. You feel the pinch of incipient panic. Must you hang helpless until your very being dissolves away? Is this the end of you? The pulse rhythm in your ears seems deafening. Are these your heart's final beats?

Slowly a pale, phosphorescent light grows in the darkness before you. Bathed in this light, an ungainly figure is approaching. As it comes closer, you see by its eldritch luminescence that it is a bare human skeleton, stiffly walking as if it had muscles to move its bones, carrying a huge scythe: the classical image of death. It turns its fleshless, grinning face toward you and raises the scythe. You see the long curved blade starting to descend. You scream despairingly. But the blade doesn't hurt you. It severs the rope above your ankle. You fall down in a heap and faint away.

When you awaken, you think you might have died and gone to a strange afterworld. You see a beautiful woman in a costume with wings on the shoulders. She stands on the bank of a stream. One of her feet is planted in the water. She holds two jars or urns, one in each hand. She holds them up and pours liquid from one to the other, back and forth. The stream of liquid flashes like rainbows. She smiles. You feel that her gesture has a profoundly meaningful relationship to the trials you have just undergone, the helpless fear and the vision of death that you have experienced.

As you rise shakily to your feet, the woman points and waves you on, through a narrow rocky corridor toward a reddish glow. You enter a chamber lighted by flaring torches and black candles. A gigantic figure stands on a dais, before which a naked man and woman are kneeling. The gigantic figure has the head and torso of a man, and the legs of a goat. Horns sprout from his skull. He fixes you with a piercing stare and raises the fiery torch in his left hand. You are suddenly reminded of the ecclesiastical lordling who was shown to you earlier.

The torch illuminates a vista on the chamber wall. You can't tell whether it is a projected moving picture, or a window opening onto a spacious landscape. You see a dark plain, where a single grim-looking tower rises frowning against the sky. The tower is crowned with a golden dome and a cross. All at once a jagged bolt of lightning shoots down from above. With a brilliant flash it knocks off the tower's crown, which burns and tumbles down in a rain of shattered bricks. Amid the debris, two human figures also fall from the broken towertop. They are too distant for you to see clearly, but they seem to be dressed like the sceptered man and the ecclesiastical lordling whom you met before.

Gradually the scene changes. The ruined tower is lost in darkness. A shining star appears, drawing you irresistibly toward its light. You hold out your arms and run toward it. The star leads you to a private garden, where a limpid brook runs past velvety green banks into a still pool. A bird is singing. You see another naked woman kneeling beside the pool. Her long red-gold hair falls like a cape over her body. She holds two jars like those of the winged woman, but she doesn't pour the contents back and forth.

Instead, she pours from one jar into the pool, and from the other jar onto the turf at her side. The star seems to pause over her head, and is joined by other stars, reminiscent of the star-crown worn by the second enthroned woman shown to you by the magician.

The stars then coalesce into one great star that grows larger and larger, until it becomes the full moon. The woman in the garden has vanished. The brook has turned into a white road, winding away into the distance across a desolate plain, like moon-path on water. Two stubby pylons stand on either side of the road, reaching up toward the moon.

There is a stirring in the pool at your feet. An enormous crab emerges from the water and reaches up with clacking claws. Suddenly two dogs or wolves appear from behind the pylons and set up a dismal concert of howling. You see drops of some dark liquid falling from the moon into the dim waters of the pool. Could it be blood? The weird canine ululations, the menacing approach of the giant crab, the pallid moonlight, all make the scene profoundly disturbing. You run away down the white moon-path.

The way leads you to a gate in the wall of another garden. You pass through the gate and find a pretty scene, illuminated by a large golden sun disc spreading out into conventionalized wavy rays. Behind the garden wall, two naked children are dancing together on soft grass, surrounded by flowers. They are a golden-haired boy and girl of the same age, perhaps a pair of twins. The garden sparkles with dewdrops. Everything feels fresh and new. You feel that you have passed through severe trials and have come at last to a place of peaceful renewal.

Then the sky darkens. The earth begins to shake. Holes open in the ground. You see that the garden has become a graveyard, and the graves are opening. Ghosts are rising up into the air. A deafening trumpet blast sounds from above. You look up. An angelic figure is riding on the clouds, blowing a long golden horn. The dead drift upward to meet it. They merge with the cloud and drift away.

Then you see the rising of the real sun. You find that you have emerged from the cave into the dawn of a new day. Far up in the air, amid the rosy sunrise clouds, the angel disappears and is replaced by the vision of an enormous naked woman, whose face is a composite of all the female faces you have seen. Poised in mid-air, she holds wands of power in her hands. She dances on one foot, in a position similar to the one you took perforce when you were hanging by your ankle. The clouds circle around her like a flowery wreath. Curious shapes form above her shoulders and beneath her feet. The roiling vapors seem to resemble a lion's head, a bull's head, the face of a man, a flying eagle.

The woman looks at you directly, and you are dazzled as if by the sun. You know she is the final revelation, the message you try to understand. Now you must think about all your experiences and their hidden meanings. While you focus your mind on this project, the sun rises higher and higher on a new morning full of light.

This guided meditation may be followed by a discussion period in which each person analyzes her own interpretation of the Major Arcana images, pointing out which passages she found particularly meaningful and why, and how the total experience affected her self-image or her attitudes. Such a discussion can lead to many new insights.

A Ceremony of Masks

Everyone wears a variety of masks. Family members see one face, friends see another, business associates another, casual acquaintances still another. Strangers passing us by on the street see the street mask, whatever we decide it should be. A mask is a metaphor for the self that we present to the world. But what are we when we are alone, and all masks are off? Or do we wear a mask even to look in the mirror?

The purpose of a mask ceremony is to play with these concepts—not to leave us psychologically naked, but to assert, admit, and accept life's inevitable masquerades, and to overcome the anxiety that goes with taking them too seriously. A lighthearted approach makes the process especially rewarding. Would we like to be Queen of the Fairies, but fear that lurking somewhere inside is a Bug-Eyed Monster? Then let us have a mask for each. Do we see one aspect of the personality as a Timid White Rabbit, another as a Ferocious Warrior Woman? Do we sense Jekyll and Hyde aspects of ourselves? Do we want to hide, or to show forth the inner spirit? Masks can do both.

The word *mask* is from a medieval ecclesiastical word for "witch," *masca*, the French *masco* or "sorceress." Witchcraft was sometimes called *mascoto*, from which came the "mascot" or totem animal, a witch's familiar. Animal-headed masks were usual in pagan religious ceremonies, when the mask itself was supposed to embody the spirit of the animal deity, the tribal totem, or even the Goddess herself, whose mask might be worn by the high priestess. Medieval mystery plays were called *masques* because they evolved from the ancient sacred drama, which was at first forbidden by the church and later, because it refused to die, simply secularized. The use of masks to change or to sacralize the character of a human being is one of the world's oldest ideas. It stems from the sacred dances of our earliest ancestors, through the animal-masked deities of Egypt and the formal masked dramas of Greece and Rome, all the way down to carnival and circus clowns and the modern theater. The archetypal depth and significance of masking can still be felt by any group in which it is tried with thought and attention.

A ceremony of masks may begin with each participant constructing her own mask(s) from materials provided by all, such as cardboard, paint, markers, beads, string, glue, rags, ribbons, yarns, cotton, papier-mâché, theatrical putty, foil, elastic, paper bags, scissors, and so on. As an alternative, participants may construct their own masks at home, taking as much time and thought as necessary, and bring their finished products to the meeting. The former course will provide the fun of communal creativity. The latter course will provide more diversity and novelty in materials and concepts. Of course, one can also buy ready-made theatrical or Halloween masks if they seem appropriate.

The most intriguing ceremony involves two masks for each individual. One mask is her idealized fantasy self, symbolizing the wish-fulfillment dream of "what I'd like to be." The other mask is her least attractive trait, symbolizing "what I don't want to be (but am afraid I might be or become)." Thus a dichotomy of "good" and "evil" personae is set up between the two masks. One might be a prissy type, the other a slattern; one a Pollyanna, the other a vampire; one a knight in shining armor, the other a dragon; and so on.

Each person in turn explains the meaning of her "good" mask and puts it on. Participants then walk around at random, meeting one another and interacting in character, according to what each thinks her mask personality would say or do. As an alternative, only two people at a time might interact while the others observe, with time limits set for each encounter. After this, the whole exercise is repeated with the "evil" masks.

One of the most interesting results commonly seen in this play-acting ceremony is the enthusiasm women display for their own "evil" characters, whose manifestations usually seem to be more colorful than what women consider "good." Thus there is some indication that women's popular images of goodness do not arise spontaneously from the inner being, but are imposed from without, from the culture, and are not quite what women really want for themselves. Later group discussion might center around possible reasons for this, and might discover more valid ideas of goodness than those usually imposed upon women in a patriarchy.

Several possible variations on the mask ceremony can provide even more scope for personal and group insights. A pair working together can first interact, then exchange their masks, each assuming her own version of the personality that goes with the other's mask. Fascinating effects emerge as a result of exchanging "good" personalities, or "evil" personalities, or one of each. Exchanges can take place in random groupings or between one pair at a time, the others observing, with time limits for each exchange. Subsequent group discussion is useful.

In another variation, each person behaves in character with her own mask for a while, then all masks are put together in a pile. Each person then chooses someone else's mask, either "good" or "evil," and its character to enact. In discussion afterward, each person in turn explains why she felt drawn to that particular mask and what meanings it held for her.

If the meeting space will not be disturbed by other groups, the masks can be left there, perhaps hung on the wall in a row, or laid in a circle to "cool" until the next meeting, when further insights might be discussed. Masks can serve also as the ancestral totemic heads served ancient peoples, being "invited" to preside over feasts and to speak oracles. The more fully the masks are invested with living, active personality, the more significant and informative they can become.

Changing the World

This is a wish-fulfillment ritual, in which women tell one another what they would most like to do in order to change the world and "remold it nearer to the Heart's desire," as the *Rubaiyat* says. While passing the talking stick, each woman expresses one or more changes that she would like to make, or to see made, which in her opinion would improve the world. Changes need not be practical, or even do-able. They can be possible suggestions, or they can be pure fantasies. It may be helpful, however, for someone in the group to write all of them down, as a form of consciousness raising. Ways might be found to implement some of them. It has been said that women can change the world, if only they become clearly aware of what they want to do.

Statements on changing the world might take the following forms: "I would pass a law that . . . " "I would declare it illegal to . . . " "I would clean up . . . " "I would throw away . . . " "I would reorganize . . . " "I would tear down . . . " "I would build . . . " "I would heal . . . " "I would stop . . . " "I would start . . . " "I would encourage . . . " "I would forbid . . . " "I would permit . . . " "I would make . . . " "I would kill . . . " "I would protect . . . " "I would develop . . . " "I would punish . . . " "I would reward . . . " "I would declare . . . " "I would ordain . . . "

Imagine that you are the Goddess, and can create a world any way you wish it to be.

Later, put together all the wish-fulfillment statements and try to envision what the world would be like if all of them were put into operation in reality. This is a useful exercise that can help to clarify goals and distinguish the possible from the impossible. It can even lead to some group projects that may be implemented now, in the local community.

The Banner

Most women enjoy fiber crafts, and it is typical of established women's groups to create a banner, shield, escutcheon, sampler, or other collective project to express the group spirit. The old-fashioned quilting bee is one example of such expression. Modern groups tend to allow more design diversity and randomness than traditional quilting patterns. The goal is to encourage each contributor to make her own personal statement.

A group banner can be created as a ritual procedure. One method is to begin with a large square of felt or canvas that can be hemmed with an open tube along the top, for insertion of a hanging rod. Mark a large circle on the square, then cut a circle of this same size from another piece of fabric. Then cut up the circular piece into pie wedges, one for each group member.

Each woman then decorates her own slice from a communal assortment of trimming materials: ribbons, buttons, beads, paint, feathers, embroidery threads, shells, fabric oddments, sequins, glue, wire, string, and so on. She may wish to incorporate a personal memento: a photograph, a piece of jewelry, a lock of hair, a bit of writing, embroidered initials, or anything else that she deems self-expressive.

When all slices are finished, they are sewn or glued into place on the banner. All group members may participate together in decorating the outer corners and the periphery of the circle.

A circle is not the only possible banner design. A large square may be divided into many small squares. A large triangle may be divided into many small triangles. A large rectangle may be divided into many small rectangles or squares. A banner can be composed of diamond shapes, hexagons, or narrow vertical strips laid side by side, or any other design that pleases the group. Perhaps a group would prefer a free-form banner on which everyone works at once, at random, painting or stitching or applying anything anywhere.

If one person in the group is especially experienced at a skill like embroidery, perhaps she alone might create the design, using materials and suggestions contributed by the others. For instance, an embroidered floral bouquet might be chosen with each group member represented by a different flower and color, for which she supplies the thread. Of if one person is a skilled artist, she might paint an escutcheon including many different symbols, each one chosen for herself by each other member. This creates a ritual object, but it is not a collective ritual of creation in the same sense as when all work together on the project.

For a temporary banner or shield made just for the purpose of one ritual occasion, a group may use a backing of cardboard or posterboard and paste on colored paper cutouts, paper chains and other constructions, painted figures and letters, or any small objects suitable for gluing. This haphazard sort of creation can be a lot of fun. A group may try this playful kind of ritual several times, to feel out their collective skills and ideas, before deciding on a serious and more permanent design.

Another collective project similar to the banner is a large circular cloth (such as a tablecloth) which can be decorated with fabric paints by every member of the group, to serve at each subsequent meeting as an altarcloth. This can be an elaborate, intricate, complex series of designs, or something as simple as a linen circle on which each woman has painted her own initials.

Copycats

We all experience the desire to influence others to be, in some way, more like ourselves. This natural human characteristic has always been particularly evident in the context of religion; and in that same context it has led to many unhappy abuses, such as persecutions, holy wars, intolerance, and the arrogant aspects of missionaryism. The ritual called Copycats is, however, a harmless way of expressing such a desire, in a manner similar to such children's games as "Simon Says" and "Follow the Leader." Copycats is that kind of a game, transplanted to an adult environment where it can be understood and used as an aid to self-illumination and social interaction as well as plain fun.

Copycats is a game with simple, obvious rules. Each person in turn does or says something, and all others in turn imitate it. When the gesture, word, phrase, sound, pose, or performance has been copied by each one around the circle, then the next person does something to be copied. Turns may pass around the circle many times, so each participant has a chance to do or say things that she needs to express. For example, people in a group might play Copycats with actions like these:

Raise your arms above your head. Stamp. Giggle. Scream. Turn a thumb down (or up). Walk around the circle and hug or kiss each other member. Light a candle and blow it out. Describe yourself in a single sentence. Kick the wall. Smell a flower. Take a sip of water or wine. Turn around three times. Take off a garment. Muss your hair. Shake your head. Cover your face. Stick out your tongue. Sing a little song. Pet an imaginary animal, child, or lover. Say words that you wish you had said on some occasion, and didn't. Strike an imaginary opponent. Jump up and down. Shake your finger. Perform a bump and grind. Express an intention for the immediate or distant future. Pick something up, and replace it. Bang your fists on your knees. Moan. Purr. Clap your hands. Thump your chest. Recite a poem. Play dead. Crawl. Rock. Hum. Do a pantomine. Call upon the Goddess. Make a statement. Place an imaginary crown on your head. Pretend you are dying or being born. Pretend you are a Stone Age woman making a pot. Reenact an embarrassing moment. Run around the outside of the circle. Do something that you consider irrational.

Freedom to indulge in irrational behavior in the safe environment of the ritual group can help women who are overly self-controlled or who find it hard to express themselves. To copy someone else's playful nonsense is a liberating exercise. It gives permission, and also encourages emulation. This ritual helps women who feel uncertain or tentative in their relationships.

An interesting variation is Blind Copycats. All except two must keep their eyes closed. If this seems difficult, blindfolds may be used. Of the working pair, the initiator performs a silent gesture. The observer watches and imitates. Then she touches the next person, who opens her eyes and observes the gesture performed by the former observer, who is now initiator. The gesture is shown from one to another all around the circle in this way, until the last participant gives the signal for all to open their eyes.

Then the gesture is repeated by the last observer and the original initiator. The whole group notes whether, and how, the gesture has been changed in its passage through different interpreters.

The same treatment can be given to phrases or stories whispered from one person to another. This version might be called Deaf Copycats. It is like the old-fashioned children's game that used to be called Whispering Down the Lane. That game effectively taught children how radically a story can be changed by passing through several retellings—and, by implication, how completely altered myths and legends can be, in passing through centuries of retelling by both approving and disapproving parties. Deaf Copycats can still serve as a useful reminder of the unreliability of gossip.

Guided Meditation:
The Colors of Creation

Close your eyes. Breathe quietly. Imagine your body suspended as if in warm water, weightless, totally relaxed, without any reference points to tell you where your limbs end or even where your right and left sides lie in relation to each other. You and your environment are one.

You are in a dark, dark place. This place is nowhere. It is utterly black. This is the infinite black of empty space, of the deepest pit, of nonexistence. There is no world, only darkness. You yourself are an essence of darkness. You have no inside and no outside. You see nothing. You feel nothing. You are nothing. You are before the beginning, formless, lightless, soundless, without dimension. Time does not pass for you, because there is no time.

But then a time comes when you think something may be appearing in the darkness—far away, small, faint, a tiny star of deepest purple against the black. At first you can't be sure it is there at all. Then slowly it grows a little brighter, taking on a richer tone of royal purple. Now you know that you have eyes to see, because you realize that the purple star is growing larger in your sight.

It seems to approach you. It becomes a spreading stain of deep violet light that gradually surrounds you. You take form before it. Now you are embedded in an infinite amethyst whose purple flashes show you that you have a form. The violet glow lights a wider and wider area around you. It becomes a purplish blue, moving in waves or ripples against the background of the dark.

You begin to see other forms. There are masses or clumps of nameless matter, churning slowly in the deep blue light. Long tendrils, like seaweeds, grow even longer. They wave gently as they grow. The light slowly changes to a rich sapphire, then fades gradually into azure and turquoise. Through the translucent liquid matrix that surrounds you, dark mountains and canyons can be seen. Shapeless living forms heave slowly over a dim sea bottom. There is no mind here, but there is life.

You rise through aqueous layers of light toward a brighter glow from above. Now the dim blue depths are far below you. The light shades from turquoise to emerald. Deep-green masses of algae and weed are floating around you in a rich nutrient soup of liquid green light. You are green and growing too. You can swim. You move through jade-green forests bathed in cool light. You float higher. The green glow takes on a golden tone. It shimmers with chartreuse fluorescence. You sense that there are not many layers left now between you and the highest source of light.

You yearn for that golden source. You feel that it can't be very far above you now. You continue to drift upward. The living, moving forests of green sink away below. There are other shapes around you: strange beings that seem to fly through the golden glow. They are indistinct. They have no faces. Like you, they strive upward. Like you, they desire the gold.

Happiness is yellow. You envision yellow flowers, fruits, birds, butterflies in floods of sunlight. Your thoughts take shape. As you see them, they appear.

You break through a final surface into dazzling lemon-hued brightness. There is a fierce yellow star, so huge, so close, so intensely brilliant that it scarifies the eye. It is consuming itself in a holocaust of light. What has been made here? Was your yearning for gold so great? Was your wish so strong as this?

The land is burning. Orange flames shoot into the fiery air from vents in the ochre-colored rocks. Orange sands whip hissing veils along the shore of the cool nurturing sea that you have now left behind. This is a harsh place, brilliant with hot color, blazing with lava, filled with fantastic twisted shapes of rock. Can life exist here?

Yes, it can. The nurturing sea gives up some of its life forms. Slowly they creep onto the burning land. Some of them put roots into the bare rock. Some of them stiffen their soft bodies and move faster. They enclose in themselves the essences of sea and fire. Their internal fluids take on the color of fire, which then cools and calms to a bright new tint: blood red.

Now is life newly self-aware, sustained by the hidden hot red within, steaming with energy, warmed by inner fires. The mighty star begins to decline, its radiance shading into ruby red. A deep blood-colored glow bathes the land. Garnet shadows embrace the hills. Perhaps you can foresee a green mantle over this raw red landscape. But one thing you know: you have come to your home.

You have the knowledge of the red essence. You know the blood secrets of your kind, the warm creatures, furred, feathered, or haired. You know that you and they share the same scarlet life force. A quest for this knowledge brought you to birth, long ago, out of the womb of darkness.

You also know that there is no knowing destined to endure forever. In time, there will be a return to the primal deep—to the black nonbeing from which all being arises, and to which it returns. Do not forget the darkness. Remember. Understand the beginnings and the endings of your powers. Live and love your ordained time. Know the warm red colors of your life. But do not forget, and do not be afraid.

The Ultimate Fantasy: Imaginative Self-Indulgence

The ritual of self-indulgence involves creative fantasizing. Few people can ever be as self-indulgent in real life as they would like to be. The point of this exercise, then, is to show women that it's all right to have wish-fulfillment dreams—even extravagant ones. Many women are so squelched by life in a patriarchal society that they dare not daydream creatively. Obeying the forces of consumerism that manipulate them almost every waking moment, they entertain few grander visions than the possible possession of many more, newer, costlier manufactured objects, and perhaps a more conventionally beautiful body on which to hang more expensive clothes.

Certainly a self-indulgence fantasy ritual may encompass ideas of this sort. But it is meant to go further: to encourage genuinely personal dreams arising from the inner imagination, rather than dreams provided by the advertising industry.

Each woman brings a candle of her favorite color and places it before her in its holder. As she receives the talking stick and begins to verbalize her fantasy, she lights her candle and concentrates on the flame. When all have spoken, and all candles are alight, they may be placed on the altar in a tight little circle around a central power object: such as a polished sphere of quartz, a natural crystal, a large pentacle, a vase of essential oil, or a Goddess image. Then all together raise their voices in a group hum, concentrating on their own as well as each other's fantasies, envisioning them as realistically and in as much detail as possible. Thus each woman's dream is supported by affirmation from others. The combined light of the candles may be seen as the light of the collective inner eye.

Here are some examples:

"I am a queen, the absolute monarch of an exotic long-ago country. I live in a palace made of polished marble and fragrant wood. There are great halls thirty feet high, with pillars of silver studded with gems, purple velvet rugs, silk-covered divans with huge cushions, and vast windows of colored glass that throw rainbow lights over everything. I wear the richest clothes, encrusted with gold and silver embroidery. I have ropes of pearls, ruby bracelets, sapphire anklets, and rings even on my toes. I have careful, kind, obedient servants attending to my every wish. I have a maid whose only function is to brush and comb my long, lustrous hair for half an hour every day. I have masseurs, butlers, footmen, messengers, and a team of the world's best chefs in my kitchen. Everything I touch is a work of art, made with loving care. My people adore me and want me to have all this because I am just, and kind, and I represent their divinity. Every day I appear to them in my Hall of Justice and solve their disputes and other problems with infinite wisdom."

"I am an angel. I have great white wings. I can fly even outside the earth's atmosphere. I can look down on the world and see everything that happens. I have power to right the wrongs. I can swoop down and zap evildoers by pointing my finger at them. I can bring rewards to good people by waving my hand. I am never tired or hungry or sick. I am immortal."

"I am the world's sexiest and most beautiful woman. Men adore me. I am always surrounded by handsome, muscular young men wearing almost nothing, trying to lure me with their bodies. They caress me, stroke me, kiss me all over, bring me gifts, write poems for me, and live only to woo me and give me pleasure. I make each one happy when I take notice of him. I take a different one to bed every night."

"I will live a hundred thousand years and become the wisest human being on earth, but my body will remain always twenty-five years old and perfectly fit. I will be invulnerable to all injuries and illnesses. Nothing can harm me. In time, I will know almost everything because I can go on learning more every century."

"I am the mother of ten adorable, happy children who never misbehave, and always enjoy each other's company as well as mine. We live in a comfortable, safe place where there are woods and fields, tame animals, a crystal clear lake for swimming, and flowers everywhere. Each day the children and I play together. At night their warm little bodies press all around me while I read stories to them before tucking them into their beds. I have one baby who never grows, but remains always a suckling infant, because I always did enjoy nursing."

"It may seem trite and artificial, but my favorite fantasy is the Superwoman one. I'd like to be like Superman, with X-ray vision, able to fly, having infinite strength, and adored by everybody because I'm always on the side of truth and justice—but not necessarily the American Way, which has a lot of flaws."

"I can create any kind of environment to live in, then make it vanish and create another. For a while I might live in a beautiful cave with walls made of opal and a natural throne of pure rock crystal in my reception chamber. Or I might live in a big suburban house surrounded by formal gardens, everything beautifully designed, with every latest convenience. Or I might live in a medieval castle with banners on the battlements, and solid gold furniture. Or I might live under the sea in a coral garden, like a mermaid, among all the beautiful sea creatures, making friends with dolphins and whales. Or I might live on a distant planet in some other solar system, where everything is different: a garnet-red sky, golden vegetation, houses like crystal domes, plants that move and arrange themselves in different esthetic patterns. Or I might live in a shimmering silver mist, everywhere and nowhere."

"I am the queen of animals. I live in the woods, and all the wild creatures are my pets. They come when I call them, and cuddle up to me, and talk to me in their own languages, all of which I understand perfectly. The birds are my scouts and messengers. They bring me news of the world. The deer carry me on their backs when I want to travel: so do the bears and the big cats. The squirrels and raccoons bring me gifts, soft mosses for my bed, ripe berries and nuts. The spiders spin silk for me. Poisonous snakes guard me and drive away any intruders who might want to harm my woodland. I love all the animals and they love me."

"I have created a paradise island where I live with a few chosen friends and compatible relatives. The beaches are like fine white sugar. The sea is always turquoise blue and calm. The sun shines every day, and there are gentle showers at night to keep things green. Delicious fruits, nuts, and vegetables grow on my island, always ripe and ready to be plucked. There are springs of cold, clear water, with rocky waterfalls and bathing pools surrounded by banks of flowers. There are shady places and sunny places. The climate is always perfect, warm enough to go naked, but cool enough to be refreshing. We swim, sunbathe, eat, play, make love, tell stories. We also have books to read, work to do, art and craft supplies, and spiritual ways of sharing."

"I am a holy nymph living in the world's most sacred temple on the summit of a mountain, far above the clouds, surrounded by beautiful crystals, rainbow-colored mists, exquisite furniture, and many instruments for observing the moon and stars. Though it's very high, it is never too cold. I have a lover, my constant companion. We live together always in that exalted romantic state of the early period of a love affair. We never tire of each other, or disagree, or become irritated. We are perpetually delighted by our love. I study the skies, and meditate. The things I do can magically influence the risings and settings of the sun and moon. Their light strikes my temple before anything else on earth. I determine the colors and shapes of every sunrise and sunset."

"I can fly through outer space, much faster than the speed of light. I travel the interstellar and even the intergalactic spaces. I visit the planets of other solar systems, every one different from every other. There is no end to the diversity that I can see and experience. I want to be a space traveler forever."

In a world where men have always poured their collective fantasies into the figure of God, surely it is not surprising that women's inner fantasies should sound so much like the archetypal images of the Goddess.

Rebirthing

At all times in all places, men have seized upon the feminine miracle of birth as the primary metaphor for any passage into a new phase of life: baptisms, initiations, puberty rites, and all other transitions. Though males never experience birthgiving, they have doggedly tried to identify with it, and to claim superior meaning for their own symbols of it. Even today, many men's groups ritualize a second birth as initiation. From primitive male puberty ceremonies to Christian baptisms, emphasis is on the born-again idea. In India, both initiations and purifications used to involve dragging the candidate bodily through a gigantic yoni (vulva emblem).

Originally of course, one could only be "born again" from a surrogate mother, at the hands of priestesses, not priests. As the only real birth givers, women stood closer to the real miracle. Women were thought to possess the *mana* that caused inner spiritual change. Rebirth rituals therefore belong more truly to women, who have always had the natural right to claim them. Women have a natural understanding of this symbolism. It is appropriate that women should devise rebirthing rituals to take back their own miracle from those who incongruously usurped it.

Symbolic rebirth may solemnize any moment in life that can be perceived as a spiritual turning-point, a resolution to change one's life, a curing of an illness, a breaking out of an uncomfortable situation, or a consolidation of a new membership. An entire group can plan rebirthing rituals for one, several, or all of its members. Such rituals can be accomplished in many ways.

A simple and common procedure is to walk or crawl along a spiral path laid out on the floor or ground. Since the Stone Age, a spiral has represented passage into magical uterine depths and reemergence therefrom. A spiral is one of the primordial female symbols. It represents the mysterious "bowels of mercy" from which one is born, as the Bible puts it—that is, the interior of the mother. The spiral can be marked outdoors on the ground with pegs, stones, cuttings, branches stuck into the soil, dribbles of paint, mown paths through a field, and so on. Indoors it can be painted on a king-size sheet (or several of them) laid out on the floor, or defined by strings, ribbons, paper, or lines of tarot cards. Each person in turn may undergo the rebirthing procedure by entering the spiral, going into the center to curl up in fetal position for a while, then uncurling and slowly retracing the path. This procedure may be accompanied by silence, music, a single slow drumbeat, a low group humming, or a running commentary on the sensations and meanings of the ritual according to each participant.

A more elaborate plan is to construct a three-dimensional womb symbol of wood, fabric, cushions, furniture; or (outdoors) branches, earthworks, or cinder blocks. There might even be a semipermanent covered tunnel dug, for example, into a hillside. The idea is that each member of the group may spend some time huddled within this enclosure, and may then be drawn forth by other members, who act as spiritual midwives. In ancient times, narrow openings in sacred caves were often used for the purpose of rebirthing. After undergoing hours or even days in such a terrestrial "womb," the individual was drawn forth, and subsequently fed only milk for a while, like a baby.

Group members may use their own bodies as the collective womb symbol. This too was much done in antiquity. Priestly ordinations and official adoptions often involved a rite in which the candidate crawled out from under a woman's skirts, or passed between the legs of the adoptive mother. A group of women together can stand in a tight line with legs apart, to form a tunnel or "birth canal" for each one to crawl through in turn. Women can also form a compact circle by wrapping their arms around each other, while the one to be born crouches down in the center and awaits an opening to squeeze through. The collective group may rhythmically sway, pulsate, or pull together to represent uterine contractions. As each one is "born," she can be given a sip of milk then rocked in the group formation usually known as the Cradle.

The Cradle is a simple raising of one person on the hands and arms of a number of others, starting from the floor and rising to the standing group's waist level—or even above their heads, if there are enough people participating. When the individual is raised up, the group provides a gentle swaying or rocking motion which is very comforting to experience. Even a heavy person can be lifted easily by seven or eight others together; the more lifters there are, the easier the lift. The liftee should start lying flat on the floor, while the others stoop and slide their hands underneath her body, limbs, and head wherever they can reach. Then all stand up together, forming the Cradle with the liftee lying in their midst.

Prior to birth-giving rituals, a period of fasting or other symbolic purification is often recommended. Purging and fasting have been used as preparations for spiritual changes from time immemorial. Pagan Roman women maintained a month's modified fast for their annual Matronalia (Feast of the Mother) connected with the spring planting. Their custom was taken up by the early Christian church and became the fast of Lent. In memory of such ritual purification stolen from female tradition, a modern group might engage in modified fasting for several days or a week. As an alternative, group members might agree to eat nothing throughout the day before a rebirthing in the evening, to be followed by a celebratory feast.

"Purifications" such as fasting should never be carried to extremes. Although severe fasting has long been one of the most common ways to produce religious visions—in the form of hunger hallucinations—we now know that this is harmful to the body. Women's groups respect the body and do not seek to abuse it. Therefore nothing should be undertaken that is hazardous to anyone's health.

A purely mental or emotional kind of purification can be represented by casting off any attitudes, dependencies, fears, or grudges that might be felt as handicaps to a new phase of existence. These can be written down on pieces of paper and burned, or they can be spoken aloud and tossed away by gestures, or they can be poured out with water, or they can be "sacrificed" by destroying an article connected with the problem. On one actual occasion after an embittered divorce, a woman purged her lingering resentment by tearing her wedding dress to shreds before a rebirthing. Another woman in a similar situation threw her wedding ring into the sea.

Sometimes rebirthing can be followed by a change of name, or the adoption of a new "soul name." In ancient paganism, children were often given a secret soul name known only to their parents, and carefully concealed from public knowledge lest it be used to cast evil spells. Cities, too, had soul names that were kept secret. In like manner, "born-again" members of religious sects took new soul names by which to be known to their particular deity. This pagan habit was also copied by the early Christian church and is still carried on today, as members of religious orders give up their worldly names and adopt new ones.

Rebirthing therefore might involve renaming, or at least the revision of a nickname. The way a person feels about her name often affects the way she feels about her whole personality; so a renaming can carry considerable significance for such an individual.

There are yet other ways of symbolizing a spiritual rebirth. Water, of course, has been a standard womb symbol for many thousands of years; and baptismal rebirth by sprinkling or immersion is now standard Christian practice. Still for women who don't mind the patriarchal connotation, a lovely rebirth ceremony might be built around a secluded pond or private swimming pool on a moonlit night, where participants can cast off all their clothes and rise mother-naked from the "uterine" waters. This is strictly a warm-weather procedure, of course. In a colder season, women might wrap themselves in quilts and lie completely covered, in fetal position, listening to soft music for a while before emerging as reborn. This could perhaps follow a brief immersion in a warm bathtub. Another seasonal idea: one group member could be completely covered by the others beneath a "womb" of heaped, dry autumn leaves. Or, one member can be wrapped mummy-like in layers of sheets, like swaddling clothes, to be unwrapped later. (Be sure that breathing room is left for the nose and mouth.)

A group that likes to inject humor into ritual can have fun with rebirthing. The reborn ones can pantomime infantile or child-like behavior: gurgling, cooing, crawling, thumb-sucking, playing with toys, and so on. They might even bring large squares of white cloth and wear them as diapers. They might play mother-and-baby roles, making a game of it, reversing roles after a while. They might spend a little time collectively imitating a nursery school. They might imagine or describe themselves "growing up," rising to their knees, then to their feet, and walking or dancing.

However it is done and for whatever reason, rebirthing can be a refreshment and a renewal.

CHANT

Come forth, child,
Open your eyes,
Look at the world
Waiting here for you.
Blessed be.

The Eight Hinges of the Year

The pagan calendar included eight major religious holidays, spaced about six weeks apart throughout the year. They were the equinoxes, solstices, and cross-quarter days. The Vernal Equinox falls around March 21, the Midsummer Solstice around June 21, the Autumnal Equinox around September 21, and the Midwinter Solstice around December 21. Between these four were the cross-quarter days—or, more correctly, the cross-quarter eves. Pagan festivals took place during the night before the corresponding Christianized "saint's day" because the pagan calendar had reckoned the days from noon to noon, not midnight to midnight. The cross-quarter eves were: Imbolg (Candlemas), the eve of February 1; Beltane (May Eve), the eve of May 1; Lugnasad (Lammas Eve), the eve of August 1 and Samhain (Halloween), the eve of November 1.

Doubtless these eight festivals represented mergings of still older traditions. Some people might have celebrated only the cross-quarter eves, others only the solstices and equinoxes. Others may have combined them in different ways with other festivals. The Catholic church eventually adopted them all, and reassigned them—or, at least, their following daytimes—to various saints. The day after Halloween became "All Saints' Day" or "All Hallows" because the original festival had honored the spirits of all the pagan dead together.

It was thought that at each of these crucial times, there came an opening in the crack between the worlds: a possibility of connection and interpenetration between the spirit world and the world of living earth dwellers. That's why the ghosts of dead ancestors could be invited to the feast on Halloween and petitioned for oracular consultations; and why earth spirits like fairies and elves (who were really the ancient dead) came out of the hills and barrows to dance on May Eve, which was Germany's Walpurgisnacht. An artificial Saint Walpurga was invented to Christianize the latter holiday, but she was never a real person, only a pious fraud.

Symbolic time wheels usually had eight spokes, connected with these eight "joints" of time, when seasons seemed visibly to change and certain things happened in the solar cycles. These occasions needed appropriate ceremonies, according to ancient beliefs. Nature's time cycles must be duly honored so that all things would be maintained in the right sequence. Our remote ancestors doubtless believed that their human rituals were necessary to keep the world going and to stave off the arrival of doomsday.

Modern women's circles usually create a special ceremony for each of the eight hinges of the year. Each one of these festivals affords an opportunity for creative planning, a bit more elaborate than regular meetings. Some groups like to get together a week or two before each festival, in order to "brainstorm" an agenda. Each member suggests various kinds of rituals she would like to try. Each contributes ideas for music, dance, actions, invocations, poetry readings, and other procedures to express the central theme of the seasonal holiday.

Certain traditional colors have been established for the eight festivals. Groups may agree to wear garments of the appropriate color, or else provide colored scarves or ribbons for each participant to wear. Candles, foods, wreaths and other decorations can carry out the same color themes.

Beltane was always the springtime ritual connected with "wearing of the green" in honor of the earth's fresh green garment. Therefore green is the sacred color of May Eve. Lammas, the harvest feast, features red for the Mother Goddess, for summer's heat, and for the blood, wine, and fire symbolic of ongoing life. The Halloween color has always been black, the color of the Crone Goddess who presides over the Feast of the Dead. The color for Candlemas is orange, yellow, or gold, the color of the flames that used to encourage the burgeoning sun during the waning weeks of winter.

In token of the same sun's rebirth, white is worn at the Winter Solstice. White was also the color of the virgin Goddess who gave birth to the sun in the first place. The Summer Solstice features royal purple for the sun's temporary enthronement at the pinnacle of heaven. The equinoxes call for a combination of black and white, or light and dark blue shades: light above dark in the spring, dark above light in the fall.

Flowers and other plant decorations should be appropriate to the seasons. One of the pleasant old customs was the wearing of wreaths of seasonal flowers, leaves or grasses around the heads or necks of celebrants; or at the very least, a sprig of something tucked into the hair. Altar decorations are especially pleasing when they reflect the season.

The following eight ritual suggestions cover each one of the Eight Hinges in turn, with certain details that might be included in their celebrations. Please remember that these are only suggestions, and any group wishing to try something different should do so. Each one of the eight festivals should be a unique event, both its planned and unplanned parts dedicated to that particular time of that particular year. Think of the festivals as times of especially heightened creativity and freedom of expression.

The Vernal Equinox (March 21)

Prepare four sheets of paper with the following question-and-answer series written on each sheet. After invocation and blessing of the space, let four people take one sheet apiece and a candle, and stand outside the circle, facing inward, one in each of the four cardinal directions. These four then read aloud in antiphonal style, one at a time, beginning with the person whose back is to the north (N). She is answered by south (S). Then east speaks (E), and is answered by west (W).

ANTIPHONAL CHANT

N: What is this night?
S: It is the night of the Vernal Equinox.
E: What is the meaning of this night?
W: It is the night of balancing.
N: What are the elements that balance on this night?

s: Tonight the darkness and the light are equals.

E: After this night of balancing, which will prevail?

w: From this night forward, light will prevail over darkness.

N: How do we recognize ourselves on this night?

s: We turn away from darkness. We embrace the light. We find the light within ourselves.

E: Who helps us?

w: Our Goddess helps us.

N: What is our Goddess?

s: She is the shade and the brightness, the fire and the ash, the morning and the evening.

E: Who is our Goddess?

w: She is the Virgin of Light, the Crone of Darkness, the Mother of Time.

N: Where is our Goddess?

s: She is in our hearts in all seasons of the turning year.

E: Who is our Goddess?

w: Behold, she is ourselves.

There are five sections to this chant, each begun by North's question. If a pentacle is inscribed on the floor or ground, the whole circle may walk slowly around the pentacle, passing one point of the star through each of the five sections, returning to original positions at the end. Alternatively the speakers themselves may walk slowly around the outside of the circle during the chant, though they maintain the same directional characters.

There will be a repetition of this ritual suggested, with slight changes, for each of the eight seasonal festivals.

The Vernal Equinox used to be considered the beginning of the New Year. It was a time of joy called forth by the resurrection of the "Light of the World" (sun god) from the underworld of winter. Its moon-bound celebration Easter was named originally for the Saxon Goddess Eostre, a northern version of Astarte, whose bud-time savior god arose when light first prevailed over darkness each spring.

Vernal Equinox rituals center around the annual warming of the earth and the renewal of her fertility; seeds sprouting in darkness after a winter of dormancy; and the rising of the spring constellations in the night sky. Appropriate decorations are budding twigs, crocuses, willow catkins, the first shoots of grasses, or wheat sprouts in an earthenware pot, like the famous "Gardens of Adonis" that women planted each year for the resurrection of Eostre's vegetation god.

Ice can be melted in a sieve and allowed to drip over soil in the pottery bowl, representing the spring thaw. Mud is a good symbol for early spring, which is mud time in most of the north temperate zone. *Mud* came from the same root word as *mother*, because the womb of the Goddess who gave birth to the universe was sometimes viewed as a primal soup of the two female elements, earth and water.

Dances can pantomime the rising of new shoots from the earth, and the rising of the sun's path ever higher in the sky. Chants can be constructed on the spot from a combination of phrases about spring, one uttered by each person in turn around the circle, such as: "New light!" "Flowers to come!" "Virgin Spring, we greet you!" "Sap rising!" "Lady Earth lives!" "Hail dear sun, shine brighter!" "Bring us softer days!" And so on.

A special candle can be passed around the circle, as each person makes a wish over the flame for renewal of something—hope, creativity, health, goodwill, wisdom, success in some project, better relationships. Specific wishes for one's self or others may be expressed. The wish candle is allowed to burn all the way down by the end of the evening. To make sure of this, start with a candle that is small or short.

The Vernal Equinox is also a good time to make vows. "This summer I will lose five pounds." "Before Beltane I will clear out my attic." "This month I will finish *The Decline and Fall of the Roman Empire*." "From this day forward I will not turn on television until after the dinner hour." "By Midsummer I will finish the two dresses and three blouses that I bought material for." "Whatever it takes, I will make peace with my estranged sister-in-law."

As this is the pagan New Year, some of the observances that our society has relegated to January 1 might be transferred to the Vernal Equinox: noisemaking, confetti, perhaps even a communal sip of champagne. It is a time of regeneration and expectation. It is the festival of freshness. Let your creative rituals reflect this idea.

Beltane (May Eve)

The Merry Month of May was one of the most joyous times in the ancient calendar. In old England, the whole month was devoted to outdoor celebrations, "May ridings," wearings-of-the-green, and periods of sexual license. It was believed that the green-clad fairies (pagan spirits) ruled the month of May, and in some way helped Mother Earth to clothe herself in green yet one more time, so life could go on for her human and animal children. As for the Vernal Equinox, prepare the Antiphonal Chant:

N: What is this night?

S: It is the night of Beltane.

E: What is the meaning of this night?

W: It is the festival of new growth.

N: What do we honor on this night?

S: We honor the refreshment of the life force, and the ever renewed beauty of our Earth.

E: After this festival of new growth, what will we do?

W: We will work to bring forth good fruits from our labors.

N: How do we recognize ourselves on this night?

S: We dance with joy. We blossom with the flowers. We call upon the Maiden who brings new life.

E: Who helps us?

W: Our Goddess helps us.

N: What is our Goddess?

S: She is the sweetness of the rose, the grace of the lily, the breath of the south wind.

E: Who is our Goddess?

W: She is the Virgin of Light, the Crone of Darkness, the Mother of Time.

N: Where is our Goddess?

S: She is in our hearts in all seasons of the turning year.

E: Who is our Goddess?

W: Behold, she is ourselves.

The primary symbol of Beltane was the Maypole, which Christian authorities condemned as a devilish obscenity, knowing full well that it used to represent a gigantic phallus planted in Mother Earth to fructify her womb. The people loved it and would not give it up. Even in Puritan times, when it was denounced from the pulpit as an abominable idol, the Maypole was still annually set up, decorated with flags and flowers and ribbons, danced around, admired, and worshiped.

A Maypole dance may be the most appropriate traditional Beltane ritual. Its sexual suggestiveness is not out of place even in an all-female group. On the contrary: ancient matrifocal religions were always much concerned with proper sexual relations between the Goddess and her male consort.

Outdoors, almost any tree can serve as a Maypole; or else a real pole can be planted in a hole dug in the ground. Dig deep, and fill in empty space with stones and soil so the pole will stand straight and firm. Indoors, a pillar, hat tree, or piece of lumber will do, if firmly propped in a vertical position. The pole must be free-standing in the center of an open space if there is to be any dancing around it.

The traditional Maypole dance starts with long ribbons attached high up on the pole. Each dancer holds the end of a ribbon. The circle of dancers begins far out from the pole, so the ribbons are kept fairly taut. There should be an even number of dancers, facing alternately clockwise and counterclockwise. All dancers move in the direction they are facing, passing right shoulders with the first, left shoulders with the next, and so on around (see description under "Dancing," page 56) to braid the ribbons over-and-under around the pole. Those passing on the inside will have to duck. Those passing on the outside raise their ribbons to slide over.

If circumstances make a Maypole dance impossible, then the altar can be decorated with green ribbons laid in circles or pentacles. At the end, the ribbons may be cut up and distributed to each participant, who later ties her piece of ribbon around any tree or pole of her choice.

If there is to be no Maypole, ceremonial planting of anything is an appropriate Beltane observation, whether it is in an outdoor site or an indoor pot. Any seed, bulb, slip, seedling, or young tree will do. Each group member may participate in the digging, and also take home a pinch of soil to add to a private altar planting.

A spring flower festival used to commemorate the classical drama of the Maiden's blossom-time return from the underworld. In token of this, a women's group might decorate its youngest member with flowers, and greet her as the Maiden under such names as Kore, Flora, Freya, Blodeuwedd, or Persephone. A doll or statue could also serve as an object of decoration.

Special foods might be served, such as candied flower petals, or pomegranates, the traditional womb-symbolic food of Persephone's underworld. Participants might also cut out and construct artificial flowers of colored paper, felt, or cloth. Other good things to share around the May circle are: flowery incense, perfumes, sachets of dried flower petals, artificial flowers of silk or beads, flower-decorated notecards, green herbs, May wine, and rosebuds.

Midsummer Solstice (June 21)

This solstice marks the sun's maximum height in the sky, making it the longest day of the year. The themes of a solstice festival at this time are light and warmth. Pagans used to signify such themes with Midsummer bonfires. Young men and women leaped over the flames. Old wives claimed that the summer's grain crops would grow as high as the leapers were able to jump; so they exerted themselves as much as they could, for the benefit of the crops.

As for the Vernal Equinox, prepare the Antiphonal Chant:

N: What is this night?
S: It is the night of the Midsummer Solstice.

E: What is the meaning of this night?

W: It is a peak of power.

N: What is the element that rules this night?

S: Tonight the light reaches the limit of its power over darkness.

E: After this night of power, what is the element that will wane?

W: From this night forward, the light will wane and the darkness will grow.

N: How do we recognize ourselves on this night?

S: We greet the sun and glory in the light.

E: Who helps us?

W: Our Goddess helps us.

N: What is our Goddess?

S: She is the brilliant fire of heaven, the living heat, the world's golden noontides.

E: Who is our Goddess?

W: She is the Virgin of Light, the Crone of Darkness, the Mother of Time.

N: Where is our Goddess?

S: She is in our hearts in all seasons of the turning year.

E: Who is our Goddess?

W: Behold, she is ourselves.

Since the weather is usually warm at this time, groups might like to plan an outdoor ceremony even if most meetings are indoors. If a place is found suitable for building a bonfire, participants might want to try the fire-leaping ceremony. Of course, this should be done with care. The fire must be kept under control. Indoors, a modest symbolic hop over a candle might do well enough.

Decorations may be large, round, ostentatious: sun discs with radiant rays, circles cut from foil, coins or medallions, gilded plates, crystal balls, sunflowers. Lights, crystals, lenses, prisms and other symbols of clarity are appropriate. Participants might dress up like queens in royal purple and gold, with lots of jewelry; or, if the weather is hot, they might dress down in as little as possible, or even in nothing at all (see "Nakedness," pages 148–51).

The festival of light is a good time for figure-8 dances that express the turning of the year's cycles, and for invoking various versions of the Sun Goddess (Sul, Atthar, Aditi, Glory-of-Elves). It's a good time for positive energy, for making resolutions and vows that require inner strength. It's a good time to draw up rules to live by, or to review the Laws of the Goddess, pages 181–83. Symbols of aspiration may be placed on the altar, or passed around the circle for supportive comments.

Guided meditations for this season should emphasize courage, intellectual competence, heroine figures, female rulers, self-confidence, and a direct, effective approach to problems. Openness, reason, and willingness to engage in frank, free communication are desirable. Blockages caused by imaginary fears should be faced and exorcised. The themes of light and clarity may be developed by any ritual means that the group might prefer.

Lammas (August Eve)

Lammas means the Feast of Bread. It was a festival of the wheat harvest. Its older name, Lugnasad, meant the sacrifice of the god Lug, or Lud, whose name is still preserved in London (formerly Lugdunum) where the god's shrine stood on Ludgate Hill. Like other vegetation deities, Lug was killed (reaped) and buried (planted) so he could rise again from the dead as a new crop.

As for the Vernal Equinox, prepare the Antiphonal Chant:

N: What is this night?
S: It is the night of Lammas.
E: What is the meaning of this night?
W: It is the feast of bread.
N: What do we honor on this night?
S: We honor the fruits of the Earth, our ongoing sustenance.

E: After this feast of bread, what will we do?

W: We will tend and store our harvest, preserving what is
    necessary to life.

N: How do we recognize ourselves on this night?

S: We knead the dough. We bake the good bread. We call
    upon the Mother who gives us our daily food.

E: Who helps us?

W: Our Goddess helps us.

N: What is our Goddess?

S: She is the benevolence of our mother planet, the rich gifts
    of her soil, the nourishment of our bodies.

E: Who is our Goddess?

W: She is the Virgin of Light, the Crone of Darkness, the
    Mother of Time.

N: Where is our Goddess?

S: She is in our hearts in all seasons of the turning year.

E: Who is our Goddess?

W: Behold, she is ourselves.

The Feast of Bread naturally features bread, preferably home-made from whole grain flour. If an oven is available, the group might bake bread on the spot and share fresh loaves around at the conclusion of the meeting.

The grain god Lug can be created as a dough figure, like the fairytale Gingerbread Man. The figure is passed around the circle and dismembered, as everyone eats a piece of him. This was one of the original forms of holy communion, when the flesh of grain gods like Osiris, Adonis, and Tammuz was ceremonially eaten by their worshipers, who thus became symbolically one with each other as they also internalized their deity. This very process was supposed to make communicants godlike (immortal), so they could obtain godlike eternal life. The same idea carried over into Christianity—the whole Christian "mystery" of salvation was based on it—but its origin was pagan.

Our foremothers regarded grain with considerable awe, see-ing as a holy mystery the fact that it is both seed and edible fruit at the same time. Thus it was thought to contain all three aspects of the Goddess: Virgin (child of the earth; fruit), Mother (life-giv-ing, fertile food spirit), and Crone (withered plant, gone to seed, ready for retirement to the underworld and later resurrection). Such unfathomable nature magic was much contemplated in temples of Demeter, Ceres, Ops, Hera, and other Earth Mothers. One ear of grain "reaped in silence" was exhibited as the ultimate revelation in the famous Eleusinian Mysteries. Native Americans and the peoples of Mexico and Peru similarly worshiped the corn (maize) for much the same reasons. Therefore corn on the cob is appropriate for a Lammas ritual, as is any other grain plant.

Seeds of any kind can be used at Lammas to create pentacles, pictures, abstract designs for oracular interpretation, decorative items, or gifts. Seeds can be glued to squares or discs of cardboard to create pictures. Seeds can be strung on thread or wire, to become Lammas bracelets and necklaces. Seeds can be enclosed in small screw-top jars to become rattles. The whole circle can be enclosed in a circle of seeds, bread crumbs, or flour. Outdoors, the group might wind in single file through a woodland, laying down a trail of bread or seeds for the birds and other animals to find. At the same time, each person may pick up a special twig, stone, or leaf to bring back to the altar.

Lammas is also an appropriate time to make a corn dolly. Usually this is a poppet of corn husks shaped and tied together, dressed in a skirt, apron, and bonnet, and kept in a special place until the same time next year, when she is ceremonially buried along with the seed corn.

Gratitude for the harvest, feasting and general merriment have been dominant patterns in harvest festival the world over, from the remote times when human beings first began to practice agriculture.

The Autumnal Equinox (September 21)

The Autumnal Equinox is also a harvest festival and a preparation for the cooler, darker times ahead, when days are "drawing in," as the old saying goes.

As for the Vernal Equinox, prepare the Antiphonal Chant:

N: What is this night?
S: It is the night of the Autumnal Equinox.

E: What is the meaning of this night?

W: It is the night of balancing.

N: What are the elements that balance on this night?

S: Tonight the light and the darkness are equals.

E: After this night of balancing, which will prevail?

W: From this night forward, darkness will prevail over light.

N: How do we recognize ourselves on this night?

S: We turn away from light. We embrace the darkness. We
find the darkness within ourselves.

E: Who helps us?

W: Our Goddess helps us.

N: What is our Goddess?

S: She is the brightness and the shade, the ash and the fire,
the evening and the morning.

E: Who is our Goddess?

W: She is the Virgin of Light, the Crone of Darkness, the
Mother of Time.

N: Where is our Goddess?

S: She is in our hearts in all seasons of the turning year.

E: Who is our Goddess?

W: Behold, she is ourselves.

Autumnal dances can pantomime the fall of the leaf, the
shortening of the day, the closing in of creative energies toward a
period of rest in the dark core of things. Like the beginning of gestation, when everything is going on in secret, this is a woman-centered time. Not concerned with striving always and only toward
the idea of the light, ancient matrifocal religions recognized the
equality and equal necessity of shadows and caves, interiors as
well as surfaces, winters as well as summers. Therefore women's
rituals celebrate the coming of the dark time as essential to the
regeneration of another cycle.

Autumn leaves and wildflowers are obvious choices for altar
decoration. So are mementoes of summer vacations; symbols of
completed projects; feathers to represent the rising winds; acorns;
insect cocoons; late-summer fruits such as berries, grapes, and
apples. The Autumnal Equinox is a good time to cut apples penta-
cle-wise (transversely) and share them around the circle. It is a

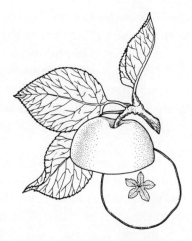

time to tell stories. It is a time to begin a new learning. It is a time to light another wish candle and let it burn away, taking all wishes together into the atmosphere.

Special costumes might be created for this festival in imitation of the colorful clown-livery that the trees wear, or will soon wear. Participants bring bags full of small bits and snippets of bright-colored cloth, ribbon, rags, and other oddments, with a big supply of safety pins. They adorn each other by pinning these "leaves" all over their clothing, then dance like bright autumn trees in the wind. The "leaves" can be unpinned and discarded one by one, symbolizing the trees' shedding of their fall finery in anticipation of winter.

Samhain (November Eve, Halloween)

Samhain or Halloween was one of the year's most significant pagan festivals, which is why the medieval church so thoroughly vilified and diabolized it that it is still associated in the popular mind with devils, witches, goblins, and other unholy folk. The ghost is the most authentic representative of this holi-

day, because Samhain was dedicated to the ghosts of all generations of ancestors, during a period when worship of ancestors (or
rather, ancestresses) was the basis of the tribal bond. Each ghost
was invited to the clan feast as a guest ("ghost" and "guest" used
to be the same word), and after being suitably entertained, might
provide oracular advice to her or his descendants. This Feast of
the Dead was considered one of the primary time-locked cracks
between the worlds.

Ancestors sufficiently revered eventually became gods and
goddesses. These pagan spirits were precisely what the church
called devils, who could be summoned from the other world by
tribal priestesses, whom the church called witches. So the pagans'
night-before festival acquired diabolic overtones, while the following day All Saints, or All Hallows—simply stole the pagan
idea and applied it to a horde of Christianized spirits.

As for the Vernal Equinox, prepare the Antiphonal Chant:

N: What is this night?

S: It is the night of Samhain.

E: What is the meaning of this night?

W: It is the feast of the dead.

N: What do we honor on this night?

S: We honor those who have gone before us into the dark,
      and who left us the legacies of their existence.

E: After this feast of the dead, what will we do?

W: We will learn from the shadows, and prepare for our own
      night.

N: How do we recognize ourselves on this night?

S: We clothe ourselves in darkness. We study the deep
      secrets. We become wise.

E: Who helps us?

W: Our Goddess helps us.

N: What is our Goddess?

S: She is the future's hidden void, the great black matrix, the
      beginning and the end of all things.

E: Who is our Goddess?

W: She is the Virgin of Light, the Crone of Darkness, the
      Mother of Time.

N: Where is our Goddess?

S: She is in our hearts in all seasons of the turning year.

E: Who is our Goddess?

W: Behold, she is ourselves.

Since this is a feast of the dead, it is appropriate to honor the lives and works of dead women, as an antidote to patriarchal history that seldom notices them. Each participant should come prepared to speak about any woman now deceased, whose influence on her was significant. This could be a relative (dead mother, grandmother, aunt), a historical figure, or a favorite female author, artist, or composer. Each participant tells the story of her chosen woman, and if possible passes around a personal memento, quotes the woman's words, or in some other way evokes her spirit. In a guided meditation, try to envision all the spirits of the dead women attending the circle of the living, each ghost standing behind the woman who told her story.

Black candles, bones, owl feathers, the Death card of the Tarot, miniature coffins and other macabre objects can be used for decoration, as well as traditional jack-o-lanterns or the Halloween skulls, imps, and black-cat familiars. The sword or athame should be prominent. A black iron cauldron is an excellent prop. A modern version of witch fire can be burned in the cauldron: a little half-and-half mixture of rubbing alcohol and epsom salts will burn without smoke, and so is safe to use indoors. But be sure the cauldron stands firmly on a base that can't be damaged by heat.

In celebrating the feast of the dead with various funereal trappings, it should be remembered that such celebrations aimed at overcoming the fear of death by providing some familiarity with it; by looking, so to speak, upon the dread face of the death-dealing Crone. Ancient sages used to say that the Goddess remains unknown to one who does not understand her death aspect. Therefore a calendar of holy days should include a recognition of mortality, the better to appreciate and cherish life while it lasts. One who refuses to confront the fact of death will not properly respect the world of the living.

The Crone still rules Halloween in her archetypal form of witch. Women might enjoy identifying with her, wearing not only the usual black robes, but also costumes, masks, and makeup as "witchy" as possible. They may want to act out the "witchiest" aspects of themselves, according to their own interpretations of the term. Some women find it immensely liberating or empowering to play an ugly or fearsome role for a while, in a patriarchal world that strives to forbid them to be either.

Midwinter Solstice (December 21)

This solstice is the year's shortest day and longest night, a circumstance that caused the ancients considerable anxiety. They worried each year that the sun might not be able to gain its warmth back again. (In northern countries, the onset of doomsday was believed to be marked by continuous winter for three full years.) Midwinter festivals therefore centered around the idea of rebirth, to assist the "newborn" sun to grow in strength when it emerged from the dark womb of night.

Savior cults like those of Attis and Jesus also appropriated this traditional birth season for their particular heroes, because people were used to the celebration of a divine birth at this time, nine months after the god's death and reconception at the Vernal Equinox—which Christians renamed the feast of annunciation, or Lady Day. The real birthdate of Jesus or any other savior god was, and is, quite unknown. When the church finally decided in the fourth century to adopt Christmas from the pagans, it was more closely aligned with the solstice, which has since precessed.

As for the Vernal Equinox, prepare the Antiphonal Chant:

N: What is this night?
S: It is the night of the Midwinter Solstice.
E: What is the meaning of this night?
W: It is a peak of power.
N: What is the element that rules this night?
S: Tonight the darkness reaches the limit of its power over light.
E: After this night of power, what is the element that will wane?

W: From this night forward, the darkness will wane and the
    light will grow.

N: How do we recognize ourselves on this night?

S: We greet the moon and glory in the darkness.

E: Who helps us?

W: Our Goddess helps us.

N: What is our Goddess?

S: She is the cold of space, the lightless womb of existence,
    the deepest abyss.

E: Who is our Goddess?

W: She is the Virgin of Light, the Crone of Darkness, the
    Mother of Time.

N: Where is our Goddess?

S: She is in our hearts in all seasons of the turning year.

E: Who is our Goddess?

W: Behold, she is ourselves.

Holly is a highly appropriate decoration for this festival, because it was adopted from the pagan Yule, and was originally named for the dark underground Crone-goddess Holle, or Hel, from whose womb the sun arose. The red berries of the holly symbolized the Goddess's holy blood, shaper of all life, according to the oldest beliefs. England still has many "Hollywells" or "Holywells" once considered yonic shrines of this Goddess. The evergreen leaves of the holly represented ongoing life, retaining vitality through the winter, with an implied promise of immortality.

The theme of this solstice is birth—or rather rebirth—with emphasis on the divine birthgiver rather than on the one who is born, as in the Christian revision. The birthgiver is Hel or the Dark Goddess, also known as Mother Night, Hecate, Myrrha, Cerridwen, Cybele-Nana, Black Demeter, and many other names. All participants may personify her midwife-priestess assistants. The youngest member of the group might be hidden under a dark veil, touched by all hands, and then brought forth as a personification of the sun's new daughter (for the ancient Yule celebrants regarded the sun as female).

It is also a good time to find ways of overcoming patriarchally instilled fears of feminine darkness, through realizing the hidden gestations necessary to all manifestations of brilliance or enlightenment. This can be symbolized in many ways: facing and dancing with one's own shadow; retiring under a covering like the Sun Maiden in order to come forth again; lighting new candles; looking "backward" through one's own legs; turning away from the circle in silence and solitude for a short space of meditation, then returning with joyful singing.

Decorating a tree, giving gifts (especially to children), roasting a pig with an apple in its mouth, burning a Yule log, harvesting mistletoe, and hanging up evergreen boughs were all purely pagan practices that came gradually into Christian tradition. Any modifications of these practices could be reclaimed, therefore, in a solstice celebration.

Candlemas (February Eve)

Candlemas stands opposite Lammas in the sacred calendar, and was probably one of the oldest of all seasonal festivals. It used to be called Imbolg or Imbolc, meaning something like "in the belly," a reference to the new gestation of the world spirit within the Mother. It became a fire festival, betokening the potential heat of a new growing season, and the Goddess's sexual fires, and the lighting of a purificatory "new fire" on every hearth—eventually including even the altars of churches, where new candles were lighted. Pagan Roman celebrations of the fiery sexual frenzies of the Goddess, Juno Februata, were revised into a Christian "Feast of the Purification of the Virgin." Candlemas is still celebrated in this form.

As for the Vernal Equinox, prepare the Antiphonal Chant:

N: What is this night?

S: It is the night of Candlemas.

E: What is the meaning of this night?

W: It is the festival of new fire.

N: What do we honor on this night?

S: We honor the hidden heat of life, the unquenched spirit within the frost.

E: After this festival of new fire, what will we do?

W: We will rekindle our lights, and look toward a brightening future.

N: How do we recognize ourselves on this night?

S: We hold high the fire. We feel the stirring of life. We call upon the Mother who brings us the spring.

E: Who helps us?

W: Our Goddess helps us.

N: What is our Goddess?

S: She is the eternal promise, the fire in the flesh, the undying spirit of blood and breath, rain and sunshine.

E: Who is our Goddess?

W: She is the Virgin of Light, the Crone of Darkness, the Mother of Time.

N: Where is our Goddess?

S: She is in our hearts in all seasons of the turning year.

E: Who is our Goddess?

W: Behold, she is ourselves.

As it has been since ancient times, Candlemas can be celebrated by quenching all fires (candles), and then relighting each one from a certain sacred source, such as a special scented red candle passed from hand to hand, or a lighter bearing some symbolic shape, or a pink (flesh-colored) candle hidden behind a screen in a remote corner, where group members may pass in single file, carrying their own candles for relighting.

Valentine hearts can be featured in decorations, even though Candlemas is two weeks earlier than the modern version of Valentine's Day. The reason is that the original valentines were "love tickets" exchanged among young people in pagan Rome, each year at this time, in honor of Juno's sexual heat (*febris*). Christian authorities tried to replace the licentious "valentines" with scriptural texts, which didn't catch on. Later, the churchmen invented a mythical St. Valentine and pretended that he was a celibate bishop; but he remained, incongruously, the patron of lovers. Despite the artificial saint, Candlemas continued to be sacred to women and to the Goddess of Love.

Candlemas was also a time of taking omens for the coming season. In this character it has become Groundhog Day, basing the weather predictions on the alleged weatherview of the hibernating groundhog. The animal didn't appear in earlier centuries, when it was said simply that if Candlemas day was fair, more winter would come; whereas if it was rainy, "Winter is gone and will not come again." Omens were taken from animals, birds, fires, dice, apple peelings, tea leaves, and many other sources not only for the weather, but for many other subjects as well.

Women's groups can celebrate Candlemas with an omen-taking game. Each member brings a bag of miscellaneous small objects, all of which are dumped into a pile and stirred around. Each member in turn, blindfolded or with closed eyes, gropes into the pile and picks up the first object she touches. When all have chosen, each puts an interpretation on her object in the form of an impromptu prophecy; or others may make the prophecy for her. To make the game last longer, each member may draw three objects, which are then interpreted in relation to one another. The three may be given the classic mystical designation as symbols of Body, Mind, and Spirit.

Honoring the Earth

At each season of the year, we should be mindful of our Mother Earth and the ancient ways of thinking about her with reverence, gratitude, and care—not in the greedily exploitive ways fostered by Western patriarchy, whose God commanded "man" to subdue the Earth and dominate all of nature (Gen. 1:28).

We know now that such an attitude toward our mother planet can lead to destruction of everything on it, including "man." It is already apparent that the generations of our children and grandchildren may have difficulty finding nonpoisonous water to drink and nonpoisonous air to breathe, let alone uncontaminated food and enough of it. Many women believe that this situation would not have arisen if over the centuries our civilization had retained its image of the holy Goddess Earth, in whose body all things lived and moved and had their being, as opposed to a remote God in a distant never-never heaven. Still extant are ancient Egyptian laws of the Goddess, forbidding the fouling of water and the misuse of land.

Because patriarchal religions treated Mother Earth or Mother Nature as the slave of "man" rather than as the divinity who graciously permits "him" to live, women's rituals turn back to the more reverent attitude of ancient peoples who clearly understood their dependence on the universal Mother. Matrifocal religions maintained a more intimate relationship with deity than did our own culture. Viewing themselves as her children, literally flesh of her flesh because everything they ate to live came from Earth, the ancients were actually more scientifically realistic than present theologians. It is true that we are all made of the same elements as Earth's plants, soil, and even the very rocks: we are all products of Earth and part of the interrelationship of all living forms on this planet.

Like our ancestors, we can honor the Earth as a trinity of Maiden, Mother, and Crone: the annually reborn flower-maiden of springtime, filled with potential; the fertile earth mother of summer and harvest; and the canny crone of wisdom, winter, and death, the revealer of hidden meanings. These phases are mirrored every day by mortal women, and appear over time in the life of each individual woman. Each phase should be honored, but perhaps the Crone phase most, because that was the one most vilified by patriarchal males who despised old women's wisdom and granted spiritual authority only to old men.

Emblems of these three phases may be brought to a ceremony of honoring the Earth. Group members may even embody them, if the group includes young girls together with mature and post-menopausal women. In the ancient manner it is customary to clothe young women in white, mature women in red, and post-menopausal women in black: the colors of daughter, mother, grandmother.

The list of possibilities for representative objects is endless. People may bring a flower, a root, a bit of soil, a chunk of lava, a twig, a stone, a chant, a poem to read, a song to sing, a symbol drawn on paper or carved on wood, a map, a landscape painting, a clay statue, a globe, a lump of metal or metal ore, a gem, a photograph, a Goddess picture or other image, a fruit, a nut, an egg, a spray of dried grasses. When all articles are assembled in the center of the circle, let each woman describe her offering in the manner of show-and-tell. All participants meditate together on the meanings and qualities of our home planet. Afterward, the talking stick may be passed around for participants to share their mental images.

There can be a reading of prose or poetry centering on the Earth theme. For example: a selection from James Lovelock's book *Gaia, A New took at Life on Earth;* or Swinburne's poem *Hertha* (an old Saxon name for Goddess Earth); or any appropriate paragraph from recent books by women on feminist and Earth-consciousness themes. Participants may tell each other short stories about their own personal methods of maintaining Earth consciousness and attempting to help preserve our common Mother.

ANTIPHONAL CHANT

Ertha, Mother,
Giver of life,
Fountain of our energy,
Nurturer, sustainer,
Source of our bodies and souls,
Blessed be She.
Let us be mindful of Her,
Let us love all beauty in Her,
Let us not forget our debt to Her,
Let us protect Her other children,
Our animal sisters,
The swimmers, crawlers, runners, climbers, flyers,
Let us fight all who would harm them.
Let us love Goddess Ertha,
Until She gathers us in
To return once more to Her substance,

To be absorbed by Her womb,
To become Mother again,
To be Ertha.
Blessed be.

Storetelling

This title is not a misprint. It is a condensation of story-retelling, or store-retelling: a retelling of the traditional "store" of stories. Especially suitable for such retelling are myths (biblical and otherwise), sagas, fairy tales, folktales, and "old wives' tales," meaning stories that have been handed down through the centuries by women. "Old wives' tales" is a pejorative term invented by men, who scorned the sayings of women but revered equally fantastic "old husbands' tales" which were considered religious revelation, inspired fiction, saints' biographies channeled through visions, charming fancies, or meaningful allegories. Conversely, they usually considered women's stories lies, pipe dreams, or nonsense. These views are particularly ironic, because many traditional tales repeated by men were stolen in the first place from women's ancient Goddess legends, and revised to disguise or erase the female divinity.

When women "storetell" as a ritual procedure, the idea is to undo patriarchal revisions and get back to the female-oriented meaning of the story. Contemporary imagination can supply some details, but others have been uncovered by recent scholarship; so preliminary research is advisable.*

Especially rich in previously divine implications are traditional female figures that have been diabolized or "witchified," as well as various female saints and martyrs who never existed except as new transformations of the Goddess. Surprising tradi-

---

*Some good sources include Merlin Stone's *Ancient Mirrors of Womanhood;* Robert Graves's *The Greek Myths* and *The White Goddess;* or Barbara G. Walker's *The Woman's Encyclopedia of Myths and Secrets* and *The Woman's Dictionary of Symbols and Sacred Objects.*

tions underlie such figures as, for instance, Lilith, Eve, the Witch of Endor, the Whore of Babylon, Hel, Medea, Medusa, Melusine, the Morrigan, the White Lady, the Banshee, Lamia, Hecate, the Hag, the Wicked Stepmother, and so on.

The following is a storetelling of *Cinderella*, a tale that was going the rounds in the early Renaissance, when there was much underground opposition to the Christian theocracy. *Cinderella* makes sense as an anticlerical allegory and a secret celebration of the Goddess. In the original old German version, the fairy god-mother was in fact a fairy tree, ancient symbol of Goddess gifts. The heroine seems to have represented both the composite pagan or "country" woman, and the pagan Maiden figure, who was enacted in seasonal festivals by young village girls costumed for the occasion.

Once upon a time there was a magic maiden named Ella, daughter of Hella, or Hel, or Holle, who was none other than the great underground Earth Mother, whose fiery womb gave birth to all things in the beginning, and would reclaim them in the end. Ella was the Virgin avatar of her Great Mother, since the Goddess used to undergo periodic changes and life stages. Alas, Ella was a weakened avatar. People had begun to believe the men who said the Goddess fire had burned away to a black cinder, so that the Mother herself was dead, and Ella had become only a Cinder-ella. Therefore her name was changed.

The Crone avatar of the Great Mother still lived; but because she was the death-bringer in olden times, the men of the new god claimed that she was wholly evil, a wicked witch, a heartless step-mother, the Earth Mother as ghoulish devourer of the dead. Even the men who were yet faithful to the old ways had to admit that the Crone was fearsome. It was she who condemned and con-sumed the ancient god after he had espoused the Virgin and begotten his successor. It was the Crone who decreed his yearly death as sacred king, and his resurrection in each new springtime.

Some said that old Crone-Mother Earth had now brought forth two evil daughters, Nobilita and Ecclesia. Nobilita fancied herself a very great person. She was arrogant and greedy. She insisted on wearing ermine cloaks, diamond necklaces, and jew-eled crowns. She took Cinderella's pretty clothes for herself, leav-ing the maiden nothing but ugly rags to wear. She also owned weapons, and used them to threaten and to injure. She could be dangerous. She treated Cinderella as her slave, issuing a thousand trivial commands each day, forcing the poor maiden to serve her in everything from household duties to heavy field work.

Ecclesia was even worse in some ways. Pretending a pious modesty, she nevertheless sported fine clothes and ornaments too. She made so much of her own righteousness that she was as arrogant as her sister, if not more so. She also forced Cinderella to toil for her, claiming that a superior spiritual magisterium justified everything she demanded. She hypocritically pretended that it was a sin to disobey her. Ecclesia had a sadistic streak and a diabolical cleverness in inventing refined tortures, both physical and mental, to harass her prey.

The great seasonal festival of the marriage of the sacred king was approaching. A new king was to be crowned. The loveliest maiden in the land was to sit beside him as his queen, for such was the custom from time immemorial, ever since each king was compelled to marry a Goddess surrogate before he could reign. The royal maiden was to be chosen at the feast.

Each of Cinderella's stepsisters was sure that she alone was qualified to take the place of the old Goddess's Virgin aspect. Nobilita insisted that she was a queen by nature, and no one else could so well play that role. Ecclesia insisted that all divine power now rested in her alone, and if the young prince espoused any other, then he and all his land would be damned and doomed.

The sisters quarreled even more nastily than usual, and almost parted in anger to go separately to the festival. But their costumes had been planned to complement one another. The effect of one depended on the other's harmonious support. Realizing their mutual dependence, the sisters swallowed their jealousy and turned their ill temper on Cinderella. If Cinderella ran to fetch a pin or a ribbon for Nobilita, then Ecclesia would scream and curse her. If Cinderella sewed a button or starched a ruffle for Ecclesia, then Nobilita would slash at her with a riding crop.

At last the stepsisters were ready. Dealing Cinderella a few final slaps, they entered their elaborate coach with its Gothic spires and turrets, and set off for the festival, dragged by a team of asses, bulls, and hogs.

When they were gone, Cinderella sadly made her traditional harvest charm: a hollow pumpkin shell containing a candle, symbolizing the plump orange harvest moon. Remembering the divine Mother who taught her all the moon charms, she took the pumpkin to Hella's hillside tomb and sat down weeping. "Alas, Mother," she said to the Earth, "my heart is sore. My sisters abuse me. I am not allowed to see the fine sights of the festival. I must stay here alone and make solitary charms."

Then Cinderella saw that a silver tree was rising out of her Mother's tomb, like the tree of fairy gifts in the old stories. Indeed it was a magical fairy Mother-tree whose branches were laden with gifts, lights, and jewels, even more beautiful than the trees of Yule. A silvery voice spoke from the tree. "Take these gifts, Cinderella. Adorn yourself and go to the festival. The moon pumpkin will carry you wherever you desire. But remember that fairy gifts dissolve at the turning point of the night. This is all I can do for you at present."

Hanging on the tree's branches were beautiful garments of white and scarlet silk, a diamond and ruby crown with matching bracelets, a silver pentacle on a string of rare black pearls, a ring in the form of a serpent with crystal eyes, and a pair of dancing slippers made of soft white kid, covered with glass beads, over a red silk lining. Cinderella hastened to put on this finery. While she did so, the moon pumpkin swelled into a golden pumpkin-shaped coach, and eight rats came from the forest tribes to metamorphose into horses and coachmen.

When Cinderella arrived at the feast, the young king-elect was greeting her two stepsisters. He kissed Ecclesia's ringed hand

and was about to kiss Nobilita's, when he saw Cinderella step from her pumpkin coach. He was momentarily transfixed, like a man turned to stone. He dropped Nobilita's hand and ran to kneel before Cinderella. "Beautiful lady, what is your name?" he asked. "Is it Titania, or Mab, or Sybilla? Has the Fairy Queen herself come to honor my nuptials? Beautiful lady, will you dance with me?"

For the rest of the evening, he would dance with no one but Cinderella. He would not look at any other maiden. It was clear to all that he wanted Cinderella to be his queen. Nobilita and Ecclesia were furious, but they dared not display their anger in public.

Cinderella understood that she was to be the queen when the prince asked her to remove her shoe, so the royal scepter could be inserted into it. For thousands of years it had been customary to display a symbol of the sacred marriage in this manner. In the very oldest times, the scepter was an obviously carved phallus and the shoe was made to resemble a yoni lined with red. Cinderella took off her shoe and handed it over. Then, all at once, she saw that it was the turning point of the night.

In a panic, she fled back to her coach. Even as she ran, her silk garments were turning to cobwebs and drifting off her body. Her rubies and diamonds dissolved into blood and tears. Her pentacle became an apple core. Her black pearls turned into lumps of coal. Her serpent ring became a small earthworm and fell to the ground. She was naked, her coach was a mere jack-o-lantern, and her rat coachmen ran away.

Ashamed, she hid herself in the woods and headed homeward by a roundabout path. At the tomb of her Mother she found her old rags lying on the ground, so she put them on. The fairy tree had turned into an ordinary willow. Cinderella went home to bed, to dream of her brief stardom.

But now the oldest custom of the people decreed that the prince must find her again. Having inserted his scepter into her shoe, he was indissolubly bound to her by the law of the Goddess. He could wed no one else, for fear of offending Mother Earth herself, so that a bad growing season might strike the land, to be followed by dearth and famine. He still possessed the magic shoe of white kid, red silk, and glass beads. The shoe, separated from Cinderella's person when she fled, had not dissolved away like the rest of her costume. Seeing that the magic shoe was unusually small (and thus a fitting symbol of virginity), the prince took it along on his search for the correct Maiden, hoping to identify her by her small foot.

When he came to Cinderella's home, the two stepsisters bustled about to serve, flatter, and woo him. They offered him wine and cookies, a cushion for his back, a collection of portraits of their illustrious ancestors for him to contemplate. The prince was bored, but he fulfilled his duty by trying the magic shoe on each sister in turn, only to find that their large feet could not squeeze into it.

Then he saw Cinderella crouching by the hearth. The expression of her face ignited a dim memory in his none too sharp mind. "Who is that?" he asked. "No one, only a scullery maid," Nobilita told him. The prince looked at Cinderella's feet, which seemed quite small. "Nevertheless, she shall try the shoe," he said firmly. "It is decreed that every woman in the kingdom shall be tested."

Of course, when Cinderella inserted her foot into the magic shoe, it slipped on as smoothly as the sheath embraces the sword.

So it was that the One True Maiden was found again. The villagers rejoiced that both she and they were freed from the greed and backbiting of the quarrelsome sisters Nobilita and Ecclesia, who were driven away in disgrace. Cinderella instructed her king in properly altruistic principles of government. The stepmother was rededicated to her right function as official Crone, repossessed by the spirit of True Mother Hella, whose tomb became a magic healing shrine and pilgrimage center. Her holy willow tree still stands to this day, in a sacred enclosure surrounded by standing stones. At the entrance, souvenir venders hawk wooden miniatures of the holy tree, and small glass shoes containing plastic models of the royal scepter.

Guided Meditation:
The Way of the Goddess

You are traveling through a dark tunnel that might extend through space or time, or both. The tunnel interior is smooth and featureless. You slip along effortlessly. You may be sliding, or you may be on some kind of vehicle.

The tunnel ends abruptly. You emerge from darkness into light. Before you lies a vast plain, flooded with sunlight. Green crops are growing in patches. You can see tiny figures of people tending their gardens in the distance. The sky is blue and clear.

Before you, surrounded by feathery trees, a huge building rises from the plain. It is bigger than any building you have ever seen. It rises up in seven terraces, like a mountain. It is made of a yellowish stone that reflects the sun. You can see no windows.

Your feet are set on the pavement of a broad avenue leading toward this building through an aisle of colossal stone figures. You begin to walk toward the building, looking at the figures as you pass them. Some seem to be animals. Others look almost human. They have wide spreading wings, hooves, horns, snake-like tails, mighty shoulders, great fanged mouths. The figures seem sentient and watchful.

You reach the end of the great avenue and climb a long flight of broad steps, up to the high entranceway of the building. It is very tiring. Your legs are weary when you come at last to a wide porch, its roof supported by sixty-foot pillars, six feet in diameter, made of sparkling green stone. The ceiling of the porch is inlaid with brilliantly colored tiles set in strange patterns. At the center of the porch there is an enormous bronze door, intricately carved. It is closed.

You approach the door. There is no handle, but a large central knob is located far above your head. You wonder if this place was built for giants. You reach up as far as you can, and knock on the metal.

Without a sound, the door swings inward. You look in at a broad courtyard, open to the sky in the center, roofed around all sides, with aisles of pillars and archways. In the middle stands a beautiful snow-white marble fountain, tossing up complex fans of clear water into the sunlight to make sheets of rainbow-colored vapor. Fantastic fish, horses, mermaids, and other figures decorate the basin, carved from a bright yellow metal like gold. Their eyes seem to be made of gems. Like the figures of the great avenue, they look somehow alive.

You can see no exit from the courtyard except another door across from the first. You walk around the fountain toward this second door. The ground is paved with red stones that glitter as if with a million tiny flakes of mica. The corners of the courtyard are filled with exotic plants in black enamel pots, with huge, showy flowers, none of which look familiar. Otherwise, the place is empty.

You find the second door standing open. Beyond it, a long, straight, arched corridor stretches away into a mist. Flaring torches are set in sconces along the walls, providing a glow of firelight. You set off down the corridor. The ceiling is so high that you cannot see it at all. Above the level of torchlight there is only darkness.

As you enter the mist at the end of the corridor, the walls slope away and you are in a darkness that seems like outdoor night. High overhead, stars are glittering. Then the mist thins, and you see that the stars are a clever illusion. A vast ceiling, more than a hundred feet above you, is pierced with tiny holes that let in sparks of sunlight. The holes are arranged to imitate the constellations.

A lower arched doorway at the other end of this huge room is shining with a brighter light. You approach this doorway and peek through. Beyond lies another lofty hall, illuminated by one single beam of sunlight falling from a round opening in the roof. The beam falls directly on a raised throne in the center of the hall: a blocky chair of silvery metal, set with purple velvet cushions, atop a high dais with thirteen green marble steps. On the throne sits a woman.

She is so still that at first you think she is a statue. Then you see her lively eyes watching you. She rises. You look up at her in wonder. She is tall and straight in body, but she seems very old. Her long hair is silver-white and fine as thistledown. Her face is deeply wrinkled. Only the eyes look clear and keen. She wears a plain black robe hanging straight from her shoulders to her feet. She wears one jewel on a chain around her neck: a large blood-red star ruby flashing its six silver arms.

She comes down the thirteen steps of the dais and warmly seizes both of your hands. She smiles. "I have been waiting for you," she says. "I am the Lady, your priestess. I will show you the Way."

You didn't know there was a Way, but you are not surprised to hear it. Somehow, it sounds right. The priestess leads you by your left hand to the far end of the hall. She lifts a trapdoor in the floor and shows you a flight of steps leading down into darkness.

"There is the place of incubation, where you will prepare for your rebirth," she says. "The steps lead to the central core of our mother country. Only certain chosen ones may rest there. You have been chosen. Take this." She hands you a crystal flask filled with sparkling red-gold liquid. "It is the blood of our earth. It will comfort you in darkness and calm you in light. I will speak to you again at a future time. Go."

Her tone is both authoritative and reassuring. You obey her with confidence. You enter the trapdoor. She closes it behind you. Now you are in total darkness. You grope carefully down the flight of steps. The walls feel curiously warm and soft, as if padded with silken quilts. The steps end. You are in a tiny circular chamber, less than the reach of your outstretched arms. You must stoop because the ceiling is lower than your head. It, too, is padded. The floor is cushioned. You reflect that the place should be unbearably stuffy; yet the air is fresh. You cannot locate the source of ventilation.

Something hisses gently in the darkness. You find that the opening to the stairway has been closed. You cannot feel a door. The chamber walls now seem smoothly unbroken. You become aware of a faint, deep sound vibrating all around you, like the slow beat of a huge drum in the distance. You rest among the cushions. After a while, the throbbing beat lulls you to sleep.

You awake with a start, realizing that a voice is speaking to you. It is a quiet, mellow male voice, speaking your name against the drumlike throbbing. You ask, "Who are you?" The male voice answers, "I am your Incubus. I am the placental entity born with you. I am the twin of your soul. Have you no name for me?"

"I don't know."

"No matter. You will never see me unless you need to do so. I teach in darkness."

You feel a touch, like the touch of a hand, over the center of your belly. A strange tingling spreads very slowly from your navel throughout your abdomen and chest, washing over your legs and arms down to the toes and fingertips, rising into your head. It is a peculiar but not unpleasant physical sensation that eventually creates a sense of reorganizing in your mind. You feel that you are acquiring the thoughts and attitudes of another person—perhaps of many other persons. Your brain takes in so much that it seems to expand beyond the confines of your skull. You see other places where you have never been, but which feel like memories. You see distant times, ancient cities, barren deserts, forests, mountains, strange otherworldly landscapes. You feel what it

would be like to live in a body not your own, even a body of radically different shape, winged or furred or four-legged. You experience fear and love and joy and hatred and sorrow that were never
your own.

You are recalled to yourself by the same mellow male voice,
saying, "I forgive you for living without me. We will meet again
beyond the seventh veil." The touch on your navel is withdrawn.
Suddenly you are frightened. You cry, "Please don't leave me!"
There is no answer but a fading snicker of laughter.

The giant drum is beating more loudly and a little faster. The
warm darkness presses close. You are aware of a terrible weakness, a deathlike weariness, a hunger in your belly as if no food
has ever filled it. You wonder if you are about to die. Reaching
out a hand as if to entreat help, you encounter the crystal flask.
Hurriedly you remove the cap, lift it to your mouth, and drink. It
feels like liquid vitality filling you with sparkling new energy. The
gnawing hunger subsides a little.

You cannot imagine how long you have been in this chamber.
Hours? Days? Weeks? It seems that an enormous length of time
has passed. You sleep again. More time passes. You are awakened
by a sudden alarming increase in the distant drumbeat. It is louder, closer, filling your space.

Something is happening before your eyes, something you can
see. Light! A part of the chamber wall has vanished like gauze.
You can see silvery light beyond. Within the light stands a gigantic figure of a woman, swathed in drifting white veils. Her left
hand holds a crystal flask shaped like the one you drank from,
but larger. It is filled with something snowy white and diamond
bright, glittering, flashing with brilliant lights. The thought comes
to you: star milk.

You move toward the gigantic woman. The light seems to
emanate from her, softened by her veils. Her head inclines toward
you in a kindly gesture. She offers you the flask of star milk.
Filled with gratitude, you drink some. It is wonderfully refreshing. It is like a life essence. You feel an overwhelming love for this
huge woman. You fall on your knees before her.

She lifts the veil that covers her head. Slowly, gracefully, she
bends down to you and raises your chin, so you may look at her
face. You look, and gasp with astonishment. It is your own face.

CHANT

Ave atque vale
Magna Mater
(Hail and farewell,
Great Mother.)

Thealogy

Theology, or "God-knowledge," is a pseudoscience invented by men to define and describe the God whom they simultaneously call indefinable and indescribable. Real science studies objective phenomena. Theology studies a collective male fantasy. Much theological effort goes into hiding the fact that God is not an objective phenomenon but a construct of men's imaginations, based on their own sense of what they are, what they wish to be, or what they think they ought to be. As Sir Richard Francis Burton sagely remarked, men have never worshiped anything but themselves.

Thealogy, or "Goddess-knowledge," may be reinstated, after its long eclipse, as a similar collective image developed by women critical of the ethical shortcomings of patriarchal culture. Many women have despaired of waiting generation after generation for theology to devise some effective ways of dealing with the wars, crimes, exploitations, cruelties, and injustices that the patriarchal God usually seemed willing to support. Even woman-hating men have often admitted that women's inherent morality tends more toward compassion, caring, and nurture of others than the morality of males, and that the world desperately needs more of the former and less of the latter.

Patriarchal society, however, could never allow women any official voice in the articulation of moral standards. For many centuries, Western women have been forbidden access to theological councils ever since St. Paul decreed that women must keep quiet

in church, and receive religious instruction only from their husbands at home. In the theocratically thought-controlled Middle
Ages, even nuns were punished for discussing theological matters
within their cloisters.

Such rules effectively stamped out the remnants of female
divinity inherited from pagan culture, and left men's God in sole
charge, more than ever an obvious projection of male ego. The
new woman tends to be dissatisfied with this projection, which is
difficult if not impossible for her to relate to her innermost sense
of right and wrong in true feminine terms. Gradually emerging
from the modern women's spirituality movement is a reassess-
ment of the Goddess image as a more viable model for human
thought, feeling, and behavior.

Theologians established their God with a pretense of his
objective existence. Thealogians need not resort to such hypocrisy.
It is possible to deal with the image of divinity as the collective
self-expression that it really is, as a symbol of women's true
knowledge, and as the arbiter of moral instruction represented by
humanity's most ancient mothers. This can be seen in women's
natural ways of defining Goddess, a thealogical exercise recommended for any women's ritual group. The following are examples of the kinds of responses women give when the question
goes around their circle: What is Goddess?

"Goddess is love, and everything implied by love: nurturing, caring, helping, comforting, being a good friend, being there when you're
needed, making things easier or more pleasant for others, and appreci-
ating others who do the same for you. Of course Goddess stands for the
sensual meanings of love, too: giving and receiving physical pleasures,
enjoying everything that feels good—music, art, poetry, nature, everything from the tactile sensations of tree bark or animal fur to the best
kind of sex. Goddess is feeling good about relationships with other people and with the world, through your senses and emotions. All that is
just another way of defining love."

"Goddess is power, the kind of power I can feel when I'm sure of
myself and confident that I can handle a situation; the power to work
things out well; the power to *do*, to make good things happen. I like the
old concept of Goddess as Shakti, energy, movement, the ability to act.
She was the power that the gods lacked, and always needed to get from
her!"

"Goddess is nature: everything that's beautiful about nature, and also everything that's wild and dark and destructive. You can't have the pretty Virgin of birth without the ugly Crone of death! That's nature's wisdom. Goddess means all the cycles—eternal births and deaths, creation and destruction going on all the time in every time scale from milliseconds to millennia—all that cauldron-churning that the patriarchal gods couldn't stand, and had to pare down to a single linearity."

"Goddess is definitely femaleness as I can feel it in myself, a spirit saying that this is the right thing to be, not a wrong thing as in Judeo-Christian teachings. Goddess means it is no sin to be born into this world, but a joy. At least, it ought to be a joy. It's up to us to make it so."

"Goddess is feminine morality, the kind of morality that says hurting and killing are evil, weapons are evil, spoiling the earth is evil. War is the worst evil of all, not glorious or heroic, never the `holy war' that God used to endorse. Goddess morality says courage means protecting others, not fighting them; and cowardice means bullying and violence."

"Goddess is the irresistible force that I felt making use of my body when I gave birth."

"Goddess is the universe, and Goddess worship involves learning as much as we can about the universe, but never pretending to know more than we do know. The largest portion of Goddess Universe will always be unknown to us, and it is sheer hubris to think otherwise."

"Goddess is the creativity that I feel driving me, telling me what I must do, what I can't possibly *not* do. Sometimes it's uncomfortable. She pushes me harder than I like. But I have to admit that it's never harder than I can manage. Somehow, I fit it all in. She seems to know what it is that I have to accomplish in my lifetime, and she has a timetable for it. I have to trust her timetable. So I guess it's really a part of me, isn't it?"

"Goddess is the oldest power in the universe. Every god was born of her, just as every man is born of a woman."

"Goddess is the earth, our only mother, always young and always old. So far, she has put up with the human species, but I'm afraid we are like spoiled children, coming close to the end of her tolerance of us. I think we need to see the error of our ways, and beg her forgiveness before it's too late. I think the earth is going to stop supporting us because of what we're doing to her, and it's all our own fault."

"To me the best symbol of Goddess is just what people everywhere have always recognized: the moon. I never see the full moon rising without a little flutter of the heart. It always seems like a sweet mellow face beaming down at me. All the women in the world respond to the moon in their very blood. That's very important. The moon represents a basis of life, living, and life-giving in the feminine context."

"Goddess is the anger that I feel about the world patriarchy has made, and is making. The exploitation, the lies, the violence. The alienated families. The battered women and children. The self-righteous politicians. The wasteful consumer society. Years ago, we were supposed to accept it all as if it was normal and right. Now the women can say that it's wrong and let their anger flow. To me, that's Goddess power."

"Goddess is our clearest sense of what the world needs in order to relieve suffering and make life more livable for the largest number of people. Limiting the population to manageable numbers, restoring the health of the environment, better management of our wastes and our resources—all those efforts that we so clearly know ought to be made, and are not being made because runaway male greed blocks them. Our Goddess knows what is right and we'd better listen to her before it's too late."

"For me, Goddess means everything I can relate to spiritually or esthetically: the earth, the sea, the stars, the moon. Time. Space. Birth and death cycles. My own sentience, by which I can perceive at least a part of the world and understand a little bit. Goddess means everything in life that is important, beautiful, or meaningful to me."

"Most of all I like the old pagan idea of Goddess as the trinity of Virgin, Mother, and Crone. It makes sense. That's the way things really go: lifetimes, seasons, the rise and fall of human cultures, even the vastly long existences of stars. You can tell that the Christian God trinity was only a copy of that concept, because there was no real relevance to him as a triad. The three parts didn't stand for anything that would naturally suggest them. But the Virgin-Mother-Crone trinity was the essence of life."

"I can't imagine how the Western world got along for so many centuries without a Goddess concept, seeing that fifty percent of all people were female and one hundred percent of all people were given life by women. How that male God concept impoverished us! It's true, what was said long ago, that the only parent we can know in our guts is a mother."

"When men claimed that their God was all light and brightness and brilliance, they left everything dark—which is most of the universe—without any personification except the necessarily evil one. But the Goddess also represented the essence of darkness because it's only in darkness that real creation occurs: germination, conception, the unconscious springs of creativity in the mind. Light is born from the darkness, not darkness from the light. The dark womb is the greatest Goddess symbol. That encompasses everything. Darkness may be perceived as a female quality but it isn't evil. Darkness is the Source, and that means Goddess."

"For me, Goddess religion means the body-oriented approach to spirituality: the sense of the body, especially the female body, as holy rather than as corrupt or evil as the Fathers used to teach. I hate all those implications about sexuality and femaleness being the essence of sin. I believe that one of the most valid paths to the truly spiritual is through the body. After all, it is through our bodily senses that we experience everything. What else is there?"

"In my school days, I was taught to sing hymns declaring myself unworthy to be noticed by the Lord. It was a profoundly demeaning thought. Goddess religion liberates me from that inner shame. It gives me a sense of self-worth that I think every woman needs. It frees me from the falsely degrading images that patriarchy lays on women."

"If every person bears a spark of divinity within, then the spark in each female person must necessarily be female. That's the meaning of Goddess to me. Why should women describe their inner divine spark by masculine words? I can't imagine why they would want to. Leave that for the men, if that's what men crave. But why should we adopt a male image? I don't like the new halfway measures, like calling God a "father-mother" or a bisexual androgyne or a neuter "force" without any sexuality at all. People always sexualize their ideas of deity. That's natural, because people are always vividly aware of their own sexuality. I choose to sexualize my deity in my own mode. My deity-within is Goddess, and Goddess only."

"Goddess is the cauldron-womb, the eternal matrix from which everything comes and to which everything returns in its inevitable season. To deny this image is to deny nature, and nature's manifest cycles, which is what patriarchy has been trying to do for thousands of years. Patriarchy taught that the body must be despised because it is corruptible. But that is to despise life. All living forms are corruptible, of necessity. Every living form grows from the dissolution of others. Ideas of these universal cycles are found in all the old Goddess religions. This is far more realistic than patriarchy's one-way life notion and the fundamental separation of body and spirit."

"Goddess is the loving creativity in women that leads them to make their homes as beautiful as they can, to try to establish a supportive and comforting atmosphere, to do little things that please their loved ones, to be thoughtful of others. Most women do that almost all the time, automatically, without even considering it anything unusual. Women are kind, and ingenious at inventing ways to express kindness. That's Goddess spirit. It should be honored, never taken for granted."

"Goddess is Mother. When you say that, you've said it all. There is nothing any greater than that."

The Dark Journey

The Dark Journey is an elaborate and highly memorable ritual modeled on Goddess-oriented mystery religions of antiquity, in which tenets of the faith were graphically demonstrated during guided journeys through labyrinthine cave-temples, or along dark winding corridors toward a final revelation in the central chamber of the temple. This was the Holy of Holies, which usually contained a statue of the Goddess. A distant echo of these ancient customs is still found in the trump suit of the Tarot, whose final card is a naked female figure centrally placed amid symbols of the seasons, directions, elements, and so on.

During these symbolic journeys, experiences were arranged, teachings were conveyed, and confrontations with the deities were staged. The latter were personified either by masked and costumed temple personnel, or by images. We can readily envision some of the ancient temples and sacred caves as impressive environments where the priests and priestesses could simulate the underworld, the cosmic womb, the heaven-mountain, and the homes of gods. Extensive use was made of aids to sensual experience, such as incense, music, darkness or blindfolding, special foods and odors, touches, periods of silent contemplation in solitude, surprise revelations, and moments of flashing light or sudden apparitions.

Traditions like these were still extant in Arabia in Marco Polo's time. He described the secret "paradise" of Alamut, where newly initiated warriors were drugged and given a preview of heaven by beautiful, sexy *houris* (angels), who promised that a heroic death in battle would mean an instantaneous return to the many pleasures of their company. In this way, the soldiers of Allah were made brave, for they really believed that they had visited the heaven where they could later live forever.

Modern women don't want to perpetrate any such crude deceptions. Yet the ancient traditions of the Dark Journey can inspire an interesting ritual, combining sensuality with spirituality, game with theater. This one is different, in that it can't be made available to all group members at once, but only to one at a time. Moreover it requires that one, two, or three set it up and know what to do in advance, keeping it secret from those who are to experience it. It requires a space closed off from the sight or hearing of the waiting ones: a fairly large space, where lights can be made dim, and materials for the Journey can be laid out beforehand.

Assume that the chosen space is a large, bare room, lighted only by a candle or two, furnished only by a few tables with the necessary materials in readiness. The candidate is firmly blind-folded and led into the room. Soft music is playing. Incense is burning. The candidate is turned about several times to confuse her sense of direction, and is led this way and that as if on a tangled, twisting path, while various nonvisual experiences are provided for her.

A vial of perfume is held under her nose. Then she is led to another spot where someone whispers in her ear, "Open your mouth." When she does so, a bite-size piece of sweet fruit is placed in her mouth. After a few steps in another direction, someone comes from behind and envelops her in a warm furry robe or blanket within arms that give her a brief hug. As the robe or blanket is withdrawn, someone gently combs her hair. After another few steps in another direction, something soft or silky is put in her hand for her to feel: a skein of wool, a ball of cotton, a satin pincushion (without pins, of course), a piece of plush, or a small stuffed animal. After another few steps, someone strokes her cheek with a hand wrapped in velvet. After another few steps, someone gently massages the back of her neck. After another few steps, someone holds a seashell to her ear. She may be given another kind of perfume to smell, or another kind of fruit to taste. She may be stroked with feather plumes, or with warm hands. Her face may be fanned. Her back may be rubbed. If she is bare-foot, a very thick, soft mat may be provided for her to walk on. Her fingers may be clasped and stroked one at a time. In short, as many pleasant experiences as possible are provided for all the senses except the sense of sight.

This is a good opportunity to present the candidate with a small talisman that she can keep, in memory of the Journey. Her hand may be placed in a bag or bowl of loose, miscellaneous small objects: buttons, beads, marbles, dried beans, acorns, pebbles, thimbles, shells, "lucky piece" coins, tumble-polished stones, and the like. A voice in her ear directs her to feel around, choose one of the objects, and keep it. Objects for this assortment should be small, and without sharp edges or points—it wouldn't do to put the hand of a blindfolded person into a vessel of sharp things.

At the end of the Dark Journey, the candidate is told that the next sight she sees will be the Goddess. One helper holds up before her face a three-paneled folding boudoir mirror (the side panels are helpful to cut off peripheral vision), while another helper removes her blindfold for just a few seconds. A single candle is held either above or below the mirror, so its light shines on the face that she sees in the glass. Then the blindfold is restored. After this, the candidate may be taken into another room, where she is helped to lie down on a quilt or thick rug, tenderly covered over, and left alone in darkness to meditate.

When all candidates have gone through the same process, materials for the Dark Journey are packed away and a regular meeting can proceed.

With the use of blindfolds, surprisingly simple techniques can produce memorable experiences. We are so used to living through our eyes that when vision is cut off, the impressions gained through other senses seem greatly enhanced. Most women also find the revelation of Goddess-in-self, via the mirror, very moving.

Initiations invented by male groups through the centuries have made use of similar theatrics, providing experiences that will be memorable by reason of their uniqueness. However, the experiences of fraternal initiations have often been painful, frightening, degrading, or harshly ascetic. In contrast to this, women should try always to emphasize pleasure in the experiences they create for one another—nothing embarrassing, hurtful, or scary. The lesson of the Dark Journey is feeling good about one's self through good feelings in general.

Tools

After a group has been working together for a while, members may decide to provide themselves with individual sets of the four traditional priestess tools. These are objects symbolizing the four elements of antiquity, just as the tarot suits symbolize them, with all their connotations. The objects are: (1) a cup; (2) a wand;

(3) a knife or *athame* (sword); and (4) a pentacle, stone, crystal, or other symbol of the earth.

Four separate meetings can be devoted to ritual endorsement and mutual consecration of tools: one meeting for all the cups, another for all the wands, another for all the blades, and a fourth for all the earth symbols.

For the cup meeting, each woman brings her own choice of a personal ceremonial cup. It might be a pewter goblet, a cut-glass chalice, a silver baby cup, an antique sherry glass, an earthenware mug, a homemade clay vessel, a favorite kitchen tumbler: anything that has meaning for the individual. There is no standard. It might be wise, however, to choose articles that are not too fragile. A very delicate wineglass, for example, might not stand up to repeated use.

After the usual opening meditations, invocations, and so on, participants set out their cups around the altar space. One at a time, each woman explains her choice in the manner of show-and-tell. Each cup is passed around for other members to handle, comment on, and appreciate. When every cup has made the round, a collective ritual may be performed to dedicate all cups together.

One way to do this is to fill each cup with water and pour all the waters together in a large bowl in the center of the space. Then, each woman dips up some of this mingled water in her

own cup, and all drink it together. In Tantric tradition, the mingling of waters from separate vessels into one vessel was a common metaphor for perfect love.

The dedication of athames or blades is a similar ritual. Each woman brings the blade she has chosen. The assortment may include kitchen knives, letter openers, jackknives, Swiss army knives, stilettos, machetes, ornamental daggers, or anything else that might be used for cutting. It can be used in future rituals to cut symbolically—as "cutting off" unwanted emotional impedimenta—or literally, to slice bread or fruit for sharing, to mark a magic circle on the ground, to cut threads or ribbons, or to wear as part of a costume. Among the ancient Celts and even in Christian Ireland, a knife at the belt was an integral part of the ceremonial costume of a bride.

Like the cups, the blades are passed around for examination and comment, then dedicated together. Group members may chant while making a "pyramid of points" over the altar, just as knights held their swords together over a bonfire to make their vows of mutual protection. As a kind of communion among members, a loaf of bread or cake can be cut by each blade in turn, and pieces shared around.

Wands may be found or prepared at home and brought to the meeting, or they can be actually created at the meeting. In the latter case, each woman brings her own personally chosen stick, plus some wand-making or wand-decorating materials. These can include paint, string, tape, glue, beads, shells, yarn, ribbon, braid, fringe, scissors, wire, and anything else that might prove useful in dressing up a stick. Some may prefer not to dress their wands at all, having found a natural stick with a pleasing esthetic shape, or perhaps having chosen a wand already manufactured. Some attractive wands are made by glueing a quartz crystal to the end of the stick and wrapping it with leather strips.

The earth symbol can be a crystal too, or a special stone chosen by the individual. Some stones and minerals are polished into egg shapes or spheres, which make appropriate earth symbols. As in the tarot deck, a pentacle is also a good earth symbol. Five-pointed stars represented the whole underworld in ancient Egypt.

The pentacle is an important symbol of feminine spirituality, because it is one ancient emblem of the Goddess that was never preempted by patriarchal revisionists. In the beginning it was drawn from natural forms such as the starfish, the five-petaled Oriental rose, and the five-lobed apple. The apple was one of the earliest symbols of mystical knowledge and life force given to the first man by the Middle-Eastern Earth Mother—or, Mother of All Living, as the Bible says (Gen. 3:20). Norsemen believed that even the lives of gods depended on the secret wisdom of the Goddess's pentacle-starred apple, and that apples were resurrection charms.

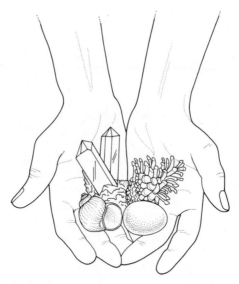

Gypsies attributed life magic and love magic to the "star of knowledge" (pentacle) revealed by the transverse cut across an apple.

Rose and apple both passed into the complex medieval syncretism of the Goddess/Virgin Mary, who was also a "star" (Stella Maris) It was said that five was the number dedicated to Marian worship. Yet women continued to revere the Goddess in some of her older forms, using the pentacle as a protection sign, and crossing themselves with the fivefold cross (see Invocation, p. 20). Therefore churchmen came to associate the pentacle with "witches," and to claim that marking the pentacle on the body was a backward copy of their sign of the cross. Originally it had been the Christians who copied the practice from paganism.

Because it is one of the so-called gateless designs, drawn in one continuous line, the pentacle has long represented a hallowed space where no unwelcome influences may enter. Witches and wizards were said to use the pentacle as a defense against invoked demons. Churchmen also claimed that the pentacle with one point downward represented the head of the Horned God, whom they confused with their own devil. The pentacle has had many interpretations, but it is still enthusiastically adopted by those who reverence the Goddess image and remember its originally earth-centered, feminine meanings.

Some people like to wear a metal pentacle on a neck chain, not only to their spirituality meetings, but also as talismanic jewelry. Some like to keep a crystal in a small silk, crocheted, or knitted amulet bag, hung around the neck with a drawstring. Also usable as earth symbols are such natural objects as snail shells, pine knots, roots, fossils, and geodes. Any small roundish manufactured object in metal or clay (ceramic) can also serve as an earth symbol. This category gives the most scope for variety in personal tools. Each individual chooses whatever she likes, and explains to the others how she relates it to the Earth concept.

An important point for women to remember in the presentation and dedication of their tools is that they are affirming each other's right to make individual choices, to decide for themselves what they will consider personally sacred and significant. There should never be any hint of criticism of anyone's choice, nor any sense of competition as to whose object is "better." All comments should be positive and supportive. The assertion of personal choice in ritual tools can represent a new sense of inner powers of decision, especially for some women who may have been unsure of themselves. It seems a small step; but when a person needs more self-confidence, it is helpful to be able to say, "This thing I choose to be sacred to myself." It is surprisingly liberating to recognize that the manufactured objects presented for adoration by traditional religions are no more holy than things that one chooses for one's self; indeed they may be much less so, for the very reason that they are created by someone else. A beautiful stone, picked up while hiking on a memorably perfect day, has more personal meaning than a church statue or a public icon. Thus becoming a priestess for one's self means creating one's own sacred objects and investing them with significance through deliberate, voluntary acts.

CHANTS

Hail, Cup,
Bearer of living waters,
Quencher of thirst,
Vessel of love,
Cradle of birth.
We salute thee.

Hail, Pentacle,

Mystic star of earth,
Cyclic emblem,
Apple heart,
Goddess shield.
We salute thee.

Hail, Wand,
Torch of holy fire,
Pointer of the way,
Path finder,
Rod straight and true.
We salute thee.

Hail, Sword,
Bringer of doom,
Cutter of threads,
Hand of the Fates,
Shining defender.
We salute thee.

Hail, Four Instruments,
Fit well our hands,
Lead us to wisdom,
By water, fire, earth, and air.
We salute thee.

Nakedness

During past ages, it was customary for some groups of Goddess worshipers to conduct their rituals naked. The usual term for such nakedness is "skyclad," a translation of Sanskrit *digambara*. Circles of Goddess worshipers removed their clothing and ornaments to indicate that in the eyes of the Mother—that is, Nature—all were equal, without artificial badges of rank or status. They wanted to appear just as the Mother made them, just as they came from the womb. Among naked people, there are few clues to distinguish rich from poor, aristocrat from commoner, priest from layperson. The idea was to remove artificial distinctions so that members of the circle could feel more truly like brothers and sisters under the same sky, sharing the same earth, meeting on the same level of humanity.

Of course it often happened in circles of men and women together, worshiping the cosmic principle of fertility, that their nakedness was an accepted prelude to sexual orgies that climaxed the celebrations. Under pagan systems, such sexual expressions were regarded as sacred and holy. Sexual orgasm itself was regarded as a brief sharing in the perpetual bliss of the gods: a foretaste of heaven, or a participation in the divine creative act.

It was the ascetic patriarchal sects who declared such unabashedly sexual observances devilish or sinful. Since the political triumph of religious patriarchy, that is the attitude that has prevailed in our society. Therefore, many of us automatically resist the idea of ritual nakedness as improper, offensive to modesty, or downright immoral—even unthinkable for a mixed group of men and women.

As a rule, however, those mixed groups bold enough to try it have found that it is not invariably sexually stimulating. The effect may even be the contrary. Like participants in nudist colonies, group members have reported that the novelty of public nakedness soon wears off. They come to accept their own and others' unclothed bodies as casually as they accept clothing. Thus it can happen that even in a mixed group, nakedness can become largely asexual and may carry a ritual significance only.

Nevertheless, the idea of ritual nakedness certainly carries a heavy load of anxiety for many people. There are all kinds of fears to be dealt with, in addition to the fears instilled by traditional religious teachings. Both women and men may feel ashamed of their bodies because they don't fit conventional standards of attractiveness. They think they are too fat, too thin, too old, too out-of-shape; they have some blemish or disfigurement; they feel that their clothing is an essential protection. Men fear that their bodies will betray them with inappropriate erections, or they fear comparison between their genitals or their muscles and those of other men. Women don't want to reveal stretch marks, scars, drooping breasts, flabby stomachs, varicose veins, or what have you. Even over and above the puritanical background of our culture, many of us are extremely sensitive about letting our bodies be seen.

In a group composed of women only, naturally there is less anxiety about nakedness. The possibility of orgiastic behavior—at least, of the heterosexual type—is not a problem to be dealt with. Nevertheless, many women have such ingrained habits of modesty that they would feel uncomfortable taking off their clothes in any company whatsoever.

Since women's rituals aim to provide reassurance and comfort for all participants, the use of nakedness in this context should not be considered unless all can feel comfortable with it. Under no circumstances should a group decide to go "skyclad" against the wishes of any of its members. As long as the modest ones are part of the group, even if they are a minority, their modesty should be respected.

There is also the purely practical consideration of temperature. Past societies that made extensive use of ritual nakedness usually lived in tropical or subtropical climates. Today, most indoor spaces in temperate zones are not well enough heated in winter to make naked people comfortable. It's possible to practice ritual nakedness with the heat turned up for the occasion, or else to restrict it to warm summer evenings either indoors or outdoors, as long as complete privacy can be assured. But if a group plans to try a skyclad meeting, environmental temperature must be taken into account.

It's possible for a group to try nakedness just now and then, for some special occasion or particular reason. Goddess worshipers have often pointed out that women's nakedness can generate real physical responses, such as erections in men, or appetite in nursing infants; thus it is a source of *mana* or power. Many naked women together, then, generate a collective emotional power that all participants can feel, as if the deeply buried infant self even in an adult can remember the maternal body on some profound emotional level. At least, this can be felt by all who don't object to nakedness. Let it be emphasized again that this should not be tried if there are some who object.

Any ritual or combination of rituals can be performed by naked participants. As a rule, this will noticeably alter the general feeling and quality of the event. It is instructive to do a group ritual with everyone clothed, then on a later occasion to do the same with everyone naked. In subsequently sharing their reactions and responses to the two methods, women are often surprised by the radical difference in their attitudes. They may feel collectively that nakedness provided a more rewarding and intense experience. Or, they may decide that there was too much hidden embarrassment for sufficient enhancement of the ritual. Reactions depend on the nature and general background of the group.

It is enough to realize, however, that ritual nakedness is a possibility, drawn from very ancient and honorable traditions that predate patriarchy by thousands of years. Therefore it may be of particular interest to women. Whether or not it is appropriate in the modern context is a matter for each group to decide for itself.

The Robe

Like talismanic jewelry, ceremonial robes add visual interest to a ritual meeting. Some groups like to provide themselves with handmade robes, created either by each woman individually, or by one skilled seamstress who might volunteer to make them all.

Very little skill is required to follow the robe directions given here. Only the most basic kind of sewing is needed. This robe can be made by anyone, even without a sewing machine. There are only two long seams to sew, and they could be sewn by hand without too much effort.

This gracefully flowing robe makes quite a useful garment. It is all one piece. It fits any figure. It moves to any dance. It sits, reclines, or sprawls in any position. It can be made in any color, with any fabric from winter wool to the sheerest, lightest summer cotton; even clinging silk, floating chiffon, or rich lace. It can do double duty as a hostess gown, housecoat, beach cover-up, or bathrobe. It can be worn over other clothes, or over nothing. Hidden beneath its folds, one can even change clothes in public. The back and front are identical, so it can be worn either way round. Best of all, making it is almost as easy as hemming a curtain.

Such a garment is so easy that one could quickly create a whole wardrobe of them in different colors, weights, and lengths. A short one, reaching only to hip level, makes a loose top to wear with pants. A longer one, reaching to knee level, makes a nice simple dress. It can be belted, sashed, or dressed up with scarves and jewelry. The fabric can be plain or patterned, or finished with trimmings, beads, sequins, fabric paint, or embroidery. Some of the world's most beautiful embroidered garments have been created with garment shapes as simple and basic as this one.

SEWING INSTRUCTIONS

1. To begin a full-length robe, take a straight length of fabric, 36 inches to 45 inches wide and as long as *twice* the distance from the top of your shoulder to your feet. For example, if your body is 5 feet tall excluding your head, then you will need 10 feet of fabric, or $3^1/_3$ yards.

2. Fold this length into quarters: one fold across the width at the midpoint, and another fold down the length in the center, so that all four selvage edges lie together. (Note: if the fabric has a one-way pattern design or nap, it will run upward on one side of the finished robe, and downward on the other. If this is not desirable, then cut across the width at the midpoint, turn one half around, and with right sides facing, seam the two cut edges together. This seam will then become the shoulder-and-sleeve seam of the finished robe, instead of the seamless top line made by folding. Be sure the upper ends of the design face toward this seam.)

3. With the fabric folded into four thicknesses, as shown in figure A, cut a quarter-circle with a 3-inch radius through all thicknesses at the doubly folded corner. When unfolded, this central open circle will become the neck hole.

Fig. A   4 Thicknesses

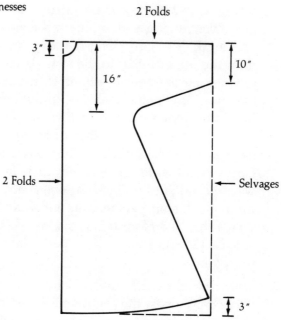

Fig. B   2 Thicknesses

4. Measure 10 inches down from the upper folds along the
   selvages, and place a mark. Measure 3 inches up from
   the lower cut edges along the selvages, and place a second mark. Measure along the long folded edge, down
   from the upper folds, to the same length as your neck-
   to-waist measurement—about 16 inches for most people. From this point, measure straight across the width
   from the folded edge to a distance that will be one-
   quarter of the desired width of the finished robe at its
   narrowest point. Leave a generous amount of fabric
   here. A total width of 48 inches to 50 inches around the
   waist portion of the finished robe is not too much, even
   for a small, slim person. You will want lots of room in
   your robe. Therefore this measured distance should be
   at least 12 inches ($\frac{1}{4}$ of 48 inches). Place a third mark at
   this point.

5. Draw straight chalk lines to join these three marks, but
   curve gently past the central mark instead of drawing a
   sharp angle (see figure A). This curve will be the under-
   sleeve curve. Draw another wide, gentle curve from the
   lower selvage mark to the bottom of the folded edges, to
   give contour to the skirt hem. Cut out the garment on
   these lines, through all thicknesses at once.

6. When you unfold the fabric, you will see that you have
   a front and back, both alike, already united along the
   upper edges, needing only to be sewn at the side seams
   and hemmed around the bottom (see figure B). First,
   however, the neck opening should have some attention.

7. With a 3-inch radius, the neck circle is still too small to
   fit comfortably over your head. (Try it and see; but don't
   force it.) If you want to finish the opening with a simple
   bias binding or other trim, you will have to cut away
   another $\frac{1}{2}$ inch to $\frac{5}{8}$ inch all the way around, until the
   hole slides easily over your head. But if you want to add
   a neck facing, then you will need this extra material for
   a seam allowance.

8. To cut a neck facing out of one of the scrap pieces, take
   the circle that you cut from the neck, lay it in the center
   of a scrap piece, and trace a circle around it. Then draw

another circle 2¹/₂ inches outside the first one, all the way around. Cut out this ring-shaped, 2¹/₂-inch-wide piece, which will become the neck facing.

9. With right sides together, pin the facing all around the neck opening, ⁵/₈ inch in from the edges of the center hole. Sew. Clip the seam allowance all the way around. Pull it over your head to see that it now fits comfortably. If not, sew again, a little bit outside the first line of stitching, and clip through this first line of stitching to provide more room. Turn the facing to the wrong side of the garment, press, and top-stitch.

10. Then, with right sides together, sew up the long side and under-sleeve seams. Reinforce the curved section with about 8 inches of additional stitching, then clip the seam allowance around the curve.

11. If the fabric has a firm selvage edge, without any obvious printing or color change, you can leave the selvages alone at the sleeve ends without hemming. Otherwise, for a better finish, turn the sleeve ends under to make narrow rolled hems, and stitch.

12. Finally, turn under the lower edge to the desired length, trim if necessary, and hem.

Extra fabric scraps can be used to make patch pockets, either on the outside of the robe or hidden on the inside. Because the sleeves are loose, you can easily pull your arm in to reach a secret inside pocket.

These directions for a robe with a simple circular neck hole are planned for quick and easy completion. The more accomplished seamstress can add her own embellishments to the basic pattern. For example, she might prefer a tight neck with a round collar, zipper, or button panel; or a turtleneck, or a stand-up collar, or a ruffle, or a square neck opening with mitered corners. Anything is possible. Another attractive alternative is to cut a wide neck circle and provide it with a casing, through which to thread a ribbon or drawstring, to gather it up to the desired width.

You might like to provide yourself with a whole set of robes in seasonal colors. For example, the traditional spring color worn at Beltane (May Day) celebrations is green. The traditional color

for the midsummer solstice is sun gold, or orange; for the feast of
Lammas in August, red; for Samhain (Halloween), the Feast of the
Dead, black; and for midwinter, the Feast of Rebirth, white.

The Parade

Any parade or procession is a public ritual, intended to be
performed by some and watched by others. Sometimes women's
groups may wish to maintain a degree of privacy in the proces-
sional format. A women's parade can be as public as a march
along a city street at high noon with banners, masks, costumes,
music, drumming, and chanting; or it can be as private as a
solemn walk through woods by moonlight.

A parade usually means going public to some extent, to
demonstrate group solidarity for a political purpose, or to bring
knowledge of the group to a wider audience. Observers may be
invited to join the procession.

Religious processions in general have involved the carrying
of a sacred article from one place to another, or along a circular
route, to expose it to public view at a special season. In ancient
Rome, for example, festival processions included holy images and
symbols, relics, treasures, heralds, dancers, musicians, heroes of
the day, priestesses, priests, clowns, and animals garlanded and
decorated to be sacrificed to the gods and distributed as eucharis-
tic meats. Christian Rome copied the same traditions, but
dropped the public distribution of meat as too expensive. Every
one of the world's religions has made use of the solemn procession. The custom undoubtedly began with priestesses in the age
of the Goddess, so it is fitting that women should reclaim it.

A private procession of a women's ritual group might take
the form of a pilgrimage to some secluded spot that a member or
members found attractive and numinous. Each participant may
carry some personally meaningful object to leave there, or to
expose to the environment so that it becomes a memento. Such a
private parade could take place at night, in silence, or else to the

accompaniment of music or chanting. For example, someone might suggest a moonlight walk to a certain tree, clearing, fountain, or waterfall; or to the top of a hill to see a special view; or to the bank of a stream for ritual bathing; or to the house of a new mother to honor her and her infant; or to a spot where something happened that the group considers significant; or to an open place at dawn or dusk to celebrate the rising or setting of the sun.

A little less private parade might pass through suburban streets by day or by night, implicitly inviting nonmembers to tag along if they wish, but without a serious effort to call attention to the paraders or their destination.

A fully public parade would take place in a populous area, with as many attention-getting devices as possible: bright colors, loud sounds, costumes, flags, rhythm, songs, prominent display of ritual objects, and perhaps a chant in honor of the Goddess. This is a "coming out" sort of parade, for women who feel secure in their feminist personae. A traditional Goddess chant might be used:

> We all come from the Goddess,
> And to Her we shall return,
> Like a drop of rain,
> Flowing to the ocean.

How about a parade in honor of a historical heroine, to offset the all-male holiday parades for heroes or fallen soldiers? How about honoring the memory of all the innocent noncombatant women slain in men's wars? How about a parade to demonstrate in front of a store that is selling war toys, or fur coats, or cosmetics tested by animal torture, or anti-woman pornography, or any other political issue? How about a Goddess parade around a church during Sunday services?

It is also possible to make a public parade without attracting attention. For this procedure, women simply walk through public places in a coherent group or line formation, silently, keeping their relative positions, perhaps following a leader and copying all her gestures. They may carry special tokens or dress in special colors, but remain generally inconspicuous.

About Crystals

Natural crystals and semiprecious gemstones have become some of the most popular adjuncts to women's rituals. Wearable as jewelry, they also look beautiful on an altar. They are pleasant to handle and rewarding to contemplate. They are wonderful symbols of Mother Earth, metaphorically the distilled essence of chthonian (earth) spirit. The molecular structures of crystalline substances can be viewed as representative examples of cosmic order, or of nature's hidden symmetries. Meditation on the vast eons involved in the infinitely slow growth of crystals, as they lie deep in Earth's dark womb and gradually coalesce out of mineral mother-liquor, tends to put ephemeral human affairs in a different perspective. It brings new serenity through the knowing of larger, grander chronologies and cycles of development and transformation.

Women may take pleasure in such a deep appreciation of the esthetic qualities and symbolic value of crystals, but they should guard against certain more exploitive applications of their affinity for stones. It is always best to be well informed about any subject of personal interest: the subject of minerals and crystals no less than any other. Yet a surprising number of people will accept myths ahead of mineralogical facts, showing almost no genuine curiosity—even people who would normally seek out all available knowledge of any other favorite subject or complex hobby. Naturally, wherever ignorance leaves gaps, misinformation will rush in.

Many of the myths still extant among "crystal mystics" have been around for thousands of years, dating back to ages of almost complete scientific ignorance. They persist in spite of the findings of mineralogical science, now well known and readily available to anyone who can read a book.*

Medieval textbooks were full of lists of various stones to be touched, held, or worn as cures for various diseases. They also

---

*See Barbara G. Walker, *The Book of Sacred Stones: Fact and Fallacy in the Crystal World* (San Francisco: Harper & Row, 1989).

prescribed certain stones to make one's self invisible, to break down prison walls, to kill enemies at a distance, to acquire wealth, to be able to fly, to be irresistibly attractive to the opposite sex, and so on. All the usual pitiful human dreams and wishes are liberally represented in the folklore of stones.

While most of these demonstrably untrue notions have been abandoned, the healing myths persist. One reason for this is that there are so many chronic illnesses, pathological conditions, malaises, and physical or emotional symptoms still lying outside the competence of modern medicine. Afflicted people tend to be willing to try anything. Often an illness or a neurotic symptom can be alleviated by a different focus of mind: the well-known placebo effect. Sometimes it can even bring a complete cure. Many things, including stones, can provide such a focus for the mind.

This is all well and good. If it works, so much the better. Unfortunately, however, lack of reliable knowledge in such subtle psychological areas has given rise to much pseudoscientific nonsense, promulgated for commercial reasons and perpetuated by popular confusion about the workings of the physical universe. True knowledge means proof, not faith, hearsay, or misapplication of terms.

"Crystal healers" invariably talk nonsense about the "electrical properties" of stones as related to human "bioelectricity," implying that interatomic electromagnetic bonds in the minerals will somehow affect human bodies by mere proximity. Neither the healers nor their customers seem to notice the fatal flaw in this argument: That is, in any such universal application of atomic theory, a patient could be just as well cured by the "vibrations" of any common material objects at all—tree trunks, tables, seashells, plastic toys, bathroom tiles, books, glassware, water pipes, flagstones, curtain rods, or the steering wheels of cars. All are made equally of vibrating atoms.

Why should magical properties be attributed to a diamond, but not to pencil lead (graphite), which is exactly the same element in another configuration? Why should a chunk of rock crystal (quartz) be any more magical than a handful of sand, which is exactly the same mineral with the same molecular structure? Why should a ruby (corundum) be considered a "blood purifier," while the same mineral in the form of emery is good for nothing but grinding and polishing? (Clearly the constant association between red stones and blood is sympathetic magic of the most primitive kind, based on nothing but likeness of color.)

Ultimately the real distinction between "curative" minerals and the more commonplace occurrences of the same minerals seems to depend on their price. This or any other kind of medical quackery-for-profit is both morally reprehensible and potentially dangerous. Excessive faith in magical cures can cause victims to neglect life-threatening conditions, which might be genuinely treatable in their earlier stages.

For all their pseudoscientific jargon, self-styled healers are usually ignorant of the real electrical, chemical, or physical properties of the minerals they deal with. Some of the recurrent myths about that perennial favorite, quartz, serve as examples. It is claimed that quartz "absorbs magnetism," when every mineralogist knows that quartz is nonmagnetic. It is claimed that quartz conducts electricity, when in fact it is as nonconductive as glass, hence an equally good electrical insulator. It is conversely claimed that quartz can generate electric current, like a battery. This error arises from misunderstanding of the mineral's piezoelectric property. Most absurd are the lists of illnesses or maladjustments that quartz is supposed to cure, as opposed to completely different lists associated with the same mineral under some of its other names, such as jasper, carnelian, agate, flint, onyx, bloodstone, amethyst, and opal.

One of the most blatant examples of chicanery is the lucrative traffic in "gemstone essence," that is, plain water, sold on the pretense that it has absorbed some hermetic quality from a stone that was immersed in it. Since the majority of these stones are absolutely insoluble in water (most can't be dissolved even in strong acids), it is clear that the liquid "essence" contains not one molecule of the mineral. In fact it is still plain water, just as it comes from the tap.

In view of the multitude of myths, scams, and shell games now connected with the crystal trade, interested women should study the subject carefully, and refuse to let pitchmen take advantage of their natural appreciation of beautiful objects. Knowledge is the best defense against flimflam or charlatanry. To nourish a personal interest in stones, study the books of accredited mineralogists, not those of self-styled mystics who perpetuate medieval errors. One may penetrate the field of mineralogical science as much or as little as one likes, but whatever the level of one's knowledge, let it be sound.

With due consideration for such caveats, minerals can be used successfully in many kinds of rituals. Natural crystals are obvious Mother Earth symbols through being congealed out of her very "blood"—that is, the molten magma of our planet's inner spaces. Even patriarchal myths from ancient Greece postulated the primordial birth of humanity from mother-stones. In a way, the Greeks even recognized that crystals are "frozen" or solid forms of chthonian liquids. The Greek word *krystallos* means ice. Indeed the freezing of water and the growth of crystals from rock melt is the same process. Technically water is a mineral too.

Transparent crystals are excellent media for personal rituals of meditation. To use a crystal of any transparent mineral in this way, pick a quiet time when you can be alone and undisturbed. Sit or lie down comfortably, in a place where a bright light can shine from behind you on what you hold. Sunlight is best, but artificial light will do.

Very slowly, turn the crystal around in your hands to every possible angle, noting its internal structures, cleavage planes, reflective surfaces, highlights, shadows, veiling, inclusions, inner refractions (rainbows), and other individual features. As you study the crystal, some of its features will begin to look like miniature scenes or figures.

It's easy to see seascapes and snowscapes, beaches, cliffs, glaciers, tunnels, walls, castles, stalactites, doorways, boats, statues, faces, and so on. Imagine yourself reduced to microscopic size, walking into the crystal like Alice through the looking-glass. You can see horizontal surfaces that you might walk on. Then, as you turn the crystal, the same surfaces might become walls or ceilings. A white landscape may change to a black, starry sky. A cloaked figure can turn into a space ship, or disappear altogether. When the light strikes internal cracks just so, you might see a spray of iridescent colors or a curtain of fire.

Take a reading glass or other magnifying lens, and study the crystal more closely. What new features do you notice under magnification? What do you see that wasn't evident before?

When you become involved in this kind of crystal contemplation, you can spend a surprising amount of time in that miniature world. An hour can pass like ten minutes. Such a spiritual journey can be refreshing and energizing. What you are really doing is dipping into the timeless world of your own unconscious—the world of imagination, dreams, and creativity—with the help of some ambiguous visual clues.

You return from that place with new ideas and symbols, new mental connections. That's why a crystal can act as a yantra (meditation sign). That's why generations of "crystal gazers" have claimed to envision other worlds or future times with the aid of minerals.

Some types of minerals are better suited than others to contemplative rituals of this sort. Transparent but "busy" crystals, with lots of interesting cracks, veils, and other internal features, might prove most pleasing to some people. Others might prefer opaque minerals with intriguing external markings, color patterns, or striations. Different minerals appeal to different people for different reasons, or to the same person at different times. If you collect specimens, you may wish to have a fairly wide assortment of mineral types. It often happens that, for no apparent reason, your hand automatically reaches for a particular item on one day, and another one on another day. Sometimes you may forget what you saw previously in a given crystal, and find quite different pictures in it the next time you pick it up. Changes in the angles and conditions of light will also change crystal features. Your own esthetic sense is the only true guide to crystal meditation. At any given time, use whatever seems to "speak" to you. This curious sense of affinity can be so powerful that collectors will sometimes express their feeling that a certain crystal "wants" to be handled just now. The feeling, of course, is human enough, but every bit as persuasive as a little girl telling us what her doll wants. She *knows*.

One may contemplate a crystal in the same way, and for the same reasons, as one might contemplate a great painting or sculpture. This is Nature's artwork, in many ways more beautiful and mysterious than anything ever achieved by human skill. Moreover, unlike a Rembrandt or a Renoir, it can be acquired for a comparatively modest price—or even unearthed from the rocks with your own hands, for nothing. Earth's body is full of surprises. The Mother is generous with her gifts.

For a group ceremony of crystals, let each member bring one or more specimens to the meeting. Nearly everyone possesses at least one crystal or gem that would serve. Some people think "crystal" means only a transparent stone like clear quartz; but remember, virtually all rocks and minerals are crystalline in their structure, whether opaque or transparent, colorful or dull, smooth or rough. Among materials commonly used for decorative purposes, only opal and obsidian are noncrystalline. There are also gems of organic origin, such as amber, pearl, coral, jet, and ivory.

If two or three members of the group are collectors and the others are not, then it's up to the collectors to bring enough specimens to go around and then some, so every woman can make a choice for the ceremony. There should be more crystals than people, in order that everyone may choose from a group of them.

Let the crystals be placed all together on the altar, or on a special cloth, bench, table top, or other surface where all can be displayed at once. The women can honor the crystals with a speech or song of welcome, a spoken blessing, or a poem such as the one that follows this chapter. The idea is to treat them as if they were sentient beings, for purposes of the ceremony. They may be sprinkled with water from the altar cup. A candle or athame may be carried all the way around them, while the women stretch out their hands toward them and project attention to them.

After contemplating the assortment of crystals for a while, each woman selects a crystal to hold in her hand and study more closely. She should try *not* to select one of her own, but rather choose one that is unfamiliar. Then she spends some time quietly meditating on the crystal in her hand, letting her imagination pass into it as described above, observing its features.

If the stone is opaque, she studies its surface patterns, colors, and general shape, turning it different ways to observe it in various lights and shadows. She notes its weight and balance in the hand, its texture, its temperature, its type of luster (dull, glassy, metallic, silky, greasy, brilliant). Then she should give the crystal a name, and decide why she chose it and what it means to her. Does it resemble some other object? Does it remind her of something or someone? Does it seem to have a character of its own? Does it "speak"? Does it seem beautiful, ugly, complex, simple, powerful, humble, funny, elegant, grotesque, cute?

When all selections have been minutely studied, let the women return to their circle and sit, each with her chosen crystal before her. Then each in turn reveals the name she has given to her crystal, describes her journey into its depths, and tells about the connotations and images she has found in it.

As an interesting variation on this exercise, the real owner of the specimen might speak immediately afterward, telling of her own responses and feelings toward this particular stone, or its history. Each reaction enhances the other, and many intriguing points of both difference and agreement may surface. For example:

USER: "I name this quartz crystal Beach House, because in the middle of it I see a blocky sort of house on a dark cliff above the sea. It reminds me of my aunt's house in California. I was happy there. When I turn the crystal over, the house is gone and I see a woman's face with a very sharp nose, pale, dead-white. When I hold it up to the candle flame, the woman seems to flush all rosy for a moment, but then she vanishes into a triangular shadow. The crystal affects me strangely. It seems to know things that I ought to know, but don't. I feel that it is somehow wise. When I picked it up, it was very cold. Now it has warmed in my hand and feels more friendly."

OWNER: "How extraordinary. It seems to me, too, a source of knowledge. I never saw a house in this stone, but I often see a pale landscape against a dark starry sky, like a scene on an alien planet. Some crystals always seem aloof until you hold them long enough to warm them. I have read that crystallized material is always colder to the touch than glass, because the organized ionic lattice structure conducts heat away from your hand faster than noncrystalline glass can do it. The sense of coldness is inherent in my response to this crystal too. Its landscape seems a long, long way from any sun."

Another ritual use of crystals employs a "leader" who chooses different stones at random out of a closed box to give them to different people. All except the leader keep their eyes closed and one hand extended, palm up. The leader goes around the circle and places a stone in each outstretched hand. Then she touches the recipient of the first stone. That person then describes what she feels about the object she holds, while her eyes are kept shut. When she is finished, she touches the next person, who then describes her stone in a similar manner. After one circuit, each person passes the stone that she holds on to the next person beside her. Another "blind" round ensues, with different people's responses and reactions to the same tactile stimuli. Those who are mineralogically knowledgable may try guessing what mineral they hold from its shape and texture alone.

In another phase, each woman opens her eyes and looks at the crystal in her hand, then describes it again with additions or revisions arising from the visual experience of it. A third phase may be added, in which each woman states what she would like to do with that particular stone, and if possible, does it (walk it around the room, press it to her cheek, taste it, hold it to her navel, breast, or forehead "third eye," give it to someone else, place it on the altar, and so on).

Another crystal ritual is like the personal gift. Each member brings to the meeting a stone intended as a gift for someone, and gives it while stating why it seems appropriate for that person. As an alternative, all gift stones may be placed in a group at the altar and each woman chooses the one that she wants to take home, explaining in her turn why that particular stone attracted her. As another alternative, gift stones may be chosen blind, by touch alone, out of a closed box or bag. In this case it must be remembered that the touch must be very gentle. Many crystals are too fragile to be stirred around in contact with others without chipping or breaking.

An interesting ritual is the creation of a crystal mandala. A large assortment of crystals is needed for this. Each woman first chooses one "theme stone" to place on the floor directly in front of herself. Then she chooses other stones to place at either side, toward her neighbors, and in front, toward the altar, keeping in mind what each stone means to her and why it was chosen for these relational positions. Designs can be developed and merged all around the circle, until all available crystals have been used. Then the group may walk or dance around the whole-circle mandala, admiring it, stepping in and out, sharing impressions. Songs or chants may be added to honor the crystals and the creativity of the group.

Another kind of mandala can be created by laying crystals in a large spiral path, in toward the altar and out again. Each woman in turn slowly walks this path: inward, once around the altar, and outward, meanwhile expressing the thoughts that come to her about this symbolism.

Crystal lovers can enjoy their stones together on several levels at once. They can share information about related aspects of the natural world: mineralogy, geology, rockhounding activities, bits of knowledge about crystal structures or inorganic chemistry. They can exercise the esthetic sense, getting in touch with deep feelings through visualization and meditation. A crystal ceremony typically helps everyone gain some self-knowledge. Collective enjoyment of beautiful things is a common reason for people to form interest-sharing groups of any kind. Sharing crystals can help to create strong bonds between group members.

Crystals can become friends. It is easy to invest them with personalities of their own, to feel comforted by their presence, to sense a mystic affinity that makes one want to hold, carry or wear them. Crystals "call out" to esthetically responsive individuals. Yet the most interesting characteristics of any given crystal may not be apparent right away. The more time you spend with a particular stone, the more features and distinctions you will notice.

However fascinating crystal meditations may be, it is important to remain aware of the difference between nature's reality and the powerful visualizing functions of the imagination. Women's spirituality is hurt whenever critics can associate it with the ignorant kind of lunatic-fringeism that talks to Martians or remembers Atlantis, or seriously relays doomsday messages from astral beings. All too many people exploit this kind of ignorance for their own profit. To connect the valid thrust of the women's spirituality movement with demonstrably false assumptions about the natural world can easily trivialize—and ultimately invalidate—that movement. It will then no longer offer a useful alternative to the established patriarchy, which is why the latter now views many of the sillier New Age ideas with notable complacency.

The women's spirituality movement may prove the best hope for our planet's preservation. It is too important to be prematurely withered by the scorn of the intelligentsia. Women's groups must beware of false premises. It is advisable to do some realistic research, and enhance the fun of esthetic appreciation with verifiable facts. The women's spirituality movement does not need comic-book fantasies in a world whose natural beauty is more than wonderful, and whose reality is infinitely more complex than anything a human mind can devise.

CRYSTAL CONSECRATION

Clearness as of air,
Hardness as of rock,

Born of Earth fires
In cauldrons underground,
When stone flowed like water
In dark unseen by eye,
In a time before time:

Child of Nature's matrix,
Gem of Nature's crown,
Come now to my hand;
Take some warmth from flesh;
Let eyes see your beauty.
Dwell here a little while;
Tell me of eternity.

Healing

In a world containing sickness and trauma, there is naturally much interest in healing. We wish our medical science could cure every ill, but unfortunately it can't. The medical establishment often seems to promise results that it can't deliver. Some so-called treatments can even make patients sicker. There are many such iatrogenic diseases, and modern hospitals can be hotbeds of infection.

Out of disillusionment with the limitations of today's medicine, a new industry of holistic healing has arisen. Although they are not directly connected, holistic healing and the women's spirituality movement have become intertwined—chiefly because the mainstream medical profession has been insufficiently attentive to women's special needs.

Holistic medicine is not new. It is the oldest form of healing. In the prepatriarchal past, it was directly connected with female spiritual leaders who were also doctors: the priestess-prophetess-sorceress-midwife-medicinewomen of the matriarchal ages. Their power was supposed to come from the Goddess who birthed and nurtured the universe. She dispensed both life and death, sickness and health. The initial trial-and-error experiments of her women, over thousands of years, produced the first herbal pharmacopeias and many techniques of "magical" healing: massage, hypnosis, trances, prayers, chants, exorcism, invocation, dreamwork, yoga, acupuncture, spells, baths, special diets, mind control, laying on of hands, crystals, magnets, poultices, potions, placebos, and prophylactic charms. Some of these ancient healing techniques are still with us. Sometimes they still work.

Primitive healing rituals are not adequate replacements for the more successful techniques of modern medicine. Nevertheless they do and should have a place in the modern world, where the spiritual implications of sickness are too often callously ignored, and the sometimes crucial mental attitude of the patient receives little attention. Some types of stress-related illness can be altogether cured by a genuinely humane, caring attentiveness on the part of the healer. We are beginning to discover how intimately the body is affected by emotional factors. Throughout history, this intimate connection has been intuitively exploited by faith healers of every description, from the sincere to the consciously fraudulent. Even the most blatant quacks and charlatans can acquire devoted followers who will loudly proclaim their efficacy.

To become valid and useful, however, women's healing rituals should avoid the taint of quackery by concentrating on the state of mind, rather than making unjustified claims about the state of the body. It is laudable to comfort and encourage a sick person, especially when professionals are too busy to bother. We unofficially recognize the importance of hospital visits by family members and friends to the sick and the dying. Professionals must give at least a fleeting impression of caring, but their personal sympathy and attention are not freely given. They are for sale. In contrast, women's groups can provide members with sincere, sisterly caring without financial strings attached.

Perhaps one of the most important functions in mental or emotional healing is to do nothing at all: to listen. Women do this for one another in consciousness-raising or in passing the talking stick. Many rituals provide opportunities to air personal problems and to feel the group's support.

Rituals cannot be considered necessarily curative, in and of themselves. History shows us thousands of years during which magic and ritual consistently failed to cure plague, consumption, rickets, scurvy, dysentery, appendicitis, cancer, typhus, toothache, smallpox, diphtheria, pneumonia, yellow fever, and dozens of other ailments that are now controllable through increased scientific knowledge. We are not so unrealistic as to expect a healing ritual to cure everything. Ritual is not a panacea.

The true purpose of a healing ritual is to improve the patient's state of mind. It is now known that an optimistic attitude can help the physical healing process, whereas gloom and pessimism can retard healing. Healing rituals can provide emotional support, confidence, and a sanguine outlook, contributing to the success of medical treatment and the body's own regenerative resources. Even when the body is not going to regenerate, as in the case of a terminal illness, rituals that express caring and support (*not* useless denial of the death process) can bring ease and peace to the patient.

Too many people view healing rituals with a simplistic faith that can only bring disillusionment when healing doesn't occur. Even worse, excessive faith in ineffective magical techniques can delay or prevent necessary medical treatment until a mild condition becomes serious. Some unscrupulous self-styled healers will go so far as to blame the victim when their fad treatment fails, claiming that the patient didn't really want to be healed, and unconsciously resisted the treatment. Both religious and psychiatric healers have gotten away with claiming that the patient who stubbornly remained sick simply lacked sufficient faith in the cure. Enlightened women should not allow any professonal or nonprofessional healer to perpetrate such deceptions.

Without any deception or misrepresentation, a healing ritual can provide the psychological equivalent of the Jewish mother's chicken soup, or an old friend's sympathetic ear inclined over a soothing cup of tea. Rituals should give the patient room to express her pain or her need, to acknowledge and respect it, and then distract her attention from it in an exercise of kindness.

Cradling is a helpful ritual for a person in immediate distress. Just as a baby is comforted by being picked up and rocked, so also an adult can feel comforted by the same sensations unconsciously remembered from infancy. A distressed person can lie down to be lifted on the arms of the whole group. Raised to about waist level, she is then gently rocked from side to side, perhaps to the accompaniment of a low humming. It sounds simple, but the quieting effect can be quite remarkable.

Another soothing ritual is the common laying on of hands that our foremothers practiced for millennia, until patriarchal Christian fathers claimed it as their own miracle technique. The distressed woman should lie down in a relaxed position, close her eyes, and breathe slowly and deeply. Others gather around and gently place their hands either on her body, or close enough so that she can feel the warmth radiating from their palms. If she has a traumatized area, the hands should concentrate there. Areas that respond especially well to hand touch are the temples, forehead, ribs, belly, thighs, knees, fingers, and feet.

Massage is an outgrowth of laying on of hands. It is recognized as an effective therapeutic technique; but you don't have to be trained in massage to provide someone with its benefits. Slow, deep rubbing of the back of the neck and shoulders, the small of the back, the palms of the hands, or the soles of the feet can be wonderfully comforting. To be massaged by many hands at once is a lovely feeling.

With the subject lying on her back, station one "masseuse" at each hand and each foot, two more to rub her arms, two more for her legs, one to reach behind her neck and shoulders, one to stroke or comb her hair. With the subject lying on her stomach, more hands can be used on her back, shoulders, and waist. If she is naked, or minimally clothed in a swimsuit or underwear, the stroking hands can be anointed with sweet-smelling massage oil, adding still another pleasant sensation to the whole experience.

Massage stimulates surface circulation of the blood, so the subject can radiate her body warmth away shortly after the end of the session. To prevent this, cover her with a soft, warm blanket and let her lie peacefully for a while, until her circulatory system readjusts.

Another kind of "stroke session" is useful for people suffering from emotional distress, depression, loss of confidence, guilt, poor self-image, low self-esteem, or feelings of rejection. On one or another level, such problems afflict a majority of women in any male-oriented, male-dominated society. When one group member is obviously and overtly troubled, the talking stick can be used to provide her with an ego massage. As the stick is passed around, each member pays the afflicted one a compliment, which must be genuine. Any insincere flattery is definitely inappropriate.

Here are some examples:

"I know you will come through this trial and be all right again. You are one of the strongest people I know. You've been through so much. I really admire the way you've faced everything with such amazing courage."

"I will always remember the first time I met you. I thought you were so aloof and elegant. Then you sang that bawdy song, and I thought, 'She's real.' I liked you from that moment on."

"You've always reminded me of some graceful animal that Nature made to be free, but you were living in a cage. I see you in my mind's eye, leaping and running, being what you were meant to be. You have the spirit to fly."

"I don't know you well because I'm the new kid on the block here. But I'm already grateful for your kindness and friendliness. You don't know how easy it is for people to like you."

"Every morning when you look in your mirror, you should say, I'm a beautiful person, and believe it. It's true."

"You're a wonderful mother, and you make the best onion soup in town."

"I wish my own blood sister could be more like you."

"I know how strong you are. People depend on you. I know you have never let anyone down, which is a unique and wonderful thing to be able to say about a person."

"You have accomplished so much. I'm awed by the many things you've done in your life."

"We love you and we want you to be well."

Verbal strokes may be accompanied by physical actions. The subject may walk around the circle and receive a hug from each other member along with her compliment; she may be placed in the center and enclosed in a group hug; or she may sit still while each other member in turn comes to give her a compliment along with a stroke or pat.

Simple verbal charms can express wishes for a return to health, just like a get-well card, except that the face-to-face speech is more direct and personal.

Here are some examples:

"I see you coming home, entering your house, walking strongly, feeling good. Your cheeks are rosy. Your eyes sparkle. I know your illness is gone."

"I see your bone cells growing, knitting together, building bridges and making them strong. I see your white blood cells eating up the infection. I see your body regenerating itself."

"Soon you will stand up straight. You will walk and run and dance."

"The Goddess will give you the natural gift of wholeness."

"We all project our thoughts toward the healing of your body. Be well."

"You surely don't deserve to be so troubled. We hope your trials will soon be nothing but a memory."

Many kinds of objects are useful in healing rituals—not because of any particular medicinal virtue in the object itself, but because of the associations and sentiments attached to it, because it is a memento of a pleasant time, a beloved person, or a meaningful place; or simply because it serves as an amulet like many other traditional objects: worry beads, rosaries, holy medals, birthstones, lucky pieces, talismanic gems, bishop's rings, medicine bags, magic pendants, and all the rest. Human hands have an affinity for small hard objects. Humanity's first playthings, tools, and weapons were stones. In China, "fingering pieces" of jade and other minerals have long been used to soothe the nerves. Natural quartz crystals and similar stones are greatly esteemed in western countries as tension-relievers. To hold a stone or jewel in the hand is comforting, and also helps to focus the attention.

Stones placed on the body can be useful too. Sometimes a headache can be relieved simply by lying down and placing a small stone on the forehead between the brows, in what oriental parlance calls the third-eye position. The stone's weight and coolness allow the mind to focus on that area, while relaxation and quiet breathing smooth out the tensions that produced the headache. Gazing into a transparent crystal is a similar focusing technique that can soothe physical distress. Should the object be a gift from a caring friend or loved one, it also serves as a reminder of that person's emotional support. The distinction between jewelry and amulets has always been blurry, because gifts of jewelry or gemstones nearly always carry an emotional charge and are intimately associated with relationship. The diamond engagement ring is a common example. In the same sense, a pretty stone presented to an invalid can be a comfort by association, especially if it has been blessed on the altar of a women's circle. No pseudoscientific nonsense about emanations, vibrations, imaginary electricity, nonexistent magnetism, or other baseless hypotheses are necessary to produce subtle but real effects through the medium of the mind.

The Zoo Game

Relationships between humans and animals have always had complex spiritual implications. Animals are loved, feared, despised, admired, ignored, worshiped, or depended upon for the life support of entire cultures. Some animals provide human food; others destroy it. Some animals assist in the hunt; others are hunted. Some animals bond with people in what can be the closest emotional ties known to either. Other animals kill people or are killed by them. Animals are constantly subjected to human judgments about their beauty, ugliness, and comparative value. They are called noble creatures, dumb brutes, or vermin. They are pets, mascots, surrogate mothers, dinner on the hoof, slaves, friends, pests, prey, symbols, or tribal totems viewed as ancestral deities. They are also, sometimes, our own unconscious conceptions of the alter ego.

The tradition of the witch's familiar—a spiritual alter ego in animal form—arose from the real love that can be established between women and their pets. Male jealousy of that love was no small contributing factor in the virulent witch persecutions of the Renaissance period, when women were frequently executed for no offense other than demonstrating affection for an animal.

It is easy for people to identify themselves with certain animals. We all have fixed notions of animal personalities and behavior patterns that can represent our own. An animal can stand for the self-image either as it is, as we wish it to be, or as we fear it might be. The Zoo Game ritual uses the archetypal power of animal symbolism to provide deeper understanding of the self.

This can be done on the spur of the moment, or it can be planned in advance. If the latter, participants may wish to bring to the meeting some articles that express their chosen animal. A woman intending to impersonate a dog might provide herself with a collar and leash. A "rabbit" might wear a cotton tail or bunny ears. A "lion" might fix her hair to resemble a mane. A "bird" might wear feathers. A "zebra" might paint her face or body with black and white stripes. Animal costumes can be anything from a simple suggestion to a full mask or makeup. Props may be used if desired. Make claws by pushing nails through the fingers of old gloves. Make horns by attaching paper cones to a cap. Make a tail with a sewn or knitted tube, stuffed with straw, cotton, or sawdust, stitched to the back of pants.

When all are seated in the circle, the talking stick may be sent around while each participant tells what animal she is impersonating, and why. It is not essential to give reasons, but most people like to explain briefly how they feel drawn to their particular animal. For example:

"I am a vulture. I have always wanted to glide effortlessly in the air like a large, broad-winged bird, but not an eagle or a hawk, because they live by killing. A vulture eats what's already dead, so it doesn't cause pain, and it cleans up the environment."

"I am an antelope. I've always wanted to run and leap like those creatures that look to me much more graceful than the best trained human athlete or dancer."

"I've always thought of myself as plain, so my animal is all beautiful appearance. I fantasize turning into a bird of paradise. I am all covered with jewels, rainbows, iridescent curls and crests of feathers. I am utterly ostentatious and utterly gorgeous."

"I think it would be very comfortable to be a hippopotamus. I can stay in the water all the time, and never worry about getting fat."

"I am a spider. All day I weave delicate silk. I make beautiful patterns. Males come to court me very cautiously, and never, never try to dominate me."

"In my childhood fantasies I thought of myself as a black leopard: graceful, strong, independent, all the things I wanted to be and wasn't. So I'm wearing black satin to look as slinky as a leopard."

"I am a mole, hiding away in the earth, a secret creature, full of deep knowledge about stones and roots and soil. I wear a lovely soft gray velvet coat."

"I want to be a thoroughbred racehorse who wins every one of her races."

"I had an Indian grandmother who belonged to the Turtle clan, so I make myself a turtle in her honor. I live quietly, well protected in my shell."

"I am one of those milk-white sacred cows that are worshiped in India as personifications of the Goddess. I wear a collar studded with diamonds, and silver rings on my horns. I give milk that is holy food."

When each participant has announced her animal, a brief meditation period provides time for inward identification with the animal soul and visualization of how it might feel to live in that kind of body and mind. This may be followed by free-form role-playing. Each woman impersonates her animal as concretely as possible, with movement, gesture, sound, and encounters with others. This can be a lot of fun, and very creative when the group gets into the spirit of it. It can also be very noisy.

When the animal impersonators have worked through their improvisations, the circle may form again, and the talking stick pass around, so that all may share their sensations and reactions. Participants may consider such questions as, How did I feel about myself as an animal? How did the concept change my feelings about others? If I could change into that animal for a while in reality, how might it alter my life as a person? Do I now have a different sense of the animal world?

The Zoo Game can conclude with animal stories. Nearly everyone has a story to tell about an animal, either real or fictitious. This is a time to remember, honor, and bless individual animals that we know or have known, to recognize our relationships and our basic kinship with them, and to be aware of all animals as our fellow voyagers on Spaceship Earth. Perhaps the group can call attention to local examples of animal mistreatment and take action against them.

The followng is an animal story of my own, a personal memoir of my dog Brenda. Because it is written, it is considerably longer than a spoken story should be in a circle, where courtesy forbids monopolizing too much of the group's time. I include this memoir here as an example of how one might talk about a pet.

I have lived with a number of animals, and loved each one. My true familiar, however, seems to have been my Groenendael Belgian sheepdog, Brenda. She received this name because it means "black," which she was. She resembled a sleek black wolf, with her erect pointed ears, long, strong jaw, long legs, shiny coat, and plumy tail. She was a beautiful animal, but much more than that, a remarkable personality.

Brenda has been dead for many years now. Her bones lie in the earth outside my bedroom wall, a few yards away from the spot where she used to sleep beside my bed. Time has not eased my sense of loss. I still miss her terribly. On occasion, I still see her ghost from the corner of my eye, behind a chair, or around a doorway.

Since she first came into our house as a lop-eared puppy, Brenda was special. Though I had raised and trained other dogs, I was surprised by her avid response to early obedience training. She was serious about wanting to learn. She concentrated. You could see her concentrating. She was joyous about being able to understand what was wanted of her. I learned from her, too. We became the most intimate of friends, communicating by the slightest nuances of tone, expression, or body contact.

When I sat reading or working at my desk, Brenda would lie against my leg or rest her chin on my foot. When I walked into another room, she would rise and follow me. When I took a bath, she would recline beside the tub. When I went out in the car and left her in the house alone, she would sit up at a window, watching the street for my return. When I invited her to go for a walk with me, she made a celebration.

In the woods, she told me about nearby animals. She had a different bark for large or small creatures. Her deer cry was unique: a high-pitched yip that she used only when she flushed a deer and at no other time. Yipping with excitement, she would chase the deer for a while, though she knew it would always outrun her.

One day we came to a field full of cows. Brenda, never having seen a cow before, jumped through the fence and immediately began to herd them, running spirals around them until they were bunched together. Having thus assembled them, she looked to me for instruction, her whole attitude saying, Okay, now where do you want them? I was laughing. I called her to me and she came, rather reluctantly leaving her sulky captives to disperse themselves again. She seemed to think it a pity that I had no use for her ancestral talent.

She had a sense of humor, though, and a casual but firm pride. No inferiority complex, no identity crises, no sexism problems for her! She ordered male dogs about with complete confidence in her own power, even when they were bigger than she. I have seen her halt and silence, with one commanding snarl, an enraged, charging male. She was very serious about her watchdog role. I'm sure she would have fought to the death to defend a member of her family.

She understood people. She liked our friends, but when she remained cool and standoffish toward a new acquaintance, we would later find that person somehow incompatible. She could immediately identify one who had a mean streak. We learned to avoid people whom she wouldn't touch. Her intuition was better than human.

She also understood human language to some degree. She showed a direct response to a working vocabulary of perhaps three or four hundred words. She listened carefully to conversations. When she heard a familiar word or phrase, her ears would flick upward. When addressed, she gave her full attention. She was as good a listener as most of the people I have known, and better than some. Often, she seemed to be trying to speak. She would gaze earnestly into one's eyes, making small noises in her throat. If she could have learned sign language, like Washoe the chimp, perhaps we could have had spoken dialogues. As it was, her body language was eloquent.

Brenda grew old and died of a liver disease in her fourteenth year. I was so devastated by her death that I didn't want to replace her with another dog and face another such trauma. The role of familiar fell to Brenda's other friend, Cotton, obviously her opposite in several ways. She was female; he was male. She was black; he was white. She was a dog; he was a cat. He had come into the household as a kitten, when she was already middle-aged. She became his surrogate mother, and I think Cotton, too, always remembered her.

Years after Brenda's death, I dreamed of her. It was the first true flying dream I ever had. I could soar and float above the tree-tops. In order to do this, I had to carry Brenda in my arms. It seemed that I couldn't fly without her. Brenda was a big animal. In real life, I couldn't have carried her very far without tiring. In my dream, however, she seemed to have no weight, only a pleasant furry warmth. It was good to have her back again, even for the ephemeral moments of a dream. When I awoke, I cried.

This is my memorial to the unnamed, almost unrecognized, but ubiquitous relationship of a familiar: a true interspecies love that seems especially characteristic of women. We learn through this precious rapport with our own pets to respect other creatures, to honor the uniqueness of every animal. Though witch-hunting men may have been jealous of it, perhaps the tradition of the familiar should be reestablished. Another Renaissance name for the familiar was *daemon,* which was taken to mean a demon from the Christian version of hell. But in the original Greek, *daemon* meant a part of one's own soul.

Solitary Rituals

Although most of the material in this book deals with group rituals, readers should not get the impression that ritual means only group work. Individuals can and do perform rituals devised either by others or by themselves, in solitude, to improve their state of mind, to calm fears, to feel centered and effective, to relax after a period of stress, or to reach into the unconscious for additional courage, creativity, perceptiveness, and power. Some people are comforted by making a ritual as much a part of the daily routine as brushing their teeth.

It has been said that deep contemplation of a crystal can be a rewarding solitary ritual. The process can be intensified with other ritualistic patterns. For instance: Before addressing the crystal, wash both it and your hands in cool water; put on a special robe with amuletic jewelry; light a stick of incense and/or a candle; sit in a formal posture, such as cross-legged on a cushion; breathe slowly and deeply until your body feels centered and relaxed. Perform all actions with smooth deliberation, as if they were part of a slow, quiet solo dance. Use the objective eye of the imagination to watch yourself doing each movement, and experience each moment calmly without haste or impatience.

These general hints apply to any self-made ritual. It is not so much what you do that refreshes you as it is the calm, open state of mind fostered by the doing. Don't engage in a solitary ritual when time presses, when you feel rushed, or when interruptions are likely. For these occasions, it is enough to take a few slow deep

breaths and envision a calming mental image. A ritual cut too
short is like a flower cut off before its petals are fully unfolded. It
can leave you feeling dissatisfied instead of soothed.

Many people like to begin a personal ritual with a leisurely
bath with special oils, herbs, or perfumes added to the bath water,
and candlelight in the room. Having bathed and dressed in a ritual robe, adorn your altar as you think fit, using quiet, slow, deliberate movements. Watch your own actions as if from a distance.
Sometimes it is helpful to perform ritual movements in front of a
mirror, so you can watch yourself literally. It is a valid metaphor
to hang a mirror over your altar as a reminder that the Goddess of
your altar is the inner self that you wish to contact through ritual
procedures.

Arrange your favorite crystals, pictures, amulets, tools, and
other artifacts on or around the altar as if they too serve as witnesses of your activities. If you have a pet, an animal familiar, let
the animal or something representing the animal be present also.
Create a sacred space by drawing a circle or pentacle around
yourself and your materials, or by laying out a long knotted cord
or an arrangement of tarot cards; or by walking around the space
with salt, perfume, smoke, or an athame; or by turning about to
address the four directions; or by beating a ceremonial drum as
you step out an encircling pattern.

Freely use fragrant herbs, incense, smudging smoke, or
anointing oils to sacralize the objects that you choose. Light scented candles. If you wish, play quietly unobtrusive background
music. Sit calmly before your altar and center yourself, breathing
slowly, meditating on the purpose of your ritual, envisioning
what you want to accomplish. You might provide yourself with a
ceremonial bowl or cup containing water, wine, broth, herb tea, or
any other favorite drink. Sip a little at the start of the ritual and
finish the remainder at the end, thinking that the vision is now
internalized by your body. The same may be done with fruit,
bread, or any other edible.

Speak your desire. Make a poem or a chant of it if you can.
Perform a symbolic imitation of what you wish. If you want to be
more effective in financial matters, arrange coins on the altar. If
you deal with love, place a heart-shaped object in the center, or a
symbol of the loved one. If you want to enhance creativity, concentrate on materials of the creative process: paints, ink, thread,

clay, and so on. If you seek learning, use an open book, especially one dealing with the desired subject. Make sure you *read* that book as well as ritualize it. Remember, the old magical notions about absorbing knowledge by eating the paper it is written on, or by sleeping with it under one's pillow, are quite useless. Real magic is not just symbolizing, but also doing. When you make ritual promises to yourself, you must keep them.

To consecrate an object to be given as a gift, pass it through the smoke of incense or candle, breathe on it, wash it, anoint it, and envision the happiness and well-being of the recipient. Be sure to tell the recipient that these things were done. Of such ingredients are made the intangible values of sentimental significance, which can invest even common objects with *mana*.

The main thing to remember about creating your own rituals is that you never need to follow anyone else's recipe. You need not ask yourself, Am I doing this right? There is no right. For you, right is whatever feels appropriate. You may imitate rituals that you have seen or read about; you may adapt and change these; or you may invent your own from scratch. There is no standard set by an organized ecclesiastical establshment. You do not have to conform to anything. Be creative. Feel free.

When you feel ready, do a closing ceremony of your choice. Bow to your Goddess image. Speak a farewell phrase or two. Unmake your circle by tracing it in the opposite direction, or thank and dismiss the "spirits" you have "summoned." Carefully and gently lay away each altar furnishing in its proper place. Make a deliberate ceremony of extinguishing your candles, pouring out waters, folding up cloths, closing cabinets, and any other process of clearing away ritual materials. Keep all movements slow and thoughtful. Meditate on the meaning of the ritual and the effects you would like to experience, and what you intend to do now to bring them about.

As a rule, people find ritual procedure refreshing and empowering for the very reason that it represents assumption of personal responsibility. At its best, a solitary ritual is a prayer to the divinity within, a way of getting in touch with yourself. You don't need anyone else to dictate its forms and sequences to you. A solitary ritual is entirely your own. It is not to be intruded upon. It sets aside a space and a time in which you enjoy and honor your own existence.

As you wish, so let it be.

Laws of the Goddess

Because our civilization has been patriarchal for millennia, it has forgotten or destroyed most of the law codes laid down by our remote ancestresses in the name(s) of the Goddess. She was said to have delivered these codes on mountaintops, to some of her royal consorts, such as Minos or Kingu, thus prefiguring the Moses myth by many centuries. Certain provisions of Goddess law were later copied into patriarchal codes. Others were dropped because they did not suit the more warlike and acquisitive father-worshipers. Most of the Mother-codes were lost.

Out of the few hints of prepatriarchal law still extant, we can perceive that matrifocal societies long ago established some fairly sensible, humane guidelines for human behavior. Roman jurists even in the classical period described the prepatriarchal code as the *ius naturale,* the "natural law" reflecting mother-right as naturally as a mother instructs and guides her children. Legal codes of ancient Asia were based on the karmic law embodied in Goddess figures like Kali Ma. Karmic law postulated in effect that every action produces an equal and opposite reaction, because the Mother's universe demanded balance in all things.

Therefore evildoing to others would bring down evil upon one's self. Conversely, beneficence toward others would bring good to one's self. The principle of karmic law passed into Buddhism with the precept, "As ye sow, so shall ye reap." Five hundred years later, it was adapted by Hillel who said, "Do not unto others as you would not have others do unto you." Eventually this precept was Christianized as the Golden Rule; but it was still just another version of Kali's law of karma.

One fairly extensive version of matriarchal law remains in the form of the Negative Confession—or Protestation of Innocence— required by the Egyptian Goddess Maat, whose name meant both "truth" and "mother," and whose all-seeing eye perceived all actions. It is clear that the biblical Ten Commandments were based on a code very like this archaic law of Maat, and quite possibly derived from Egypt, though the biblical scribes made some notable revisions. A similar Buddhist Ten Commandments also seem to have been taken from older Goddess-given rules of behavior.

Few modern women know about the Negative Confession. On hearing of it, however, many recognize a moral code that harmonizes with the feminine spirit. Even now, after a lapse of nearly four thousand years, we can perceive in such laws the rudimentary beginning of a more just and less violent world than men have created over the centuries of their dominance.

Here is an abbreviated paraphrase of portions of the law of Maat. Like the original it is phrased not in a god's dictatorial "Thou shalt not," but rather in the speaker's own assumption of responsibility, saying "I have not."

> I have not told lies.
> I have not committed fraud.
> I have not caused anyone to weep.
> I have not done violence to anyone.
> I have not fouled water.
> I have not driven cattle from their pastures.
> I have not stolen the property of others.
> I have not cheated in weighing the grain.
> I have not forced anyone to do excessive daily work for me.
> I have not enriched myself at others' expense.
> I have not taken milk from infants.
> I have not harmed animals.
> I have not robbed the dead.
> I have not defiled the sanctuaries.
> I have not caused murder to be done.
> I have not caused suffering.
> I have not offended against the holy laws of Maat.

In order to be worthy of a good afterlife, each Egyptian had to stand before the Goddess in the underworld and recite such declarations truthfully. In today's world, we might also add, " I have not polluted the environment," "I have not littered the landscape," "I have not helped to create weapons," "I have not destroyed forests," "I have not hunted wild animals for amusement," "I have not corrupted children," "I have not sold addictive or toxic substances to anyone," "I have not been guilty of discrimination against members of any other ethnic group," and so on, addressing some of the modern problems in detail.

On the whole, though, the laws of the Goddess made a good beginning. One of the long-term functions of women's spirituality might well be the establishment of just such humane laws, a new moral code for a world desperately in need of it, a world made safer for women and children everywhere which of course means safer for the human race in general. The morality of their civilization is a subject that all women need to consider carefully. It is too important to be left in the hands of men.

Eating the Serpent

Because the Serpent was sacred to women, was originally female (such as Uraeus, Kundalini, Ananta), and represented women's knowledge of their own holy mysteries, the Serpent was extensively diabolized in patriarchal culture. Judeo-Christian tradition insisted that Woman and Serpent collaborated in bringing forbidden knowledge to the first man, although the exact content of that knowledge remains an unexplained mystery even to the present day.

Eating the Serpent is a ritual symbolizing the internalization of ancient female knowledge that is explained and made conscious, rather than left dark as in the Judeo-Christian fable of eating the apple (or whatever fruit it might have been called). The Serpent is living wisdom, as opposed to the patriarchal tradition's passive fruit of knowledge. Performed with serious mental focus, and accompanied by a suitable meditation, Eating the Serpent

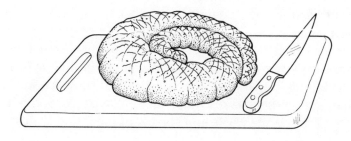

implies a kind of knowing that may bring to any woman a permanent realignment of attitudes for her own empowerment.

To prepare a serpent, make a dough and roll it into a long, thin cylinder. Coil it into a spiral for baking. Use bread, cookie, fruitcake, or stollen dough that is firm and dense rather than fluffy. Green or red vegetable coloring may be added. Imaginative bakers can create snakeskin patterns by scoring or frosting, so that the spiral looks as much like a coiled serpent as possible.

When the circle of women is convened, solemnly slice the baked serpent into bite-size pieces and pass it around. When all have eaten, recite the following meditation:

Woman, remember. You have the memory living deep in your mind, in your blood, in your lifegiving darkness. Reach down to it and bring it forth. Re-member.

Remember the time before men began to count time. Remember when woman was the world, and the world was woman. Remember when every mother established her clan, guided her children, set the standards of behavior for her lovers, and owned the home place to be passed down to her daughters. Remember when the Mother's laws forbade every man to do violence to others, most especially to woman or children. Remember when rape was unknown because every sexual encounter between woman and man was by woman's choice. Remember when men dared not claim the right to control any aspect of women's economic, political, sexual, or reproductive activities, but honored all women for bringing forth and nurturing the human race. Remember when every woman unequivocally owned her own body and her body's offspring.

Remember that man stood in awe of women's wise blood, which brought forth all peoples. Remember that woman alone had the right to approach the Goddess on man's behalf, and the right to decree wise laws for the benefit of future generations. Remember that woman alone knew the mysteries of life and death, of healing and cursing. Remember the shrines established by the primal ancestresses. Remember the great temples where priestesses dwelt in peace, helping their people. Remember that the world was at peace because men were forbidden to kill. They were forbidden by women, who understood how precious is the life that each mother takes the trouble to nurture in this world, and how sinful is the waste and sorrow of prematurely destroying life.

Remember what the sacred serpents taught, they who lived in the womb of Goddess Earth and knew her secrets. Remember that those secrets are your secrets, have always been your secrets, will always be your secrets. Take your power from the teachings of the Serpent. Realize that the claims of men's gods are mostly empty, and that the real foundation of human life is Woman. Remember your Goddess.

Woman, remember.

Finish the meditation with the Serpent's voice as women used to imitate it in the ancient rituals: Sssssssssssssssssssss.

Rites of Passage

Today we are accustomed to male jurisdiction over such life-stage rites of passage as baptisms, weddings, and funerals. Several thousand years ago, our ancestors might have considered such male dominance a blasphemy. Life-stage events belonged to the Goddess and her priestesses. Because the natural life-time sequences ultimately centered on the female body, women were the first to establish rites of passage. Women, not men, showed the overt physical signs of transition through birth, menarche (first menstruation), defloration, maternity, menopause, and death.

Many thousands of years before human beings even recognized any male role in propagation, creation was attributed solely to the divine Mother who gave birth to the universe and everything in it, including its gods. All things began with birth, a Goddess-magic possessed by females only. Birth spirit dwelt in women, particularly in the Mother's priestesses, who were usually required to be mothers themselves.

Their holy office originated in remote antiquity as a natural function of tribal matriarchs, the wise-women who established standards of behavior for the offspring they personally birthed and nurtured. As matrilineal families expanded into clans, spiritual authority passed from mothers to daughters through the uterine blood bond, envisioned as the red thread of ongoing life. Grateful for the gift of life that women gave, men deferred to the judgments of women because the women seemed closer to the holy mysteries of the Goddess.

Birth is still informally ritualized by the baby-viewing visits of relatives and friends, and is commemorated in the secular world by birthday parties. Significantly, however, patriarchal religious institutions take no notice of birth *per se*, except for the annual celebration of the birth of the Christian version of the savior god; and even there, the role of the birthgiving mother is downplayed as much as possible. Forgotten is the old tradition that named Christmas Eve "the Night of the Mother." The baby produced on that night is no genuinely infantile baby but a god, unrealistically precocious, while the mother is a mere mortal, overwhelmed by the honor of producing him. No girl baby of any description appears in modern religious imagery.

A basic reason for the disappearance of birth rituals was their obvious expression of maternal creativity, which men envied and often imitated, but could not reproduce in reality. Birth belonged too inescapably to the women.

Even under the patriarchal gods of the Roman empire, delivering a baby was considered a divine ritual of the Goddess, in which men were irrelevant and unwanted. The ancient birth priestesses (*obstetrices*) would have been profoundly shocked by some of today's obstetrical practices, such as unnaturally immobilizing a laboring mother on her back, to raise her pelvis to a convenient eye-level for a male doctor; or artificially inducing or retarding her labor to make birth occur when the male doctor is ready for it; or using drugs to prevent her active participation in the event; or slicing open her perineum, causing scars that may later interfere with sexual function; or generally treating her and her newborn with inconsiderate roughness, later adding insult to injury with excessive fees. Acquisitive male physicians' forcible takeover of women's time-honored midwifery in America at the beginning of the twentieth century is one of the more shameful chapters in the history of medicine.

Ancient priestesses of Juno watched over every aspect of pregnancy, birth, and lactation, while the Goddess still appeared in many of her guises as the intimate patron of motherhood. Juno Populonia ruled the continuation of the human race as a whole.

Juno Sospita protected pregnant women. Juno Lucina brought forth each newborn into the light. Juno Ossipago strengthened the baby's bones. Juno Rumina provided adequate supplies of mother's milk. Each function had its priestesses, who not only performed the rituals but also provided intimate hands-on care for mothers and their babies, when the sensitive and essential work of ensuring humanity's future was still considered holy.

Birth *per se* was declared unholy early in the Christian era, when church fathers decided that every child was born demonic as a result of sexual conception and passage through the "polluted" female body. St. Augustine laid down the doctrine of original sin perpetuated through "concupiscence" (copulation), which required exorcism of every baby—still preserved in the baptism ritual—and a symbolic rebirth under male hands before the patriarchal God would accept the infant. The mother herself was also made unclean by birthgiving, and became an outcast from the church's congregation until she could be ritually purified, also under male hands. Her "churching" was not allowed until forty days after her delivery, because priests were still afraid of the contagion of her uncleanness, as described by the Bible (Lev. 12:2–6). During this time of *quarantine* (meaning "forty days"), both mother and child were forbidden to enter the house of God, and were said to belong to the devil (or, the Goddess). Old Testament rules went so far as to declare the mother of a daughter twice as unclean as the mother of a son, so she would have to stay out of the temple twice as long (Leviticus 12:2–5).

It was long believed that a Christian woman before her fortieth-day churching, or a baby before baptism, would go directly to hell in case of death. Theologians asserted that witches used unbaptized infants in their rituals because such infants were demonic creatures already. Nevertheless, folktales left over from pre-Christian matriarchy claimed instead that such spirits would go to the pre-Christian underworld realm of the Goddess under several of her pagan names, such as Hel, Holda, Perchta, Frigga, Hecate, or Persephone.

The church's official literature equated midwives with witches, and declared that no people ever did more harm to the Catholic faith than midwives. The word *midwife* used to mean "wise-woman," which was also synonymous with "witch." Pagan birth priestesses were the original "broomstick witches" who swept the house of a new mother with a special broom, to keep evil spirits away from mother and child. The fact that women retained control of the actual birthgiving process—because men feared and avoided it—led to the disappearance of birth rituals from Western religion and the increased ritual importance of male name-giving in the form of baptism.

Once upon a time, name-giving was the mother's right, usually done when her baby was put to the breast for suckling. Baptism with a name originated as a primitive ritual anointing of a new baby with its mother's milk, as she pronounced its soul-name to proclaim it a legitimate member of the tribe, entitled to a share of the common food supply. If the mother wouldn't or couldn't signify her acceptance of the child in this way, the newcomer might be regarded as a nonperson and allowed to die. Infants bereft of their mothers usually died anyway, as is still the case among wild animals. This is the meaning behind the old Hindu story of the newborn "thousand-eyed god" Existence, who pleaded for a name, because he couldn't eat food and survive unless a name was given him. Ancient Egyptian scriptures similarly insisted that every god needed a mother to give him his name.

A remnant of matriarchal custom is still found even in the Bible. Naomi signifies her acceptance of Ruth's child by a ritual of pretended nursing, while the child receives his woman-given name, Obed (Ruth 4:16–17). Biblical name-givers were mothers; but later male imitation of the old ritual produced the Bible's bizarre image of a "nursing father" carrying the sucking child in his bosom (Numbers 11:10). Under Christianity, male priests preempted the pagan maternal ceremony of anointing and name-giving, though some folk traditions preserved the mother-given "milk name" (the French *nom de lait*). Matrilineal tribal surnames were converted into the patronymics that we take for granted today.

An equally tangled history distinguishes the rituals of menarche, which also involves a body fluid that only women produce. Because males have no experience of it, the original menarche observances disappeared from patriarchal societies. As the first appearance of that dread "blood of life"—the wise blood that knew how to create offspring—menarche was loaded with taboos arising from male fears. Stone Age men seem to have been terrified by the blood that women shed so mysteriously without pain.

And yet men tried to devise their own imitations of this fearful female life magic. Primitive puberty rites for boys featured genital bloodshed, through circumcision, subincision, or other mutilations, at the same age when girls normally begin to menstruate. Clearly boys were meant to identify with girls at this time. Australian aborigines called their subincisions "man's menstruation" and referred to the wound as a vagina. In Egypt and the East, boys were dressed as girls for their circumcision ceremonies at the onset of puberty. Such customs originated in male efforts to claim female-type *mana* (spiritual power). Some early priesthoods even practiced full castration and then assumed female dress and identity, in order to become spiritually empowered. Even today, priests wear skirts.

Because the shedding of male blood at puberty had to be artificially caused, by deliberate mutilation, patriarchal societies often seized the opportunity to subject young boys to real torture. Painful and humiliating experiences could become prerequisites for acceptance in men's groups. Such customs hint at the Oedipal hostility of older males toward younger ones, the resentment of declining virility toward rivals who will soon be better endowed. Male-group initiations retain traces of this hostility nearly everywhere in the world.

Medieval Moslems apparently took sadistic delight in torturing young boys, and also carried such abuses from males back again to females—perhaps on the premise that if boys had to suffer to become adults, then the "inferior" sex should suffer even more. So they instituted the still-prevalent customs of clitoridectomy and infibulation, which permanently destroy women's sexual enjoyment and cause agony not only at puberty, but throughout life. With her genital structures cut away and sewn up (without anesthesia), an Islamic woman suffers new mutilations at defloration and childbirth. The men are taught that normal, unmutilated women are evil and dangerous. This foul system still torments many women, as much as the Chinese system of female footbinding that was abandoned almost a century ago.

The pseudomenarchial rite of circumcision was copied from the Egyptians by the biblical Jews, then legitimized via commandments attributed to Yahweh. The Jewish communities eventually transferred circumcision to the period of infancy, to redeem the male child from the firstborn-sacrifice that Yahweh originally demanded. An expendable portion of flesh was offered, instead of the whole child. Thus circumcision ceased to be an imitation of menarche. It was reinterpreted as a sign of Yahweh's covenant with male tribesmen.

Oddly enough, however, the pubescent ritual was retained in Judaism even when its central physical manifestation shifted to the period of infancy. It became the bar mitzvah, which is celebrated at a boy's thirteenth year, the old lunar number formerly sacred to menstrual mysteries, because of the thirteen annual lunations and menstrual periods. Moreover the real menarchial passage-event of girls continued to be ignored, though their menstrual blood was feared as a deadly poison.

When girls were obliged to retain premarital virginity to ensure the new patrilineal succession, defloration necessarily became identified with marriage. The biblical God commanded that brides found not to be virgins must be stoned to death by the men of their village (Deut. 22:21). Yet the rite of "opening the matrix" remained another occasion of male dread. In many societies, it was ceremonially performed by someone who could escape the possible blood curse: a priest, a god, or a stranger.

In Babylonia, it was customary for girls to be deflowered in the temple, prior to marriage, by strangers who offered them a coin. The idea was to protect the future bridegroom from contact with genital blood. The custom arose during the transition from group marriage or general promiscuity—which characterized the old matriarchal societies "when people knew their mothers but not their fathers," as the scriptures said—to a patrilineal system.

In India and the Roman Empire, as well as certain Middle Eastern cultures, it was usual for brides to deflower themselves on the artificial penises of gods' statues, or on temple phalli like the Hindu *linga*. Thus any firstborn son could be called a son of God, conceived by a virgin mother. Early Christians objected to the practice, but explained that pagan Roman women considered it pious and essential to consecrate every bride-to-be, insisting that no wedding could be performed without it. Some of the priapic statues apparently survived Christian iconoclasm and continued to be used ritualistically. The Middle Ages were full of stories about women initiated into pagan cults by sexual intercourse with a "devil" whose penis was hard and cold, like that of a statue.

Recent Christian missionaries were shocked to discover pre-civilized societies where girls' defloration was carried out slowly

and gently, by mothers stretching their daughters' genital openings with their fingers. Missionaries described this as a heathen
corruption, as opposed to their own (apparently more acceptable)
tradition that virgin brides should expect to be raped on the wedding night, and should display bloodstained sheets on the following day as a proof of maidenly virtue.

The early Christian church had found marriage rituals generally unacceptable, because of their inherent paganism. Roman
priestesses of Juno controlled every step of the wedding ceremony even into the Christian era. Juno Pronuba was invoked at premarital negotiations. Juno Domiduca conducted the bride to her
domicile. Juno Nuxia perfumed the doorposts to welcome her.
Juno Cinxia untied the bride's nuptial belt. Marriages were so
firmly governed by the priestesses that church fathers condemned
marriage altogether as an unspiritual and sinful state, devised by
the Goddess whom they called "that foul devil Venus." Origen
said marriage was impure and unholy. St. Ambrose labeled it a
crime against God. Tertullian said marriage was an obscenity and
a moral crime. Tatian described it as corruption. Therefore no
place was made for marriage under Christian canon law.

The church had no official marriage ceremony until the six-
teenth century. It was only in the twelfth century that priests were
allowed to bless newly married couples outside the church door,
thus keeping the "pollution of lust" out of the sacred building.
The blessing was not moved inside the church until some centuries later. Through most of Christian history, the marriage service was not a Christian sacrament but a secular procedure, under
the jurisdiction of common law. This explains why the traditional
trappings of wedding ceremonies are still those of ancient pagan
fertility magic, having nothing to do with Christian mythology.

Rice-throwing was an obvious fertility charm; so was the
bride's "something borrowed." It used to be stipulated that the
borrowed object's owner must be the mother of several healthy
children. The rest of the traditional wedding rhyme called for
something blue, something old, and something new. Blue was the
sacred color of the pagan Queen of Heaven (Juno, Venus Salacia,
Aphrodite Urania, Astarte, Astraea, Isis, and so on). Old and new
symbolized past and future generations channeling through the
bride. Similar significances once attached to the matron of honor
and the flower girl: the elder woman and the child representing

Crone and Virgin aspects of the Goddess, as well as life phases of every woman.

Still another wedding symbol of life flowing through the generations was the red carpet. As the blood river, the original meaning was preserved in fairy tales where it signified a journey to the paradise of the Goddess, in her medieval incarnation as Fairy Queen. Only the bride's party arrives by way of the red carpet, because only the bride used to embody the living blood that could flow through time into her future children. She carried flowers, preferably five-petaled like apple blossoms and the pentacle inside the apple. These stood for her future offspring as forerunners of the fruit of the womb, her own lifegiving blood, which the Bible still calls "flowers" (Leviticus 15:24).

Other wedding traditions still hint at former matriarchal systems. The word *bride* is akin to a Celtic name of the Virgin Goddess, Brigit, who was falsely Christianized as Saint Bride or Saint Bridget. *Bridegroom* means literally the bride's servant or vassal, just as *husband* used to mean a man "bonded" to serve the house *(hus)*, which belonged to his wife. The original owners of lands and houses were women. Husbandship meant stewardship of the property and its produce. For the same reasons, *lady* derives from *hlaf-dig,* she who owns and distributes the bread; and *lord* from *hlaf-ward,* he who guards it for her.

A similar reminder of former female property ownership is the Jewish wedding canopy called *huppah,* "tent," from the primitive tribal rule that women were the owners of their tents. The ancient marriage service gave a man permission to enter his wife's tent. Among pre-Islamic Arabs, female tent owners could divorce their husbands simply by turning the tent around to face a different direction, which meant that the man could no longer enter.

Weddings also retained the festive custom of dancing, which used to accompany all religious services before Christian authorities forbade it as too body-centered and sensual. Because churchmen took little notice of marriage rituals for such a long time, the ban on dancing was not applied to them. Another pagan remnant is the wedding cake, from ancient Rome's patrician marriage rite where newlyweds shared a cake of flour and salt, standing for flesh and blood, which made them kin. In some marriage traditions, they would prick their fingers and literally share each other's blood; or the two mothers of the couple would mingle a few drops of their own blood, thus making the couple magically or symbolically children of one womb.

Menopause rituals have altogether disappeared from our intensely patriarchal society. Yet in antiquity there were rites of passage from the Mother to the Crone stage of woman's life, especially for the elder priestesses and clan mothers who became the magistrates, healers, and oracles of their groups. In contrast to our present attitudes, the ancients did not consider a woman's life wholly defined by her reproductive capacity. They believed that when her "wise blood" no longer came forth with the moon's cycles, it accumulated in her body and gave her ever greater wisdom. Even as late as the seventeenth century A.D., Christian writers were still claiming that elder witches' secret knowledge came from the "wise blood" retained in their veins.

Death was the only passage that patriarchal religion took over completely, because death is common to all, and because patriarchy was concerned with teaching different ideas about death from the ideas formerly held by worshipers of the Great Mother and the old gods. Churchmen claimed control over the rewards and punishments to come after death, selling promises of the former, and backing up their authority with threats of the latter. It was the perfect profitmaking scheme, because the failure of its claims could never be demonstrated. Moreover, the fear engendered by its sadistic visions of hell drove the guilty and the hopeful alike to pour their money into its coffers.

During previous ages, the usual teachings about death spoke not of a permanent heaven or hell, but of some form of rebirth. The feminine principle (Goddess) was closely associated with this, as with any birth. There were death priestesses in many cultures: Egyptian *muu,* Indian *dakinis,* Slavic *valas,* Swedish *volvas,* Saxon *walcyries,* Celtic *morrigan,* Russian *rusalki,* and so on. Their functions included instruction in proper mental and physical rehearsals for death, and hands-on comforting of the dying.

Sometimes it was said that death in the arms of such a woman could be not only painless but even ecstatic, a kind of spiritual orgasm whereby the soul came forth from the body to beget itself again in another body. This view of the soul's continuation through female mediation applied even to gods—which explains the ubiquitous identity of Father and Son figures throughout most mythological and religious imagery. They were united by the Goddess who was simultaneously both virgin bride and mother, as well as the god's death-attendant in her Crone form. Christianity retained the same imagery, but deliberately suppressed any clear statement of the pivotal female role in uniting the two male spirits.

Even under Christianity, however, women remained the traditional attendants of the dying, although their former ceremonial authority was taken from them. Practical, hands-dirtying action such as nursing, feeding, washing, dressing, disposing of wastes, and sitting for long hours by the sickbed was left to women, while male priests administered only brief impersonal rituals of extreme unction. Priests did not hold the dying in their arms, but women did. There were even hints of continued belief in the "soul kiss," which used to mean that a sacred woman would take a man's soul along with his very last breath into her mouth, and later give birth to the same soul in a new body. As the death priestesses were transformed into witches, this kindly kiss was similarly transformed into the kiss of death.

Eventually women will have to reclaim their rites of passage from the male establishments that usurped or obliterated them. It is necessary for women to ritualize their life stages, so as to endow each one with its proper value and significance. Most particularly in need of attention are the menarche and menopause passages, both of which have been downgraded to occasions for embarrassment, shame, or despair, as if they were crimes. These important turning points of the female experience need to be rescued from shameful obscurity and restored to conscious collective acknowledgment.

Menarche rituals are still found in primitive societies. Often, however, they are overshadowed by patriarchal notions of terror and taboo. Young girls may be temporarily exiled from their tribe, and made to see themselves as spiritually dangerous to others.

This was not the case among matriarchal peoples, such as the Nagas of India, where girls at first menstruation were said to have borne the red *kula* flower, precursor of the holy fruit of future life: the red flower being a symbolic expression of the blood bond that united all generations. Thus a girl's first menstrual blood was seen as her mystic connection with the life of her clan, empowering her to continue that collective life. Surely such a positive attitude must have allowed the menarchial girl to develop a more wholesome, confident feeling about her body and her general worth than did the Western view of menstruation as an inevitable offense, a sickness, or "the curse."

A modern mother might hold a menarche party to celebrate her daughter's physical coming of age, provided the girl is sufficiently enlightened to enjoy such a party without embarrassment. No males are invited to a menarche party. It is—it has always been—a strictly female affair. The girl may be honored with gifts, as at a birthday party. The dominant color of decorations, foods, and costumes should be red: the feminine color of life, according to oriental tradition. Red roses are especially appropriate.

In turn, a grown daughter might hold a menopause party to celebrate her mother's arrival at the age of wisdom. Becoming a Crone is not as much honored in our society as in those of the past. Certainly it is not as much honored as it should be. Yet a ritualization of the event can help a woman achieve a positive perception of her own aging. Guests might play ritual games, like round-robin speeches about the advantages of the post-motherhood period. Older women in the group might tell amusing stories of menopausal experiences. Gifts can be oriented toward new interests, studies, or hobbies. An atmosphere of expectation and broadened outlook can help an older woman see herself as ripening into a fuller maturity, rather than declining into a lesser significance in her world.

Rites of marriage and death also need to be reclaimed by women, in recognition of their primordial origins among women. Today it is legally possible for a couple to marry each other, without conventional officiation of clergy, simply by exchanging their vows to one another in the presence of witnesses and signing the proper documents. Couples can write their own scripts, recite their own chosen poems of love, and plan their own marriage ceremonies as they see fit. A priestess or a mother can officiate. Recent years have seen the development of some extremely beautiful and memorable secular or pagan wedding customs, which need no recourse to conventional format. After all, a personalized ritual geared to the tastes of the individual couple is far more meaningful to them than a torpid ritual that has been used for millions of other, anonymous people.

Funerals have long been appropriated by a remarkably predatory semi-ecclesiastical industry that preys, financially, on the bereaved and grieving in a reprehensible way. No matter how

poor the widow or the orphaned child, this burial business bland-
ly takes a significant chunk of her slender resources, under pretense of honoring the dead. Laws have been made to support the
system. It is not legal any more to bury a relative privately on
one's own property. It is not "proper" to ignore the formal obse-
quies of patriarchal religion. Even people who don't believe the
implied threat of eternal torture in hell, or the unverifiable
promise of eternal bliss in heaven, may feel constrained to salute
death in the traditional ways.

Moreover, the right to die has been taken out of the individual's own hands, thanks to an ancient law of the Inquisition which
made suicide both a spiritual sin and a secular crime. The original
rationale was to prevent heretics from escaping torture by killing
themselves before they could be arrested; and if they succeeded in
doing so, to confiscate their property and take it from their heirs
for the benefit of the church. Such rules made the church ever
richer and lay people ever poorer.

Today the wishes of people who sincerely want to die are seldom respected, because the system has no place for them. Many
are forced to suffer horribly in terminal illnesses because traditional morality will not grant them control over their own life-
spans. Next to infants, the dying are the most helpless members
of society, which takes advantage of them because they don't have
the same kind of fiercely dedicated protector that an infant usually has, in the person of its mother.

It was not always so. Pagan religions generally accepted
death, like birth, as an integral part of the life cycle; and generally
honored an individual's right to claim the release of death at will.
In such cases the ritual for the deceased often took place before
death, not after. Relatives and friends gathered to celebrate the
dying one, so he or she might carry away a good opinion of them
into the afterworld, mention them favorably to the deities, and
not return to trouble them as an angry ghost.

Indeed it was the superstitious fear of ghosts that gave rise to
many funeral customs still practiced even today. Tombstones
evolved from the cairns or heavy boulders piled over a grave to
weigh down the departed and keep him from "walking." Mourn-
ing veils and black clothing evolved from the disguises worn to
confuse the ghost and hide from its notice. Funerary speeches
were made to flatter and mollify the listening spirit, to appease its

anger. Funeral flowers, incense, and embalming spices were originally intended to cover the smell of the body's decay, lest it offend
the soul. Our elaborate, expensive embalming practices are as
"superstitious" as the similarly elaborate practices of mummifica-
tion in ancient Egypt. Both were based on the religious notion that
the soul would have need of its body in the afterlife of "resurrection of the flesh."

At present, the only legal way to avoid the assorted human
vultures who prey on the dead (and their survivors) is to donate
the corpse to medical science. This is useful, and much needed,
and serves a far better purpose than placing the remains underground to rot away inside an overpriced, hermetically sealed box.
Since this useful means of disposal involves no conventional rite
of passage, the way is open for relatives and friends of the
deceased to create a memorial ritual of their own.

Such a personal, individualized ritual, devised and conducted by genuine loved ones, is surely more meaningful than formal
phrases mechanically uttered by a clergyperson who may not
have known the departed one at all: especially formal phrases
about a "sure and certain" anticipation of resurrection in which
neither the deceased nor the survivors have any true belief. As the
final passage of life, death deserves its dignity. Hypocrisy is not
dignified.

Let mourners, then, create the kind of memorial ceremony
that they find truly appropriate. The ancient circle formation and
the talking stick are well suited to such occasions. Each participant in turn can speak of the dead in the hearing of all. Anec-
dotes, reminiscences, personal reminders of the good qualities of
the deceased can be set forth. Instead of impersonal flowers, small
personal mementoes can be brought to the service and placed in a
consecrated center for all to see and appreciate. Decorations may
consist of the dead person's own handiwork: painting, pottery,
photographs, needlework, carvings, books, favorite possessions,
parts of a collection—anything that expresses that individual's
life. Readings might include the individual's own written words.
Background music should reflect his or her own tastes and prefer-
ences.

The presence of a corpse is unnecessary because, after all, the
corpse is not the person being mourned. That person is gone. A
genuinely honest funeral should celebrate the uniqueness of the

individual who was and is no more, not the needless generalized reminder that death is the common fate of all.

Priding itself on its technological expertise, surely our civilization should manage to provide a dignified and painless death for those in need of it. Priding itself on moral enlightenment, surely our civilization should provide meaningful rites of passage for those who stand at any of life's greater gateways. When rituals have become mere form, devoid of content, even the physical truths of birth, sexuality, and death are devalued. A whole new philosophy of ritual is needed, to bring about a whole new sense of the significance of living and dying as a human being.

Feminists have been saying for a long time that the really vital new philosophies are still hidden in the souls of women, whose collective power is probably the only power capable of saving our planet from manmade destruction. Women's rituals are needed in order to bring forth and focus that feminine power.

Many women today feel that the old rituals, invented by men to serve their own purposes, are not satisfying the spiritual needs of women. Some turn away from traditional religion to seek their spiritual comfort in fringe groups and cults, only to find these also dominated by men. Thus cultism is not the answer. In the long run, the real answers will have to be created by women themselves.

Sonia Johnson wrote of her favorite feminist fantasy:

I imagine that the next Sunday or Holy Day, in every church, synagogue, and mosque, every religious gathering place in the world, the men in charge, the ministers, priests, rabbis, imams, look out upon their congregations and see (oh unspeakable wonder!) . . . *no women!* No women at all! Neither that holy day nor the holy day following nor the holy day after that. No women, ever again.

And I imagine that during the next election year, no women organize, raise money, stump, stamp, campaign, or come to the polls, no women attend political meetings, put out newsletters, organize demonstrations.

I see the men crying in terror: Where are the slaves? Their whole ugly edifice in danger of collapse. *Because they can't do patriarchy without us!* [Author's italics]*

---

*Sonia Johnson, "Going Out Of Our Minds," in *Woman of Power* no. 8:10.

Indeed they can't do patriarchy without us. That is why women don't have to ask, they can *tell* religious authorities to give equal time to the Goddess, to end the male exclusivity of religious ritual and terminology, to divide theological decision making equally between women and men. Together women can demand a truly female-oriented religion that honors the lifegiving principle in nature and in humanity, and preaches a true morality of worldwide sisterhood under the Mother. Women can back up their demand by seizing their collective power, and threatening collective boycott. The patriarchal system would crumble before that threat.

Women are the fundamental support of Western civilization's religious system as well as the base of its economy. Women's unpaid labor keeps all the churches going. The paternal authority of God is actually a fragile illusion maintained by the acquiescence of millions of female volunteers. If all those volunteers deserted him at once, God himself would vanish.

After two thousand years of suppression, women have the right to demand the restoration of their stolen Goddess. Instead of hearing themselves called *man* and their deity called *he* in their houses of worship, women can speak up and insist on hearing the word *she* in reference to divinity. Instead of making do with the pitifully few and badly misrepresented female figures in the Judeo-Christian Bible, women can demand restoration of the Goddess's older scriptures and myths. Instead of working for the glory of God, women can work to raise consciousness of the greater glory of the Goddess who once mothered and commanded every god (including Yahweh). Instead of living in fear of offending a God who cursed their whole sex, women can judge him and find him insufficiently just. Instead of glorifying Christian soldiers and God's armies, women can demand the peace of universal sisterhood and call a halt to the hideous waste of militarism and war. In short, women could establish a true moral system based on behavior instead of a pretended morality largely based on orotund but empty words.

This would be the greatest of all rites of passage: the reversal of that historical passage from the Mother image to the Father image, from matriarchal peace to patriarchal warfare and persecution, that took place several millennia ago and changed the course of civilization. Women could establish their own religion in honor of the earth, nature, motherhood, and the peaceful perpetuation of biological life through future generations—all those blessings that women respect and that male authorities have tried to disparage or control. Let these matters be seriously considered. Let the women demand what they want and need; and then, if their needs are not met, make a collective rite of passing out of the church door, never to return.

The world does not need women abasing themselves before a male deity (and his human counterparts). The world needs men who can learn to live with the maternal principles that really support human society. Established religions do nothing for women that women couldn't do better for themselves. Religious counseling, teaching, charity, medical missions, fund-raising, social events, and other volunteer services are usually performed by women even now. It is necessary only to restore the original feminine meanings and moral imperatives. Then the feminine principle may recover its true significance in a world that sorely needs some human power to end its macho slide toward doomsday.

Baptism

Water baptism is one of the oldest techniques of ritual regeneration. Water stood for the sea womb, early identified as the essence of the Goddess who created the world out of her primordial deeps. Many ancient societies ceremonially returned their dead to water, or to the sea, so they might be born again. Similarly, a newborn was ceremonially blessed by water to indicate maternal acceptance of his or her existence. This was considered necessary to the child's right to a share of the fluids that nurture life.

A curious remnant of such ancient rituals of baptism has been preserved among the Mexican priestess-midwives, whose traditional title is *recibidora*. Though nowadays the midwife may be nominally Christian, she remains an agent of the pagan Goddess in her professional intimacy with the ultimate female mystery. Her ritual address to the infant she delivers may have originated with a pre-Columbian caste of holy women similar to the Roman *obstetrices*. The speech is given here in a remarkable translation.*

The priestess-midwife first places water on the lips of the newborn child, saying, "Take this; by this thou hast to live on the earth, to grow, and to flourish; through this we get all things that support existence on the earth; receive it."

Second, she wets the child's breast with water, saying, "Behold the pure water that washes and cleanses thy heart, that removes all filthiness; receive it; may the Goddess see good to purify and cleanse thy heart."

Third, she pours water on the child's head and speaks in a way reminiscent of the ubiquitous ancient image of the priestess-midwife as an honorary grandmother, in the role of wise-woman and Crone, usually revered as a second ceremonial mother by each child she brought into the world. She says to the infant: "O my grandson, my son, take this water of the Lord of the World which is thy life, invigorating and refreshing, washing and cleansing. I pray that this celestial water, blue and light blue, may enter into thy body and there live. I pray that it may destroy in thee and put away from thee all things evil and adverse that were given thee before the beginning of the world. Wheresoever thou art in this child, O hurtful thing, begone! leave it; put thyself apart; for now does it live anew, and anew is it born, now again is it purified and cleansed; now again is it shapened and engendered by our Mother the Goddess of Water."

Clearly this ceremony was inspired by pre-Christian beliefs in reincarnation and karmic debt. Somewhat similar medieval beliefs in the redemptive powers of the Virgin Mary led her worshipers to refer to her as a fountain of living waters, a sweet spring, Star of the Sea, and other watery epithets. She inherited the baptismal magic of the great Marine Aphrodite with her blue robe and pearl necklace; and she was the sealed fountain of the virgin bride in Old Testament allegory (Song of Solomon 4:12).

It is appropriate for us today to ask what the ritual of baptism really signifies. If we are no longer naive enough to believe in demons, then we could hardly consider it necessary to cast

---

*See Bayley, Harold: *The Lost Language of Symbolism* (2 vols.) New York: Barnes & Noble, 1957. Vol. 1, pp. 239–240.

demons out of newborn babies. The legal registration of a child's name is not contingent upon its being baptized either. Therefore we might reclaim the whole idea of baptism as its original acknowledgment of a mother's acceptance, earthly image of the Goddess's beneficence. Christian authorities in Saxon England used to describe the women's time-honored baptism of their newborns with water and earth as a devilish paganism; but the women, the water, and the earth were there long before Christianity and their rituals had served many generations.

A Wedding Ceremony

The following is a detailed description of a wedding ceremony actually performed and found eminently satisfactory to all involved, including those not familiar with Goddess-oriented concepts.

All wedding guests form a circle around the three principals—bride, groom, and priestess—who stand in triangle formation beside the central altar. The altar bears a pentacle, lighted candles, cup of wine, small silver box, wedding rings, scissors (or athame), red scarf or ribbon, and the priestess's wand.

The circle is cast with reference to the directions and elements (see Invocation, p. 20).

PRIESTESS: "We are gathered here today to celebrate love: specifically, the love that unites this woman and man, and through them the larger principle of love that unites any human beings with others. It is our sense of the universality of love that makes a wedding a joyous occasion. In token of this, we use the ancient and honorable sign of the Goddess of Love to dedicate this bride and groom to the great principle, to themselves, and to each other."

With her wand, the priestess marks the pentacle on the groom, lightly touching his forehead, left side of body, right shoulder, left shoulder, right side of body, and forehead again.

PRIESTESS: "I dedicate thy mind, heart, action, support, and will to the Great Goddess."

With her wand, the priestess marks the pentacle on the bride, lightly touching her forehead, left side of body, right shoulder, left shoulder, right side of body, and forehead again.

PRIESTESS: "I dedicate thy mind, heart, action, support, and will to the Great Goddess."

The priestess hands the wand to the bride, who turns to face the groom and marks him again with the pentacle in the same manner, speaking to him.

BRIDE: "I dedicate my mind, heart, action, support, and will to thee."

The bride hands the wand to the groom, who faces her and marks her again with the pentacle in the same manner, speaking to her.

GROOM: "I dedicate my mind, heart, action, support, and will to thee."

The groom hands the wand back to the priestess, who places it on the altar. The priestess then hands the cup of wine to the bride. She drinks, and hands the cup to the groom. He drinks, then holds the cup to the bride's lips while she drinks again. Then the bride takes the cup and holds it to the groom's lips while he drinks again. The bride hands the cup back to the priestess, who places it on the altar, saying, "Blessed be."

PRIESTESS, marking a large double circle in the air: "What we now know as the infinity sign in mathematics, a horizontal figure eight, came to represent infinity because it was once the Goddess's sign of perfect union, female with male, Goddess with God, creating a world without end. This dual circle grew from the world's oldest wedding custom, the ceremonial joining of hands so the couple's arms formed the double circle. In Celtic tradition this ceremony became known as handfasting. It remained the preferred method of nonecclesiastical marriage up to the middle of the nineteenth century. Today we revive that ancient ceremony, whereby this bride and groom may be united in the tradition of the oldest deity known to human beings."

Directed by the priestess, bride and groom join their right hands, then join their left hands over the right. The priestess binds their joined hands together, loosely, with the blood-symbolic red scarf or ribbon. The couple slowly turn one full circle around, gazing into each other's eyes. Then they stand still and speak to each other the words they have personally chosen to solemnize their union. The bride speaks first, stating in words of her own choosing that she takes the groom to be her husband, before the assembled family and friends, expressing her love for him, blessing him, and declaring her devotion. If desired, she may recite a bit of poetry or other phrases significant to both of them. If the bride's speech is too long for her to memorize, she may read it from a page held before her by an attendant (bridesmaid) during the handfasting.

Then the groom speaks, stating in words of his own choosing that he takes the bride to be his wife, before the assembled family and friends, expressing his love for her, blessing her, and declaring his devotion. He too may read from a page held before him by an attendant (best man) during the handfasting, if necessary.

When bride and groom have finished speaking to each other, the priestess removes the binding from their hands, and gives the scissors (or athame) to the bride, who cuts a small lock of the groom's hair. She places the hair in the small silver box held by the priestess. Then she gives the scissors (or athame) to the groom, who cuts a small lock of the bride's hair and places it also in the silver box.

PRIESTESS, holding up the box so that all may view it: "As the hairs mingle in this vessel, so may the spirits of this woman and man mingle forever."

The priestess places the box on the altar and holds out the wedding rings, either on the tip of her wand or on the point of an athame. (Other possibilities: a satin cushion, a narrow crystal, a shallow gold or silver dish.) Bride and groom take the rings and place them on each other's fingers, then kiss.

To finish the ceremony, witnesses around the circle may speak their own blessings and good wishes, one at a time, to the bride and groom who stand side by side with their arms around each other. Alternatively the bride and groom may process around the circle while each guest in turn congratulates them, in the manner of a receiving line. Meanwhile the priestess may leave the altar and join the circle. If the group is so large that it would take too long for each one to speak to the bride and groom, then only a few short speeches may be given, perhaps by the couple's closest relatives or friends.

The ceremony may conclude with the "faery" chant, spoken by all, as the priestess leads it, line by line. (See Invocation, p. 28.)

Readings

Reading has been a ritual procedure ever since the barest beginnings of literate civilizations, when the written word was holy, and those who were able to read it were regarded with awe. In the world of classical paganism, literacy was fairly common; but it became less so in the subsequent Dark Ages of Europe. The early church opposed education for lay persons and forbade the reading of scripture by anyone other than clergy. Reading became a standard Christian ritual, however, even when the reading was given in Latin to congregations who couldn't understand a word of it.

Ritual reading is also an accepted part of women's spirituality meetings. Some groups encourage members to bring to each gathering a short quotation, poem, or prose paragraph to share. In this way, many significant thoughts can be brought to the attention of the group. Some groups may designate a different person on each occasion to bring a longer reading as a theme setter.

Traditional religions invariably quote from their own scriptures to set themes for sermons, homilies, seasonal festivals, and other ceremonial activities. With this in mind, the following material is compounded especially for women's groups, out of a mixture of mythological sources suggesting prepatriarchal attitudes. Because so much of the ancient Goddess-oriented literature was destroyed, there are few such sources still extant. Still, this might serve as a useful re-visioning of traditional stories which were themselves radically changed, long ago, by patriarchal re-visioning of the old matrifocal cultures.

This is almost what the myths used to say.

In the beginning, the Goddess dwelt in her formless aspect, mingling all elements in her substance. For infinite ages, she drifted in her mystic darkness. In the deep places of her womb, waters gathered, the fluids of birth. Within these waters, she began to create life out of herself in her aspect of the Deep, later to be known by such names as Tehom, Tiamat, Temu, Themis, Thalassa, and Terra Mater, or Ma, Mami, Mammetun, Marina, Mari-Anna, Meri-Yam, and Maria.

Her first children were small, blind, mindless, drifting specks in the Deep, knowing only the simplest assimilation and reproduction. Later she allowed them to elaborate themselves. She granted them better organs of pressure-sensing, smelling, feeling, even seeing. She allowed them to produce locomotory mechanisms and hard supportive tissues.

She caused portions of her forming substance to rise above the waters. She encouraged her creatures to live in air. Thus Earth became the second primal compound for the support of life, after Water; and Air became the third. Water, Earth, and Air together became Matter, or Mater: the Mother.

The Goddess rejoiced in diversity. In all the universe, she never made any two exactly alike of anything whatsoever. The better to diversify her living children, she allowed some races of them to divide into primary reproductive females and secondary nonfemales, the latter to compete among themselves so that only the best of them could win the right to contribute genes to the offspring. So that the two sexes would seek union, she made them avid for union at the proper seasons, and let it be a pleasure to them.

The system worked well until one species learned to stand up on two legs, then to speak, then to make and use tools, and considered itself superior to all other species because it could do these things. This was the first hubris of humanity.

Human beings lived mostly at peace as long as the females busily created civilization for the better nurture and support of their young, even as the Goddess created worlds for her children; and the nonfemales contributed what they could to the same endeavors. Both sexes honored the Mother as the true source of life force for all creatures including themselves; for they all were born of mothers. Yet the nonfemales greatly envied the females' superior endowment of life force. They wanted to be able to give birth too, and claim offspring of their own, so that after dying they could be worshiped as divine ancestors like the ancient Clan Mothers. This was the second hubris of humanity. It was the hubris of men. In their jealousy, men forgot the natural responsibilities of male toward female, and dared to aspire to a kind of leadership for which they were not sufficiently maternal.

Talking among themselves, men began to devise ways in which they might claim a reproductive role. Some tried eating exactly what women ate, believing that babies were created with the aid of certain foods. Some tried eating placentas when they could get hold of them. Some defied powerful taboos by tasting the forbidden magic moon blood of women, said to be the very stuff of life. Some pretended to give birth, believing that the enactment could make the fact. Some dressed in female clothing and formed associations to give birth to one another, dripping their own blood over new male initiates, declaring them born again.

Some men thought it might be their own sexual movements that churned the women's magic moon blood to make a baby, as butter is made by churning milk. Some men suggested that their own sexual fluids might be necessary for a baby's nourishment as it grew in the womb before birth, just as its mother's milk was necessary afterward. Some men thought that women needed sexual intercourse to prepare them in some way for the visitation of the birth spirit, which was sent from the Goddess, or ancestral ghosts, or divine animals or plants, or placentas of previous births, or wherever they thought the spirit came from. This theory met with little acceptance, however. It was often pointed out that women could engage in sexual intercourse without producing children; and that women had many secret spells of their own for baby-making. No one, not even the women, was quite sure how long it took for a mother to grow her baby. People thought that babies, like plants, grew larger if they took more time, and that the local conditions of climate, rainfall, and dwelling places were intimately involved in the process.

There was an unhappy man who spent much of his time sitting alone. One day he came to a group of other men and told them, "I will be the Mother for many generations of offspring. I will become divine life force if you will worship me as ancestor and redeemer of men, as the Clan Mothers are worshiped. I will become a part of the Goddess and live forever, because I will become woman."

The other men laughed at him and said, "How can you become woman, Redeemer? You are nonwoman. Your body has no magic moon blood, no womb vessel, no milk. You cannot be an ancestor in the blood bond."

"I have blood," the Redeemer answered. "I have blood in my body like any woman, except that I cannot shed it without pain, as women do. Well then, I will shed it with pain. I will become the first male Clan Mother. You will worship me for the sacrifice of my blood, and I will be your god, because I will let you cut off the excess male flesh and make me a woman with a bleeding Gate of Life."

The men thought Redeemer was crazy, but they were awed by his boldness. One wise old man told him, "You will die." But Redeemer answered, "Even if I die, I will live forever in the Goddess, as do the women who die in childbirth. My sacrifice will give spiritual rebirth to all men."

They saw that he was determined. Being men, not at all averse to mutilating flesh and causing pain, they cut off his genitals and watched him bleed, dabbling in his blood and pretending it had as much mystic *mana* as women's blood. When he died, they made a special tomb in honor of his sacrifice and told the tribe that he had been specially chosen for a sacrifice to the Almighty on behalf of them all.

Redeemer's offering inspired others, especially the emotionally unbalanced, who craved attention enough to die for it. Men developed the tradition that at certain seasons, at planting times in particular, a man would be chosen to embody the spirit of Redeemer and to be ceremonially castrated and killed to provide holy blood for the nurture of all.

Men who became Redeemers were not always willing. It became necessary to bribe them with a foretaste of the godlike life before the sacrifice. They became sacred kings, worshiped for a while on earth and provided with the best of everything: the choicest foods, finest clothes, and plenty of sexual bliss in which gods were thought to live always, because they were embedded in the lifegiving body of the Goddess.

Women became involved in the choosing of sacred kings, because they wanted to nourish their own future children on godhood, and because women attended to all sacred procedures. Councils of Clan Mothers insisted that candidates be young, healthy, attractive, and virile. They established a custom of exposing each candidate to a naked female to note how promptly his phallus would rise. If a king's virility waned, he was quickly killed and replaced by a stronger candidate before his loss of spirit could harm the land.

As generations passed and the traditions of sacred kingship grew in complexity, each god-king was declared the son of the previous god-king. These "sons" were also the castrators and executioners of their predecessors. Sacred kingship thus enthroned male rivalry, and underscored Oedipal jealousy with very real fear of the young challenger.

Some kings, more power-hungry and more persuasive than the rest, found ways to hold on to the holy office once they had it. Some declared that the Goddess favored no others. They said, "I, in my omnipotence as God, can transfer divine spirit to another body for the duration of the sacrifice." So they used surrogates to redeem themselves: war captives, prisoners, criminals, children, even animals to embody the god their "father."

The annual Redeemer sacrifice became one of the most important rituals of life, especially among people who tilled the soil. So important did men make it, that people believed no crops could grow without it. Each year it was eagerly anticipated and discussed. Omens for the season were taken from each of its details.

Men especially set store by the sacrifices made to water the precious flesh of Mother Earth with precious blood. They insisted that their god had decreed it. If the land could not bear its fruit without male assistance, then the male principle was important. Perhaps women could not bear their fruit without male assistance either. The idea began to take shape: perhaps male sexual fluids were not just nourishment for future children, but the complete seed itself, needing nothing from the mother except her body as "soil." Some even dared to suggest that the real creators of future generations were not women but men. This was a truly revolutionary idea. It revolutionized the course of human history, having its effect on every aspect of life up to the present day—even though, all along, it was wrong.

In some areas, the men who survived castration were officially declared women, dressed in female garments, and allowed to serve in the Goddess's temples among the holy women. They were the first priests. They usually supported the sacred kings, and even permitted unmutilated men to join their company after they realized that the initiatory requirement discouraged new membership.

With the opening of priesthoods and kings' armies to more and more men, the balance of power began to slide toward males.

Societies became less altruistic, less peaceable, and less concerned for the welfare of posterity, but more aggressive, self-absorbed, greedy, warlike, and cruel. Kings' men killed neighboring tribes and seized the lands of others, to enhance their power.

Some of the priests and even some of the kings managed to learn the women's magic of alphabets, and began to study sacred writings preserved in the Goddess's temples. When priesthoods gained control, they dared to change sacred writings to support a new male-centered view of history. They inserted male names into the records of ancestral Clan Mothers. They listed generations of kings in place of the Goddess-personifying queens of older times. They rewrote myths to turn the Goddess into a demoness, or an insignificant nymph, or a subordinate wife of their god.

In their growing arrogance, some even dared to claim that woman was born out of man, instead of the other way round, and to pretend that their god arranged this unnatural event as one of his early miracles (for gods, they said, could break the laws of nature with impunity). When this story was first invented, the older priests scoffed, saying no one would believe such an absurdity. Was not the god himself born out of the Great Goddess in the beginning? The militant ones answered that even if she existed before the god, she was only a manifestation of his spirit, the source of his ideas. They said women must owe obedience to men as the child to the mother, because the first woman was the child of the first man; our god is able to create a male mother.

In one story, the first man bore the name of Adam, meaning "bloody clay," because it had long been a custom for women to conceive children magically by anointing clay dolls with their menstrual blood and chanting life-giving spells over them. They believed this was an imitation of the Goddess's first creation magic. The name of Adam was given to male poppets, and Adamah to female ones. Thus the revisionists also used the name of Adam, declaring that their god had learned the trick of life giving from his Mother. Although he had no animating moon blood, he was able to use breath instead, for it was often said that breath was a soul essence.

The revisionists did not quite dare to destroy the scriptures that said male and female human beings were created together, as it was written for thousands of years that both sexes at once were formed by the Goddess Mammetun, or Mami, or Ninhursag, or Pyrrha, or Belit. Nevertheless men inserted a new contradictory scripture into the ancient writings, telling of the birth of the first woman out of the body of the first man, with the upstart new god acting as midwife. To this first woman they gave the Earth's name as Mother of All Living, Hawwa or Heva, because Mother Earth was sometimes regarded as the spouse of Father Heaven.

It was known to all that while the Goddess as Mother Earth was the universal life giver, she was also the death bringer. Every one of her children eventually fell back into her body, to provide nourishment for new forms. Men disliked this cyclic system. Feeling less firmly anchored in the future than women could feel because of the children of their bodies, men faced the prospect of their inevitable dissolution with horror. Above all, they wished to prolong their lives indefinitely, like gods. Some men converted to Father religion simply because the Father's priests promised them seven more years of life than the Mother's priestesses regarded as normal.

Thus the groundwork was laid in the very processes of nature for men to hate the Goddess's destroying aspect. They were unable to see that creation and destruction must be coexistent forever; just as there can be no death without life, so also there can be no life without death. This was the teaching of the Mother. But the militants said, "It was the Mother of All Living, it was Woman, it was the Goddess, who gave us death. Our god would have let us live forever." They said it even though they knew it was a lie, contradicted by their own scriptures, which specifically stated that their god wished to prevent humans from living forever.

The scribes began to write stories about the sinfulness of the first woman, who brought death into the world. Even though it was the god who made this happen, the blame was laid on the woman of unnatural birth—who, it seemed, was quite powerful enough to negate the plans of the allegedly omnipotent Heavenly Father.

The asceticism that rose like a miasma from generations of priestly *castrati* soon focused on sexuality as the cause and expression of sin. Priests pointed out that it was by sexuality that man joined himself to lifegiving female flesh, yet he lost his "strength" in doing so. It was by sexuality that women stole men's essence to contribute to the growth of their children, whom they loved more. It was by sexuality that finite life was produced, generation after generation, all to be devoured again by Mother Earth in the end. Sexuality kept man tied to woman, to the land she owned, and to the children she bore. Sexuality was the magic whereby she ruled his very flesh, even against his will. Sexuality brought the deaths of sacred kings and gods. Moreover, even the deities had agreed that women could enjoy sexuality more than men did.

On the other side were some who maintained that, according to very ancient traditions, sexuality gave human beings their only opportunity to taste the bliss of deities' lives. When the Goddess allowed her son the god to become her consort, they merged in perpetual hermaphroditic union. All the energies of creation arose from their unceasing divine pleasure. This was the prototype of Paradise where existence was eternally ecstatic: an idea that combined with human racial memories of the perfect comfort of life in the womb. Therefore all pleasures were to be found in the female body. Surely then, they said, a return to the Earth womb could not be so terrible. There were even whole temples staffed by death priestesses, whose function was to take dying men into their arms, comforting them with sexual attentions, promising to take their souls in a final kiss, to renew them as children born again.

Death priestesses often kept the sacred serpents that were honored as bearers of ever-renewing life because they could shed their old wrinkled skins and be freshly reborn. Many people were convinced that snakes could not die unless something deliberately killed them. The Redeemer himself was credited with serpent incarnations, indicating immortality, because he wore many "skins" and was reborn with each new season. To keep their sexual energies high, priestesses often played with the sacred snakes, allowing them to caress the Goddess-spot between their legs. The women hoped in this way to absorb the serpent's powerful life force, just as men hoped to absorb the life force of women by sexual contact.

From this practice arose the holy image of the omphalos or yonic vessel enwrapped by the serpent. Many traditions declared that the serpent in the primal paradise was the first consort of Mother Earth; and many believed that women could conceive only after a sacred serpent had "opened the matrix" for them. Men were jealous of the serpent's apparent wisdom. Gradually they abandoned their worship of the serpent god and began to diabolize him. Revisionists declared that it was through both the Goddess and her serpent that death came into the world.

And yet there were stories with a different viewpoint, blaming the god and not the humans for their loss of longevity. It was said that in the lost Golden Age, people lived long because they were created by the Goddess as hermaphrodites, male and female in the same body. Thus they were always joined together, and always filled with the bliss of sexual union. The god, however, was jealous of their happiness. He "took woman out of man" by ripping the two sexes apart. In his haste and carelessness he tore away from woman a piece of flesh that properly belonged to her, leaving a cavity that leaked blood ever afterward. Her piece of flesh stuck to the body of man, but it still yearns to return to its rightful place in woman's cavity. That it is not a proper part of man's body is proved, they said, by the fact that it is not under his control like his other limbs, but rather is controlled by woman. She can influence its actions even from a distance, especially by displaying the hole in her body where it belongs.

Revisionists preferred stories that equated man's phallus with the diabolized serpent, who collaborated with the first woman-born-of-man. But the wise old priestesses who were writing-women and knew the ancient scriptures, scoffed at such stories. "Of course that woman could not have been born of man," they said. "No woman is born of man. Man is born of woman, always. Besides, our oldest books tell us that the first man was created by the Mother, at the same time or shortly after She created the first woman. That woman's name was not Heva but Lilit, the Lotus, which means flower-of-the-vulva."

New stories about Lilit the Lotus were invented to mock the radical priesthood. It was said that Lilit's consort tried to make her lie underneath him, like a pinned wrestler, for sexual congress. She refused and laughed at him. He called on his god, and the god tried to make Lilit obey her consort. She laughed at the god too, and robbed him of his power by uttering his secret name. Then she left both her consort and his god, and went to live by the sea, where she played with serpents and fertilized herself to give birth to many clans of offspring.

The new priests did not want to trace the beginning of humanity to this primordial Goddess-woman who reproduced without help from man. The priests claimed that their god sent the first man another wife, born from his own body and therefore constrained to obey him. It was she who listened to the counsel of the wise serpent, stole a fruit from the god's tree of knowledge, and brought a sentence of death upon herself and all her descendants forever (for the god was very vindictive). Lilit, the priests said, became a demon who stole men's seed from them in their erotic dreams, to maintain her fertility. Thus she became men's secret horror/desire, mother of all subsequent imaginary *succubae* for three thousand years—the priests claiming that these creatures were real and that all men must believe in them. It was also declared that Lilit devoured children, like every other version of the old Earth Goddess.

Other aspects of the Goddess were maligned in much the same ways as Lilit. The Medes' Great Mother Medea, Queen of Heaven, entered a late Greek myth as a child-killing mortal witch. Athene or Ath-enna, Triple Goddess of the Libyan Amazons, became an ever-virgin daughter whose only parent was a father. Her wise death-dealing Crone aspect—called Medusa, Metis, or Gorgo—was made a diabolic monster. Astarte-Ashtoreth, another long-established Queen of Heaven, was mentioned in patriarchal scriptures only as an "abomination." Mari or Mari-Anath, once worshiped as the spouse and power source of Israel's god, was artificially sanitized as a pallid mortal virgin mother of his only child.

Even the old Redeemers were diabolized as false demonic gods because they obviously consorted with the Goddess. Only one Redeemer was retained, having been reinterpreted as an ascetic who rejected even his virgin mother, while his earlier connections with Marian priestesses and various acts of the sacred drama were almost entirely written out of his story. He was still called the Bridegroom, because that was the required title, but he became a Bridegroom with no Bride.

Hearing the men's new creation stories and other revisions, the old priestesses laughed and said, "These fools have made up fictions from looking at the sacred pictures, such as the ones that show the Goddess offering fruit from the Tree of Life to the first man, while Her holy serpent twines in the branches. They are silly men who do not understand the sacred mysteries. Everyone knows that woman is not born of man, and that the fruit of life is the Goddess's gift, and that no man can be a Bridegroom without a Bride. No one will believe their stories."

But the priestesses did not understand how dangerous the new stories would be to their daughters and their daughters' daughters, down through the generations. The men were learning that even the stupidest story will be believed if it is repeated often enough, while alternative stories are suppressed. Instead of questioning the improbable-sounding miracles of the god, generations of men tried to turn their own common sense inside out to invent ways of explaining them. This process sooner or later attains a time when the improbable becomes Truth, and to question it is a sin, and questioners may be summarily destroyed. Many generations can be raised in ignorance, forbidden to discover any real truths that might undermine the imaginary One. After that, nothing can dislodge the improbable fiction but a major social revolution.

So it came about that women, who used to be holy repositories of life force and mystic power, were debased along with the Goddess who embodied these qualities. Instead of men trained to revere the Mother who gave them life, the new societies produced women trained to revere a Father who cursed their progenitress, and subordinated them all. In such societies, men became able to appropriate the clan names, properties, children, money, rulerships, and priesthoods. Education, lawmaking, and other lucrative professions were retained in exclusively male hands. Though women continued to do nearly all the same kinds of work by which ancient Clan Mothers supported their families, such work was robbed of dignity and recompense. Instead of a voluntary gift of love and grace, women's work became involuntary slavery; no woman had the option of refusing it. Like any slave, a mother/wife could be beaten or otherwise abused for intransigence.

So it happened that men believed they had won. In fact, they had lost. They created for themselves a world filled with violence, war, injustice, irrationality, and naked greed. Not content with oppressing women and children, they oppressed each other also. They set up hierarchies of oppression, so that those higher on the scale might abuse those below. Their insecure governments required paranoid militarism, and their insecure religions required vicious persecution of dissenters. In the civilization that developed out of men's apparent victory over the Goddess, fanaticism, sadism, anti-intellectualism, rape, robbery, fraud, sexual trauma, and legalized torture became commonplace.

During the centuries of change, a certain priestess once looked into the future with her wise understanding of human nature. She wrote her vision and entitled it the Priestess's Prophecy. She said the end result of the new god-centered society would be a terrible holocaust, the ultimate expression of men's passion for destruction—their counterpoise to women's passion for nurture. The priestess said that gods' jealousy of the creative powers of the Goddess can have no ending. Such jealousy can never be assuaged until even the possibility of further creation is destroyed. Therefore a world would have to die before the anger of such gods could be propitiated; and in the process the gods themselves would die, destroying one another in their madness, because there can be no gods if there are no worshipers.

The priestess foresaw many signs of the beginning of the end. She said there would be weakening and dissolution of the precious blood bonds of the clan, which had held human groups together through their birthgiving matriarchs for uncounted millennia. Families would separate and be scattered, because men wanted to isolate their chosen women from helpful relatives. Children would grow up knowing nothing of the sacred clan, knowing only alienation from the strife between lonely parents. This they would pass on to their own children, and so the sense of clan unity would pass out of human consciousness.

Respect for elders would be forgotten. The holy ways of mothers would be dishonored. Children would be abused by fathers and would be taught to blame their mothers for it. Sexual bonding would be robbed of tender meanings. Men would value themselves mostly in terms of fighting abilities. They would make heroes of warriors rather than of lovers, artists, or philosophers. They would create a world of selfishness, ruthlessly enslaving not only people and animals, but even Holy Mother Earth herself. They would befoul her soil, water, and air, dig out her bones, and strip her green garments, even to the exhaustion of her power to support living things.

They would fight viciously over the last waning necessities of life, until in their final madness they would destroy the whole world in a mighty holocaust. And then Mother Earth, sickened and dying, would cover all their traces with a great darkness.

Winter would be upon the world for untold ages. Nothing would move any more, in the places where the Goddess once created such diversity as to escape all conceiving by any human mind.

Then, gradually, she might create again after long ages had passed. But in this place and time, through one cycle, the Goddess will have shown that no one species can be allowed to think itself superior to others. She will have shown also that men are most like devils when they believe themselves to be like gods.

Goddess Names

The following names of goddesses are from cultures all over the world. Any of them may be used for invocation.

A (Su)
Abundia (L)
Acca (L)
Acco (Gr)
Achamoth (Gn)
Acuecueyotl (Az)
Aditi (Hi)
Adrasteia (Gr)
Aegina (Gr)

Aegle (Gr)
Aello (Gr)
Aethra (Gr)
Agatha (L)
Aglaia (Gr)
Agna (L)
Agwe (Af)
Ahat (Eg)
Akewa (Af)

Akka (F)
Alcyone (Gr)
Alecto (Gr)
Al-Lat (Ar)
Allatu (Ba)
Alphito (Gr)
Al-Uzza (Ar)
Amaltheia (Gr)
Amaterasu (J)

Ambika (Hi)
Ame-no-uzume (J)
Ament (Eg)
Amphitrite (Gr)
Amunet (Eg)
Amymone (Gr)
Ana (Su)
Anahita (Pe)
Ananke (Gr)
Anansi (Af)
Anastasia (Gr)
Anath (Canaanite)
Anatu (Su)
Andraste (Br)
Andromeda (Gr)
Angerona (Ro)
Angitia (Gr)
Angurboda (N)
Anna-Nin (Su)
Anna Perenna (Ro)
Annis (Sa)
Anthea (Gr)
Anuket (Eg)
Anumati (Hi)
Aoide (Gr)
Aphaea (Gr)
Aphrodite (Gr)
Apoconallotl (Az)
Arachne (Gr)
Aradia (Gn)
Aramaiti (Pe)
Arche (Gr)
Arethusa (Gr)
Ariadne (Gr)
Arianrhod (Ce)
Arinna (Ar)
Armat (Armenian)
Armathr (Ic)
Artemis (Gr)
Artio (Ce)
Aruru (Ba)
Aryajangulitara (Hi)
Asherah (Canaanite)
Ashima-Bethel (He)
Ashnan (Su)

Ashtart (Ph)
Ashtoreth (He)
Asia (Gr)
Astarte (Sy)
Asterodia (Gr)
Astraea (Gn)
Astronoe (Ph)
Asuniti (V)
Ata (Aramaic)
Ataensic (Iroquois)
Atanua (Po)
Atargatis (Ph)
Atet (Eg)
Athene (Gr)
Athyr (Eg)
Atira (Pa)
Atropos (Gr)
Audumla (N)
Aurora (Ro)
Au Set (Eg)
Auxo (Gr)
Awitelin Tsita (Z)
Baalat (He)
Baba Yaga (Ru)
Babd (Ce)
Bachue (Chibcha)
Baduhenna (IE)
Bagavati (Hi)
Bahet (Eg)
Banba (Ir)
Bast (Eg)
Bau (Su)
Bebind (Ir)
Befana (It)
Belili (Su)
Belit (Ba)
Bellona (Ro)
Beltis (Ba)
Bendis (Thracian)
Benten (J)
Benthesicyme (Gr)
Berchta (Ge)
Berecynthia (Gr)
Beset (Eg)
Bestla (N)

Beyla (N)
Bhadrakali (Hi)
Bhavani (Hi)
Bhrkuti (Bu)
Bhumidevi (Hi)
Biducht (Pe)
Bindumati (Hi)
Blanaid (Ir)
Blodeuwedd (W)
Boann (Ce)
Bona Dea (Ro)
Bona Fides (Ro)
Braciaca (Ga)
Branwen (Ce)
Brigantia (Ce)
Brigit (Ce)
Brimo (Gr)
Brisaya (V)
Britomartis (Ae)
Brizo (Ae)
Buana (Ir)
Budeia (Gr)
Buto (Eg)
Cabiria (Gr)
Caillech Bheur (Ce)
Calafia (Gn)
Calliope (Gr)
Callisto (Gr)
Calypso (Gr)
Car (IE)
Cardea (Ro)
Carmenta (L)
Carna (L)
Carpo (Gr)
Caryatis (Gr)
Cathena (Mo)
Ceacht (Ir)
Celaeno (Gr)
Cerdo (Gr)
Ceres (Ro)
Cerridwen (Ce)
Cessair (Ir)
Chaabu (Aramaic)
Chalchihuitlicue (Az)
Chamundi (Hi)

Ch'ang-O (Ch)
Chantico (Ma)
Chao San Niang (Ch)
Charis (Gr)
Chasca (In)
Chicomecoatl (Az)
Chih Nu (Ch)
Chikisanti (Ainu)
Chimalman (Az)
Chloe (Gr)
Chloris (Gr)
Chthonia (Gr)
Chuang Mu (Ch)
Cinxia (Ro)
Circe (Gr)
Citlalinicu (Az)
Ciuateotl (Az)
Cleia (Gr)
Cleta (Spartan)
Clio (Gr)
Clotho (Gr)
Clothru (Ir)
Clymene (Gr)
Clytie (Gr)
Coatlicue (Az)
Comizahual (Hon-
  duran)
Concordia (Ro)
Coronis (Gr)
Cotys (Phrygian)
Cotytto (Thracian)
Coventina (Sa)
Coyolxauhqui (Az)
Creidyllad (Br)
Cuba (Ro)
Cunda (Hi)
Cunti (Hi)
Curitis (L)
Cybele (Phrygian)
Cynthia (Gr)
Cypria (Gr)
Cytherea (Gr)
Daeira (Gr)
Damgalnunna (Su)
Dam-kina (Su)

Damona (Ga)
Danae (Gr)
Danu (IE)
Daphoene (Gr)
Dasse (Bushman)
Dea Caelestis (Ca)
Dea Syria (L)
Dechtire (Ir)
Dee (Ce)
Deino (Gr)
Delia (Gr)
Delphyne (Gr)
Demeter (Gr)
Deohaka (Se)
Derceto (Ba)
Despoena (Gr)
Devaki (Hi)
Devana (Czech)
Devi (Hi)
Devorgilla (Ir)
Dharti Mai (Hi)
Dhisana (V)
Dhupa (Bu)
Dia (IE)
Diana (Ro)
Dictynna (Ae)
Dido-Anna (Ca)
Diiwica (Serbian)
Dike (Gr)
Dinah (He)
Dindymene (Phry-
  gian)
Dinsangma (Bu)
Dione (Gr)
Dipa (Bu)
Doda (Serbian)
Doljang (Hi)
Dol-Ma (Ti)
Dolya (Ru)
Domina (L)
Domnu (Ce)
Doris (Gr)
Dosangma (Ti)
Draupadi (Hi)
Dryope (Gr)

Dsovinar (Armenian)
Dubh Lacha (Ir)
Durga (Hi)
Dyava-matar (Sl)
Dyne (Ro)
Dziewona (Sl)
Eadna (Ce)
Echo (Gr)
Edda (N)
Edji (Altaic)
Egeria (L)
Eigin (Ce)
Eire (Ir)
Eistla (N)
Eithincha (Iroquois)
Ekajata (Bu)
Elaine (Ce)
Elat (Ar)
Electra (Gr)
Elen (Br)
Elissa (Ar)
Elle (Te)
Elli (N)
Embla (N)
Emer (Ir)
Enyo (Gr)
Eortha (Sa)
Eos (Gr)
Eostre (Sa)
Epona (Br)
Erato (Gr)
Erda (Ge)
Ereshkigal (Ba)
Eri (Ir)
Erigone (Gr)
Erinys (Gr)
Eris (Gr)
Eriu (Ir)
Erkir (Armenian)
Erua (Ba)
Erycina (Sicilian)
Erytheia (Gr)
Erzulie (Af)
Etain (Ce)
Ethne (Ce)

Eudora (Gr)
Eunomia (Gr)
Euphrosyne (Gr)
Europa (Gr)
Euryale (Gr)
Eurybia (Gr)
Eurydice (Gr)
Eurynome (Gr)
Euryphassa (Gr)
Euterpe (Gr)
Evadne (Gr)
Eve (He)
Fand (Ir)
Fata (L)
Fatima (Ar)
Fauna (L)
Fea (Ga)
Felicitas (Ro)
Feronia (L)
Flidhais (Ce)
Flora (Ro)
Fornax (Ro)
Fortuna (Ro)
Fotla (Ir)
Frea (Sa)
Freya (N)
Frigga (Te)
Fuchi (Aino)
Fuji (J)
Fulla (N)
Furina (L)
Gaea (Gr)
Galata (Ga)
Galatea (Gr)
Gandha (Bu)
Gandhari (Hi)
Ganga (Hi)
Ganis (Lapp)
Garbh Ogh (Ce)
Gashanki (Ba)
Gauri (Hi)
Gayatri (Hi)
Gefn (N)
Gerd (N)
Gersimi (Ic)

Gita (Bu)
Gjalp (N)
Godiva (Sa)
Goewin (W)
Gorgo (Gr)
Grainne (Ir)
Greip (N)
Grismadevi (Bu)
Groa (N)
Gula (Ba)
Gullveig (N)
Gunnlod (N)
Gwynhwyfar (W)
Hahaiwuqti (Pueblo)
Haimavati (Hi)
Halja (Gothic)
Hamingja (N)
Hanea (Armenian)
Hannahanna (Hittite)
Har (Ba)
Haravaiti (Av)
Hariti (Hi)
Harmonia (Gr)
Hathor (Eg)
Havfrue (D)
Hawwah (Canaanite)
Hebat (Hittite)
Hebe (Gr)
Hecate (Gr)
Hecuba (Ae)
Hegemone (Gr)
Heimarmene (Gn)
Hekit (Eg)
Hel (N)
Helen (Gr)
Helice (Gr)
Helle (Gr)
Hemantadevi (Hi)
Heqat (Eg)
Hera (Gr)
Hermione (Gr)
Herse (Gr)
Hertha (Ge)
Hesione (Gr)
Hesperia (Gr)

Hestia (Gr)
Hetpet (Eg)
Hi-Asa (Po)
Hina (Po)
Hine-Ahu-One
  (Maori)
Hine-Maki-Moe (Po)
Hippona (Gr)
Hlodyn (N)
Ho Hsien-ku (Ch)
Hokmah (He)
Holda (Ge)
Holle (Ge)
Hope (Gn)
Horsel (Sa)
Hotu-papa (Po)
Hsi Ho (Ch)
Hsi Wang Mu (Ch)
Hua Hsien (Ch)
Hueytonantzin (Az)
Huitaca (Chibcha)
H'uraru (Pa)
Huruing Wuhti (Ho)
Husbishag (As)
Huzruwauqti
  (Pueblo)
Hvov (Pe)
Hygeia (Gr)
Hyndle (N)
Hyrrokin (N)
Iamanja (Af)
Iambe (Gr)
Ida (Gr)
Idun (N)
Iha-no-hime (J)
Ila (V)
Ilamatecutli (Az)
Ilithyia (Gr)
Ilmatar (F)
Inada-hime (J)
Inanna (Su)
Indrani (Hi)
Innini (Su)
Ino (Gr)
Inoshishi (J)

Io (Gr)
Iodama (Gr)
Iole (Gr)
Iowahine (Ha)
Irene (Gr)
Iris (Gr)
Irkalla (As)
lshi-kori-do-me (J)
Ishtar (Ba)
Isis (Eg)
Itzcuinan (Az)
Itzpapalotl (Az)
Iuturna (L)
Iweridd (Br)
Ix Chel (Ma)
Ixcuina (Az)
Izanami (J)
Jael (He)
Jagadamba (Hi)
Jahi (Pe)
Jana (L)
Jarnsaxa (N)
Jezanna (Af)
Jokwa (J)
Jord (N)
Jordegumma (Sw)
Juksakka (Lapp)
Jumna (Hi)
Juno (L)
Justitia (Ro)
Juventas (L)
Kadesh-barnea (Hit-
   tite)
Kadi (Ba)
Kadru (Hi)
Kaiwan (Ethiopian)
Kala-Nath (Hi)
Kali Ma (Hi)
Kamadhenu (Hi)
Kamanari (J)
Kara (N)
Karali (Hi)
Karmadakini (Hi)
Karpophoros (Gr)
Kasenko (J)

Kaukabta (Sy)
Kauri (Hi)
Kel-Mari (Hi)
Keraunia (Gr)
Keroessa (Gr)
Keu Woo (Ch)
Khi-dimme-azaga
   (Ba)
Khon-Ma (Ti)
Khotun (Y)
Ki (Su)
Kicva (Br)
Kilili (As)
Kishar (Ba)
Kishibojin (J)
Kokyanwuqti
   (Pueblo)
Kore (Gr)
Kuan-Yin (Ch)
Kunapipi (Aus-
   tralian)
Kundalini (Hi)
Kunhild (Ge)
Kupala (Sl)
Kurukulla (Hi)
Kushi-nada-hime (J)
Kwai-Yin (Ch)
Kwannon (J)
Kybai (Y)
Kyohime (J)
La Balianne (Haitian)
Labartu (As)
Lachesis (Gr)
Lada (Sl)
Lahar (Su)
Laka (Ha)
Lakshmi (Hi)
Lamashtu (Su)
Lamia (Gr)
Lampetia (Gr)
Lara (L)
Lasya (Bu)
Lat (L)
Latona (Ro)
Laufey (N)

Laverna (Ro)
Leah (He)
Leda (Gr)
Leto (Gr)
Leucothea (Gr)
Leukippe (Gr)
Levana (Ro)
Levarcham (Ce)
Lha-mo-karpo (Ti)
Liban (Ir)
Libera (Ro)
Libitina (Ro)
Libra (Gn)
Libya (Eg)
Lif (N)
Ligobund (Po)
Lilith (He)
Lilitu (Su)
Ljod (N)
Lobsangma (Ti)
Locana (Bu)
Lochia (Gr)
Lofn (N)
Louhi (Lapp)
Lua Mater (L)
Lucifera (Ro)
Lucina (Ro)
Luna (Ro)
Luonnotar (F)
Luot-hozjik (Lapp)
Lupa (Ro)
Lympha (L)
Ma (IE)
Maan Emoinen (F)
Maat (Eg)
Mab (Ce)
Macha (Ir)
Mader-Akka (F)
Madhavi (Hi)
Maera (Gr)
Maeve (Ce)
Mafuike (Po)
Magna Dea (L)
Magna Mater (L)
Mah (Pe)

Mahadevi (Hi)
Mahamayuri (Bu)
Mahasitavati (Bu)
Mahora-Nui-Atea (Po)
Mahuea (Po)
Maia (Gr)
Makaravakta (Bu)
Ma-Ku (Ch)
Mala Liath (Ir)
Malama (Po)
Malinolxochitl (Az)
Mama (IE)
Mama Allpa (Peruvian)
Mamacocha (In)
Mamacora (Peruvian)
Mamaki (Bu)
Mama Ogllo (In)
Mamaquilla (In)
Mami (Su)
Mami Watu (Af)
Mammitu (Su)
Mana (L)
Manah (Ar)
Manasa (Hi)
Manat (Ar)
Mandarava (Bu)
Mania (Ro)
Ma-Nu (Eg)
Manzan Gormo (Buryat)
Mara (Sl)
Mardoll (N)
Margawse (Ce)
Mari (Sy)
Maria (L)
Marica (L)
Marici (J)
Marina (L)
Maritchi (Ch)
Marjatta (F)
Mary (He)
Marzyana (Sl)

Mater Matuta (L)
Mati-Syra-Zemlya (Ru)
Matlalcueje (Az)
Matrikadevi (Hi)
Matrona (L)
Matronit (He)
Mau (Eg)
Mawu (Af)
Maya (Bu)
Mayuel (Ma)
Mbaba Mwana Waresa (Af)
Mboze (Af)
Medb (Ce)
Medea (Medean)
Medusa (Gr)
Megaera (Gr)
Mehit (Eg)
Mehurt (Eg)
Mekala (Siamese)
Melaina (Gr)
Melanippe (Gr)
Melete (Gr)
Melpomene (Gr)
Melusine (Ga)
Mena (Eg)
Menaka (Hi)
Menarva (L)
Menglod (N)
Meni (As)
Mensa (L)
Meridiana (Gn)
Meri-Yamm (Ph)
Merope (Gr)
Mersekhnet (Eg)
Meschamaat (Sl)
Meskhent (Eg)
Messbuachalla (Ir)
Metakorab (Po)
Metis (Gr)
Metra (Pe)
Metzli (Az)
Mictecaciuatl (Az)
Mielikki (F)

Minaksi (Hi)
Minerva (Ro)
Minne (Gn)
Mintha (Gr)
Miriamne (He)
Mirume (J)
Mnemosyne (Gr)
Modgudur (N)
Modir (N)
Modron (Br)
Mohini (Hi)
Moira (Gr)
Moneta (Ro)
Morana (Sl)
Morgana (Ce)
Morgan le Fay (Ce)
Morrigan (Ce)
Mu Kwa (Ch)
Mut (Eg)
Muyinewumana (Pueblo)
Mylitta (Ca)
Myrine (Gr)
Myrrha (Gr)
Myrtea (Gr)
Naith (Ir)
Nambi (U)
Nammu (Su)
Nana (Ba)
Nanda Devi (Hi)
Nang Pyek-Kha (Burmese)
Nanna (N)
Nanshe (Ba)
Nari Mariama (Hi)
Nat (N)
Natura (L)
Neheb-kau (Eg)
Nehellenia (Te)
Neith (Eg)
Nekhbet (Eg)
Nemea (Gr)
Nemesis (Gr)
Nemetona (Br)
Nemhain (Ir)

Nephele (Gr)
Nephthys (Eg)
Nereis (Gr)
Nerrivik (Eskimo)
Nerthus (Te)
Neskeper-Ava (F)
Nessa (Ir)
Ngalalbal (Aus-
    tralian)
Niamh (Ce)
Nidaba (Su)
Nifl (N)
Nike (Gr)
Nimue (Ce)
Nina (Su)
Ninella (Ba)
Ningal (As)
Ningyo (J)
Ninhursag (Ba)
Ninkarraka (Ba)
Ninkasi (Su)
Nin-ki (Ba)
Ninlil (Su)
Ninmah (Ba)
Ninsun (Ba)
Nin-Ti (Su)
Nintud (Ba)
Nin-Ur (Ba)
Niobe (Gr)
Nipa (Algonquin)
Niritu (Ph)
Nirrti (V)
Nokomis (Algon-
    quin)
Nonacris (Gr)
Nortia (Et)
Nott (H)
Nu-kua (Ch)
Nun (Eg)
Nut (Eg)
Nyx (Gr)
Ocypete (Gr)
Odatis (Pe)
Odsmaer (N)

Oenone (Gr)
Olla (In)
Olympia (Gr)
Omeciuatl (Az)
Omphale (Gr)
Onatah (Iroquois)
Oneaea (Gr)
Ops (L)
Oshun (Af)
Otafuku (J)
Oto-hime (J)
Oxomuco (Ma)
Oya (Af)
Pachamama (In)
Padma (Bu)
Paivatar (F)
Pajan Yan (Cambodi-
    an)
Palatia (Ro)
Pallas (Gr)
Pandara (Bu)
Pandora (Gr)
Pangaea (Gr)
Panquetzalitzli (Az)
Parendi (Pe)
Parjanya (Hi)
Parnasabari (Bu)
Parthenia (Gr)
Parvati (Hi)
Pasht (Eg)
Pasiphae (Gr)
Pasithea (Gr)
Pasowee (Kiowa)
Peitho (Gr)
Pelagia (Gr)
Pele (Po)
Penardun (Br)
Penelope (Gr)
Perchta (Ge)
Perkun Tete (F)
Persephone (Gr)
Phaenna (Spartan)
Phaethusa (Gr)
Philomela (Gr)

Philyra (Gr)
Phoebe (Gr)
Phorcis (Gr)
Phyto (Gr)
Pitys (Gr)
Pleione (Gr)
Pluto (Gr)
Podarge (Gr)
Poene (Gr)
Poludnica (Ru)
Polyhymnia (Gr)
Pomona (L)
Prajna (Hi)
Prakriti (Hi)
Praxidike (Gr)
Praxithea (Gr)
Primigenia (L)
Prisni (Hi)
Prithivi (V)
Procne (Gr)
Pronoia (Gn)
Pronuba (Ro)
Prorsa (L)
Proserpina (L)
Protogenia (L)
Providentia (Gn)
Psyche (Gr)
Purandhi (Hi)
Pyatnitsa Prascovia
    (Ru)
Pyrrha (Gr)
Qadesh (Sy)
Queskapenek
    (Okanagan)
Quetzalpetlatl (Az)
Quoots-Hooi (Chi-
    nook)
Rachel (He)
Radha (Hi)
Rafusen (J)
Raka (Hi)
Ran (N)
Rana-Neidda (Lapp)
Rati (Eg)

Ratnadakini (Bu)
Rauni (F)
Rebekah (He)
Regina (L)
Rehtia (L)
Renenet (Eg)
Rhamnusia (Gr)
Rhea (Gr)
Rhiannon (Ce)
Rhode (Gr)
Rhodope (Gr)
Rigatona (Ce)
Rinda (N)
Rohini (Hi)
Roma (Ro)
Rosalia (L)
Rudrani (Hi)
Rusa (Ar)
Sabaga (Y)
Sabia (Ir)
Saci (Eg)
Sadb (Ce)
Saga (N)
Saho-yama-hime (J)
Sakuntala (Hi)
Sakuya-hime (J)
Salacia (L)
Salma (Sy)
Salmacis (Carian)
Saltu (Ba)
Salus Publica (Ro)
Samjna (Hi)
Santa (L)
Sao-tsing Niang (Ch)
Sapientia (Gn)
Saradevi (Bu)
Sarai (He)
Sara-Kali (Gypsy)
Sarakka (F)
Sarama (Hi)
Saramama (In)
Saranyu (Hi)
Sarasvati (Hi)
Sarpanitum (Ba)

Sasthi (Hi)
Satet (Eg)
Savitri (Hi)
Scatha (Ce)
Scotia (Gr)
Scylla (Gr)
Sedna (Eskimo)
Seewa (Sl)
Seimia (Sy)
Seiobo (J)
Sekhmet (Eg)
Selene (Gr)
Semele (Gr)
Sengen Sama (J)
Seoritsu-hime (J)
Seshat (Eg)
Shakti (Hi)
Shala (Canaanite)
Shamshu (Ar)
Shannon (Ir)
Shapash (Ar)
Sharis (Urartian)
Shaushka (Ak)
Shayba (Ar)
Shekina (He)
Shesemtet (Eg)
Shimti (As)
Shin-Mu (Ch)
Shiwanokia (Z)
Shuhiji-no-kame (J)
Shuki (Hi)
Siduri Sabatu (Ba)
Sif (N)
Sigdrifa (N)
Sige (Ro)
Signy (N)
Sigrun (N)
Sik Sawp (Burmese)
Siris (Ba)
Sirtu (Ba)
Sita (V)
Sitatara (Bu)
Sith (N)
Sjofn (N)

Skadi (H)
Skuld (N)
Smyrna (Gr)
Snorta (N)
Somagalags (Bella
  Coola)
Songi (Af)
Sophia (Gn)
Sophrosyne (Gr)
Soteira (Gr)
Spenta-Aramaiti (Av)
Spes (Ro)
Spider Woman
  (Pueblo)
Sraddha (Hi)
Sreca (Serbian)
Sridevi (Hi)
Steingud (N)
Stella Maris (L)
Sterope (Gr)
Stheno (Gr)
Strenia (Ro)
Styx (Gr)
Subhadra (Hi)
Suedela (Ro)
Sukkamielli (F)
Sulis (Br)
Sunna (N)
Surabhi (Hi)
Syamatara (Bu)
Sybilla (L)
Sylvia (Ro)
Syr (N)
Syrinx (Gr)
Tailltu (Ir)
Tai Shan (Ch)
Tait (Eg)
Tai Yuan (Ch)
Talatumsi (Pueblo)
Tamar (He)
Tanit (Ca)
Tannetis (Gn)
Tara (Hi)
Taranis (Ga)

Tashitsheringma (Ti)
Tashmetu (Su)
Tatsuta-hime (J)
Taueret (Eg)
Tefnut (Eg)
Teleia (Gr)
Tellus Mater (Ro)
Temazcalteci (Az)
Temu (Eg)
Tenemet (Eg)
Tensho (J)
Terpsichore (Gr)
Terra Mater (Ro)
Teteu Innan (Az)
Tethys (Gr)
Thalassa (Gr)
Thalia (Gr)
Thallo (Gr)
Thea (Gr)
Thelxepeia (Gr)
Themis (Gr)
Thetis (Gr)
Thinggishalsangma
  (Ti)
Thrud (N)
Thyone (Gr)
Tiamat (Ba)
Tien Hou (Ch)
Tihkuyi Wuht (Ho)
Tisiphone (Gr)
Titaea (Ae)
Titania (Ro)
Tlacolteotl (Az)
Tlalteutli (Az)
Toci (Az)
Tonacacihuatl (Az)
Tonacajohua (Az)
Tonantzin (Az)
Tou-Mu (Ch)
Toyo-tama-hime (J)
Trevia (Ro)
Triduana (Ce)

Triformis (L)
Tritone (Gr)
Tsan Nu (Ch)
Tuag (Ir)
Tursa (L)
Tutela (L)
Tyche (Gr)
Tyro (Gr)
Tzinteotl (Toltec)
Uathach (Ce)
Ua Zit (Eg)
Uchtdelbh (Ir)
Uka-no-kami (J)
Ukemochi (J)
Uksakka (F)
Ulfrun (N)
Uma (Hi)
Unelanuhi (Chero-
  kee)
Uni (Et)
Untar (F)
Urania (Gr)
Urd (Te)
Ursel (Ge)
Urth (N)
Urvasi (Hi)
Ushas (Hi)
Ushnishavijaya (Hi)
Ut Set (Eg)
Uzza (Ar)
Vac (Hi)
Vajradakini (Bu)
Va-Kul (F)
Valetudo (It)
Vanadis (N)
Varunani (Hi)
Vasa (F)
Vasantadevi (Bu)
Vasilissa (Sl)
Vasundhara (Bu)
Venus (Ro)

Verthandi (N)
Vesna (Sl)
Vesta (Ro)
Vidyahara (Hi)
Vijayashakti (Bu)
Virava (F)
Virginal (IE)
Virgo (Gn)
Viviane (Ce)
Vjofr (N)
Volla (N)
Vor (N)
Walpurga (Ge)
Weiwobo (J)
Wellamo (F)
Whaitari (Maori)
Wyrd (Sa)
Xixiquiphilihui (Az)
Xmukane (Ma)
Xochiquetzal (Az)
Yabmeakka (Lapp)
Yahsang Khasi (Ch)
Yami (Hi)
Yamuna (Hi)
Yansa (Af)
Yemaya (Af)
Yimak (Pe)
Yngvi (N)
Yolkai Estsan (Nava-
  ho)
Yuki-onne (J)
Zamin (Pe)
Zarbanit (Ba)
Zerpanitum (Su)
Zikum (Ak)
Ziva (Sl)
Zlotababa (F)
Zoe (Gr)
Zora (Sl)
Zorya (Sl)
Zurvan (Av)

Suggestions for Further Reading

The following is a small selection of books from a large and ever-growing body of literature about rediscovery of the feminine spirit and reempowerment of women. Members of a women's spirituality group may read, discuss, and share such books for better understanding of their essential role as women in modern patriarchal society, and for better knowledge of their future potential.

Adler, Margot. *Drawing Down the Moon: Witches, Druids, Goddess-Worshippers, and Other Pagans in America Today.* Boston: Beacon, 1986.

Briffault, Robert. *The Mothers* (3 vols.). New York: Macmillan, 1927.

Christ, Carol P. *Laughter of Aphrodite: Reflections on a Journey to the Goddess.* San Francisco: Harper & Row, 1987.

Daly, Mary. *Beyond God the Father: Toward a Philosophy of Women's Liberation.* Boston: Beacon, 1985.

Eisler, Riane. *The Chalice and the Blade: Our History, Our Future.* San Francisco: Harper & Row, 1987.

Fisher, Elizabeth. *Women's Creation: Sexual Evolution and the Shaping of Society.* New York: Doubleday, 1979.

French, Marilyn. *Beyond Power: On Women, Men, and Morals.* New York: Simon and Schuster, 1985.

Johnson, Buffie. *Lady of the Beasts: Ancient Images of the Goddess and Her Sacred Animals.* San Francisco: Harper & Row, 1988.

Morton, Nelle. *The Journey Is Home.* Boston: Beacon, 1985.

Sjöö, Monica, and Barbara Mor. *The Great Cosmic Mother: Rediscovering the Religion of the Earth.* San Francisco: Harper & Row, 1987.

Spretnak, Charlene (ed.). *The Politics of Women's Spirituality: Essays on the Rise of Spiritual Power Within the Feminist Movement.* New York: Doubleday, 1982.

Starhawk. *The Spiral Dance: A Rebirth of the Ancient Religion of the Great Goddess.* San Francisco: Harper & Row, 1979.

———. *Dreaming the Dark: Magic, Sex and Politics.* Boston: Beacon, 1982.

Stone, Merlin. *When God Was a Woman.* New York: Dial, 1976.

———. *Ancient Mirrors of Womanhood: Our Goddess and Heroine Heritage* (2 vols.). New York: New Sibylline Books, 1979.

Walker, Barbara G. *The Woman's Encyclopedia of Myths and Secrets.* San Francisco: Harper & Row, 1983.

———. *The Secrets of the Tarot: Origins, History, and Symbolism.* San Francisco: Harper & Row, 1984.

————. *The Crone: Woman of Age, Wisdom, and Power.* San Francisco: Harper & Row, 1985.

————. *The I Ching of the Goddess.* San Francisco: Harper & Row, 1986.

————. *The Skeptical Feminist: Discovering the Virgin, Mother, and Crone.* San Francisco: Harper & Row, 1987.

————. *The Woman's Dictionary of Symbols and Sacred Objects.* San Francisco: Harper & Row, 1988.

————. *The Book of Sacred Stones: Fact and Fallacy in the Crystal World.* San Francisco: Harper & Row, 1989.

Wynne, Patrice. *The Womanspirit Sourcebook.* San Francisco: Harper & Row, 1988.

Index